AMERICANA LIBRARY

ROBERT E. BURKE, EDITOR

GENERAL JACOB S. COXEY

COXEY'S ARMY

A STUDY OF THE INDUSTRIAL ARMY MOVEMENT OF 1894

BY

DONALD L. McMURRY

Introduction by John D. Hicks

UNIVERSITY OF WASHINGTON PRESS

SEATTLE AND LONDON

Copyright © 1929 by Donald L. McMurry
University of Washington Press Americana Library edition 1968
"Introduction" by John D. Hicks copyright © 1968
by the University of Washington Press
Library of Congress Catalog Card Number 29-23512
Printed in the United States of America

PREFACE

"Coxey's army" has become a byword, a synonym for a tattered aggregation of disreputables. As in many such cases, and in spite of the comparatively recent occurrence of the events that gave rise to the phrase, its origin is unknown to many who use it. There was a time, however, when all who could read gained a great deal of information and misinformation about the subject, which caused reactions ranging from uproarious amusement to genuine alarm. Thoughtful persons who tried to look below the picturesque surface of these events saw a meaning in them but were not agreed as to what it all signified. To-day, with a better perspective, the student of the United States of thirty-five years ago can profitably examine again these strange happenings that then excited such intense interest, and try to find out what they meant. It is the purpose of this book to describe the situation that gave rise to "Coxey's Commonweal" and the "industrial armies", to tell the story of these curious crusades of the unemployed, and to attempt an interpretation of them.

A summary of parts of the manuscript in an earlier stage of its development appeared in the *Mississippi Valley Historical Review* of December, 1923. The writer wishes to acknowledge his indebtedness to the editor, Doctor Milo M. Quaife, for permission to use this material again, and to Professor Benjamin F. Shambaugh of the State Historical Society of Iowa for similar permission with regard to an article on

"Kelly's Army" in the *Palimpsest* of October, 1923; also his appreciation of the courtesy of various members of the staffs of the Wisconsin Historical Society, the State Historical Society of Iowa, and the Carnegie Library at Pittsburgh, in which collections much of the material was obtained. Mr. Jacob S. Coxey, Senior, of Massillon, Ohio, has furnished copies of a number of his publications and some manuscript letters, has made helpful comments upon parts of the manuscript relating to his financial ideas, and has given much oral information about the facts of his career. Other friends who have read the manuscript have eliminated many of its worst faults.

CONTENTS

viii CONTENTS

ILLUSTRATIONS

INTRODUCTION

Donald LeCrone McMurry, like the first of the "armies" he wrote about, came out of the Middle West. Born in Winona, Minnesota, he attended Beloit College and the University of Wisconsin, where he was awarded the Ph.D. in 1921. These were great years in Wisconsin history, with Charles R. Van Hise followed by Edward A. Birge as president, with Frederic L. Paxson and Carl R. Fish in American history, Richard T. Ely and John R. Commons in economics, and E. A. Ross in sociology. However "the Wisconsin idea" may be defined, the youthful McMurry could hardly have escaped its influence. As a historian, he specialized in problems of late nineteenth-century America, particularly labor history, in which his interest began early and continued throughout his career—bracketed in a sense by *Coxey's Army*, which appeared in 1929, and *The Great Burlington Strike of 1888,* published in 1956. Both books were pioneering ventures on subjects that other scholars had chosen almost to ignore.

When Donald McMurry wrote his account of the 1894 marches of the unemployed, the United States, with the important exception of agriculture, was enjoying an abundant prosperity. The panic of 1929 and the great depression were still around the corner. There is nothing in this book to indicate that its author foresaw any better than the outstanding business leaders of the time the economic turmoil that was so close at hand. Ironically, however, as McMurry observes in his concluding paragraphs, Jacob Coxey had scented the impending doom as early as 1928. The only reason that the coming of hard times was not generally apparent, the Sage of Massillon declared, was that the newspapers were suppressing the evidence.

McMurry's findings are thus uncolored by the existence of hard times about him as he wrote; he cannot be accused of writing the present into the past. The Bonus Expeditionary Force, with its more dramatic march in search of similar objectives, had not yet taken place. As a matter of fact, the United States had undergone no severe economic depression since the 1890's. Just before the outbreak of World War I, hard times had threatened, but the war soon turned the expected "bust" into a boom. The fighting had been over less than two years when another challenge to easy living appeared, but the postwar "recession," as it came to be called, soon disappeared (except for agriculture) beneath an avalanche of Coolidge prosperity. McMurry was thus in good position to deal objectively with the events he was to describe. Had he written *Coxey's Army* during the 1930's, he would no doubt have found it difficult not to reflect in the book his own emotional reactions to the conditions that surrounded him. Nor could he, after the Roosevelt years, have regarded Coxey's plan for issuing noninterest-bearing bonds to finance public works as particularly sensational. It was almost miraculous that Roosevelt was able to head off some similarly "unsound" scheme. Indeed, few defenders and no opponents of the New Deal would argue that its net effect was not highly inflationary.

Coxey's Army does not pretend to tell the whole story of the panic of 1893 and the four years of depression that followed it. Understandably, the author takes it for granted that his readers know the essential background of his study. Hard times had hit agriculture long before 1893, but in that year the industrial machine, too, had begun to run down. Five hundred banks and sixteen thousand businesses failed during the panic year alone. Railroad construction, long an index of prosperity, fell off drastically, and one great railway system after another went into receivership. Wages fell and unemployment rose. Samuel Gompers thought that the number of workers out of jobs reached three million by the end of 1893; by the time of Coxey's march, probably 20 per cent of the labor force was unemployed. McMurry does not fail to mention, as almost any other writer of his time would have done, that the frontier as a safety-valve for labor discontent had disappeared. More recently, critics of this hypothesis have pointed out that comparatively few city workers ever found their way to the frontier. But critics of the critics have noted also that discontented farmers, who might otherwise have sought refuge in a move to the West, sometimes flocked to the cities instead, thus joining with the recent immigrants and their descendants to glut the labor market.

McMurry makes it clear that Coxey's thinking had closely paralleled that of the Populists. The farmers, particularly those of the West and the South, had known hard times for several years before the panic broke and had tried in various ways to alleviate their distress. Activists among them had organized Farmers' Alliances through which to publicize their grievances and to seek relief. When economic pressures proved unavailing, they had tried their hands at politics and had even captured some state and local governments. But the farmer leaders soon realized that the problems they confronted were national, not local; only the national government had the power to deal effectively with the railroads, the middlemen, and the bankers whom they blamed for their troubles. As a loyal member of the Populist party, Coxey shared its doubts about the efficacy of state and local governments; furthermore, unemployment, no less than low prices on farm products, was a national problem. Like the rest of the Populists, Coxey had absorbed the old Greenback doctrines and had become an ardent believer in the soft money panacea. Since only the national government had authority to deal with the money problem, and since more money was essential to the war on unemployment, why not a march on Washington, a living petition to Congress for legislation on this essential subject?

Except for his convictions, Coxey was not the usual Populist. He was a businessman rather than a farmer, and a successful one at that. Although in 1894 he was only forty years of age, he had already amassed a small fortune from a sandstone quarry he owned and worked near Massillon. According to one theory, it was his distress over having to discharge some of his employees that led to his deep concern over unemployment and the resulting plan for a march on Washington, but the depression had by no means got him down financially. It was his substantial solvency, more than any other single factor, that enabled him to put his army on the road. Coxey was a good enough businessman, however, not to permit the cost of the march to break him; he induced others to pay the larger part of the bill. One of his indulgences as a wealthy man, and one that he apparently had no intention of giving up, was fine horses; he had long owned a stock farm in Kentucky where he bred them, and he drove out of Massillon behind his favorite pacer, Acolyte, a horse reputedly worth forty thousand dollars. According to an eyewitness, who reported much later what he saw as a boy, Coxey's phaeton was "a luxurious 'piano' box buggy, the then equivalent of today's seven passenger Cadillac."

Perhaps it was Coxey's business acumen that made him so well aware of the virtue of advertising. He saw the importance of getting his army talked about, and to this end he made the most of every means that came his way. His handsome equipage attracted attention, as he meant it to do. So also did his good-looking young wife, who followed him in another carriage, holding in her arms their infant son, whom he had thoughtfully named "Legal Tender." When it came to picking a second in command, Coxey's choice fell on Carl Browne, a professional agitator, whose eccentricities in dress and demeanor were certain always to provoke a maximum of comment. To cultivate the interest of a generation supersaturated in emotional religion, Coxey even permitted Browne to introduce religious overtones into the "crusade"; officially his organization became known as "The Commonweal of Christ." Coxey also welcomed about fifty newspapermen as companions on his march, and supplied them with exciting enough copy that nearly a third of them stayed with him all the way to Washington. A half-century later one of those correspondents, Ray Stannard Baker, devoted a whole chapter in his autobiography, *American*

Chronicle (1945), to "Marching with Coxey's Army." No wonder the marchers were talked about far more than their numbers justified—instead of the predicted one hundred thousand recruits, they started with only about one hundred men. All this publicity was quite as Coxey had intended. And if his "petition in boots" was harshly dealt with on the Capitol grounds, Coxey, after his arrest, at least got a hearing before a subcommittee of the House of Representatives, presided over by the up-and-coming young Democrat, William Jennings Bryan, who was also a seeker after publicity.

Populist acceptance of the Coxey undertaking was complete and unequivocal. Members of the party who lived along the line of march showed both the leader and the led every consideration. While Populists existed in great numbers only in the West and the South, there were a few of them everywhere, as McMurry's record makes clear. Invariably the third-partyites regarded the unemployed workers who composed the army as no less the victims of economic discrimination than the farmers themselves. The other armies of unemployed, whose activities McMurry also relates, won equally preferential treatment from the Populists, whatever the route toward Washington they had chosen. Populist pronouncements in favor of the marchers were frequent and vigorous. As Coxey's group approached Washington, Populist Senator William T. Allen of Nebraska urged his colleagues to send a committee to the "General" to hear his cause. Populist Governor L. D. Lewelling of Kansas defended the western armies of unemployed as poor unfortunates, robbed and legislated out of their right to work. Populist candidate James B. Weaver visited Charles T.

Kelly's army as it crossed Iowa, approved its program, and did what he could to help it obtain transportation across the state. Populist platforms invariably championed the reforms demanded by labor, and accepted them as their own.

One of the hardest things for the Populists to understand was their failure to get over their message to labor. They wanted, almost above all else, complete farmer and labor solidarity; it was no fault of theirs that labor rejected their overtures. They showed themselves willing, time after time, to ask for workers all the rights that labor demanded. Why, then, should not labor take up the cause of the farmers? It is possible that the rank and file of the workers might have gone along with the Populists had their leaders consented. But Samuel Gompers stated the official point of view when he warned against any entanglement with "the employing farmers." Labor, in his opinion, should promote its ends by playing off the two old parties against each other. Only Terence Powderly among the prominent labor leaders favored making common cause with the Populists, but the support of his dying Knights of Labor availed them little. What mattered was that the alive and growing American Federation of Labor let them down. Coxey and his kind accepted the Populist favors willingly enough, but the Populists got little support from labor in return.

Both the Populists and the Coxeyites were ahead of their time in thinking that the federal government should seek directly and actively to defeat the depression, unemployment included. The public works idea was by no means new, but in the United States most political and economic thinkers still regarded it with the gravest suspicion. To Grover Cleveland, Democratic President of the United States, no less than to his Republican adversaries, the depression was an unfortunate business calamity, but in no sense a responsibility of government; since the depression was the result of business operations, its cure was up to business. All the government could be expected to do under the circumstances was to keep the currency sound and the treasury solvent.

Twentieth-century leaders, among them both Herbert Hoover and Franklin D. Roosevelt, were to take a very different view of the situation. Neither of these Presidents would have regarded generous federal expenditures for the improvement of roads as particularly startling, although they would certainly have objected to Coxey's method of financing the project. They would have assumed, as nineteenth-century statesmen did not, that the federal government was under an obligation to lead the way back to prosperity. To them it was unthinkable that the government should stand idly by, leaving the whole problem of recovery to private enterprise. In a way, therefore, Coxey and the Populists had caught a glimpse of the future.

Many of the reporters who wrote about the armies of the unemployed described the marchers as tramps. This charge was inaccurate, for large numbers of the recruits were not, and had never been, tramps in the technical sense of the term. The word "tramp" was then applied to down-and-outers who tramped or bummed rides along the railroad tracks, sometimes in search of temporary employment, but sometimes also as an indolent and happy-go-lucky way of life, such as the "hippies" of our time are content to lead. Tramps begged, stole, and foraged for survival; they bedded down in vacant boxcars, vacant buildings, or vacant lots; they eluded, frightened, or won the sympathy of railroad trainmen. Naturally, such "weary Willies" were attracted to the armies of the unemployed; the handouts were good, and the company was congenial. Naturally, also, they guided the marchers away from the abominable dirt roads and toward the railways. Their presence helps explain the persistent efforts of the western armies to make their marches by train; tramps had always done it that way.

The armies, however, included not only tramps but also great numbers of men out of jobs who really wanted to work, men who believed that every willing worker had a right to a job. Such persons accepted the life of the road only because they could do no better; they were angry at having to live the way they did; they believed with their leaders that it was up to the government to provide them with jobs. In what more effective way could they make their feelings known? Perhaps it is worth noting that the civil rights protagonists of the 1960's have adopted the same manner of protest. Masses of men on the march are hard to overlook, and by appealing to the affluent as well as to the downtrodden our more recent marchers have managed greatly to amplify their numbers.

Unlike most of the other leaders of 1894 marches, Coxey did not long remain out of the newspaper headlines. He was the Populist candidate for Congress from the eighteenth Ohio district in 1894, and he ran for governor of Ohio in 1897. When symptoms of another depression appeared in 1914, he led another march to Washington, and this time spoke from the steps of the Capitol. He tried unsuccessfully to obtain a nomination for United States senator in 1916, threatened another march on Washington after World War I, and obtained an interview with Warren G. Harding in 1922. "Do not think for a moment," he told the President prophetically, "that all profiteers and grafters are confined to the Democratic Party." Harding listened to his arguments for monetary reform, but brushed them off with a genial, "You're right, Coxey," which, considering the source, meant exactly nothing.

Coxey was in Washington again in 1928 without an army, charging that there were already five million men unemployed in the United States, compared to only three million in 1894. The remedy, he again insisted, was his noninterest-bearing bond bill, and at his request it was once more introduced into the House. To Andrew Mellon, however, Coxey's proposal was only another "fiat money scheme," and the bill got no further, as usual. Coxey continued to threaten another march on Washington, and spoke in behalf of his bond proposal everywhere he could attract an audience. According to an Omaha *World-Herald* reporter:

The general is an affable gentleman, who far from looks his age of seventy-three. He is dressed like a business man, which, as the owner of a stone quarry, he is. A stand-up collar and silver-rimmed spectacles give him an old-fashioned appearance. He still has a thick head of hair, tho it is gray, and his face shows few wrinkles. His eyes are the eyes of a dreamer rather than of the man of action, the eyes of an enthusiast who sees through what he considers a world of injustice to Utopia, a Utopia to be reached by following his directions.

When the depression really struck, Coxey was in his

element. His proposals at least won a favorable hearing in his own home town, for in 1931 he was elected mayor of Massillon as a Republican, running on a platform advocating municipal ownership of public utilities and the flotation of two hundred thousand dollars in municipal bonds to aid the unemployed. The bonds were to be issued in denominations ranging from twenty-five cents to ten dollars, would bear interest at only one-tenth of one per cent, and would be used to pay the wages of men employed on city works or to provide loans to the unemployed. But when Coxey sought re-election in 1934, he lost. In 1932 and again in 1936 he obtained nominations for President by a splinter group calling itself the Farmer-Labor party; in 1932 he received 7,309 votes, but in 1936 he finally withdrew and threw his support to William Lemke. To finance his speaking tours in 1935, he drove about the country in a patent-medicine truck, from which he sold at $1.25 a bottle a concoction of his own making called "Cox-E-Lax." In 1938, still hearty at eighty-four, he again ran for Congress from his Ohio district, this time calling for a thirty-hour WPA work week, with wages at one dollar an hour, a one-year moratorium on all federal taxes, and a fifty-four-billion-dollar issue of paper money to finance the government. Never one to be intimidated by defeat, he tried it again in 1942 (aged eighty-eight). Next year he ran once more for mayor of Massillon, this time on the Democratic ticket, and with a campaign promise to have policemen escort drunks to their homes instead of to jail. On May 1, 1944, he stood on Capitol Hill in Washington and completed the speech he had intended to give there fifty years before.

Coxey hoped to live to be one hundred years old, but he failed to make it. He and his wife celebrated their sixtieth wedding anniversary on September 3, 1950, and on January 14, 1951, he died at the age of ninety-seven. But little Legal Tender, perhaps overwhelmed by his name, never even reached maturity.

JOHN D. HICKS

Berkeley, California
October, 1967

COXEY'S ARMY

CHAPTER I

The "heart-breaking nineties" were packed with grim facts that tried men's souls — hard times, business failures, mortgaged farms, and labor disturbances. Corn selling at ten or fifteen cents a bushel in Kansas was cheaper to burn than coal. The tenant farmer in the South who obtained his supplies by giving the storekeeper a lien on his crop saw no prospect of paying up his account with five-cent cotton. In the industrial centers the laborer frequently faced the alternative of a reduced wage scale or a strike — and often, after a period of idleness, the reduced scale had to be accepted. In the summer of 1892 the historic strike in the Carnegie Steel Works at Homestead resulted in a pitched battle between the strikers and three hundred Pinkerton detectives sent to guard the plant and to protect "scab" labor. In July the representatives of disgruntled farmers and wage earners met in a national convention of the People's Party to demand relief from their oppressors, the monopolists and plutocrats who loaned them money and foreclosed mortgages, or who lived in luxury while the laboring man lacked the necessities of life. In November these Populists polled a million votes for General Weaver — three times Cleveland's plurality over Harrison.

In April of 1893 the gold reserve in the United States Treasury fell below a hundred million dollars, the amount set by law and tradition as a safe fund for the redemption of the outstanding paper currency, and the watching friends of the gold standard were uneasy; in May came the failure of the National Cordage Company, which only five months before had declared a stock dividend of one hundred per cent., and the storm broke. The result was perhaps the most severe financial crisis through which this country had passed, with runs on the banks, business failures, and unemployment following in its wake.

On March 25, 1894, Coxey's army of the unemployed began its march to Washington to demand of Congress the passage of measures for the relief of starving workmen, and soon "industrial armies" from the Far West took up the long pilgrimage to the national capital. Before they had all arrived or disbanded, the strike that had started in the Pullman works near Chicago threatened to paralyze the whole railroad system of the United States; mobs destroyed Pullman cars, attacked strike breakers, and flouted the "blanket injunction" issued by a Federal Court; Eugene V. Debs, president of the American Railway Union, was arrested and imprisoned; and President Cleveland, over the protests of Governor Altgeld, sent in the United States army to end the disturbance.

It was a busy year for our little peace-time regular army, with Coxey armies stealing trains to carry them eastward, overawing local authorities who were often too sympathetic to do anything about it, even if they were able, and with truculent strikers, or mobs that passed for strikers, in open resistance to authority. These disturbances caused the most extensive troop movements since the Civil War, and Major General Schofield, in command of the army, reported that before they were over the resources of the army were strained to the uttermost to maintain order.[1]

To many good citizens these ominous outbreaks and the conditions that underlay them appeared to threaten very serious consequences. In less troublous times, secure in our knowledge of the outcome, we may smile at some of the alarmist predictions of those trying years. But it is not altogether surprising that many timid or conservative persons should have been a bit jumpy about it, and that they should have conjured up bogies of anarchists with bombs or socialists with insidious propaganda (there were as yet no Bolsheviki to affright them) or Populists with wild schemes of reform — all bent upon the subversion of the established order — or that some thoughtful and intelligent individuals should have trembled for the safety of republican institutions.

Nor was their alarm altogether groundless. The smoke in which they saw or imagined these fantastic figures arose from the smoldering fires of discontent among millions of the less fortunate classes. A blaze was soon to burst forth furiously and sweep the West and South like a great prairie fire, threatening to consume Eastern creditors, plutocrats, and the "gold bugs" of Wall Street, until, as the New York *Nation* put it after the free silver campaign of 1896, William Jennings Bryan had caused more fear without taking human life than any other man in history.

For several years before Bryan, as the leader of the silver forces, refused to permit the crucifixion of humanity upon a cross of gold, there were many strange

---

[1] "Report of the Secretary of War, 1894", 53rd Cong., 3rd Sess., "House Executive Document" No. 1, Part 2, Vol. I, pp. 3, 4, 59.

manifestations of unrest among dissatisfied farmers and industrial laborers. These workers enrolled themselves among the downtrodden because they were denied what they regarded as their fair share of this world's goods. Many who despaired of helping themselves by their own efforts alone were ready to follow any leader who proposed a plausible remedy and tried to organize a following, thereby converting an inarticulate clamor into a "movement."

Of the many picturesque and curious movements produced by the economic discontent of that period, none was stranger or more fascinating than the march of the unemployed armies. Coxey's "Commonweal of Christ" marched out of Massillon, Ohio, on a chilly Easter Sunday, with flags and symbolical banners flying, followed by nearly half as many reporters as there were "soldiers." The Western industrial armies stole trains and kept the country through which they passed in a state of anxiety or enthusiasm — again, in most cases, without taking human life. They were crusaders bent on a mission suggested by their leaders in response to their needs. The purposes actuating these organized bodies of marchers are indicative of several phases of the economic maladjustment from which the United States then suffered. They are related, on the one hand, to the agrarian movement that dominated Populism, and, on the other, to the grievances of the suffering laborers in the mining and industrial centers.

The restlessness in the less prosperous agricultural regions had been brewing for several years. Dissatisfied farmers, complaining that the burden of mortgages on their farms was greater than they could bear, and that the price of their crops was too low, joined Farmers'

Alliances and other organizations that gave them an opportunity to air their grievances and devise means of redress. They wanted, among other things, a plentiful currency that would enable them to dispose of their products at prices that would bring them a profit and leave something to pay their debts. If the Government would not print more paper money, they were ready to indorse the demand of the Far Western producers of silver for the free and unlimited coinage of their bullion into silver dollars.

Out of these conditions sprang the Populist Party, which held its first national convention at Omaha on the Fourth of July, 1892, to give voice to the complaints and the demands of the discontented. They blamed the financial system that enabled bankers and factory owners to amass great fortunes while poor men suffered, and they attributed to capitalism and plutocracy all the diabolical qualities of intentional oppressors. The platform adopted at Omaha was distinctly of the type that views with alarm.

We meet — it read — in the midst of a nation brought to the verge of moral, political, and material ruin. Corruption dominates the ballot-box, the legislatures, the Congress, and touches even the ermine of the bench. The people are demoralized. . . . The newspapers are largely subsidized or muzzled; public opinion silenced; business prostrated; our homes covered with mortgages; labor impoverished; and the land concentrated in the hands of capitalists. . . . The fruits of the toil of millions are boldly stolen to build up colossal fortunes for the few, unprecedented in the history of mankind; and the possessors of these, in turn, despise the republic and endanger liberty. From the same prolific womb of governmental injustice are bred the two great classes of tramps and millionaires.

This Populist "uprising of the people" attained the religious fervor of a crusade for the betterment of mankind. Prophets of the discontent preached various panaceas to avert impending disaster — notably the "free silver" cure for financial ailments. The Omaha platform contained a plea for the free and unlimited coinage of silver dollars, along with the demand for more paper money. Much of the Populist program, indeed, was made up of items such as postal savings banks and the popular election of United States senators which, although they seemed radical measures to the conservatives of that time, are accepted as a matter of course to-day; and the more extreme proposals were relatively mild by comparison with the more violent types of radicalism. But Populist orators (who were often much less unamiable in action than in speech) spoke as if they believed in bloody reprisals if their grievances were not redressed. Governor Waite of Colorado declaimed that it was better to wade in blood to the horses' bridles than that the people's liberties should be destroyed, and Mrs. Mary Ellen Lease of Kansas told the farmers that it was time "to quit raising corn and begin raising Hell."

At the time when this agrarian movement was organizing for political battle, the commercial and manufacturing centers of the country were passing through one of those periods of specious prosperity which usually precede industrial crises. Then came the disastrous panic of 1893. In the lean year that followed, the plight of the wage earner was worse than that of the farmer. Factories and mines closed down and business of all kinds stagnated. Hundreds of thousands of wage earners were thrown out of work, and by the end of the year 1893 the ranks of the unemployed were swollen to two million men or more.[1]

Jobless men without visible means of support flocked from the outlying districts into the cities in search of work, only to find that there was not enough employment for the workers already there. The less skillful and the shiftless suffered first, but after a few months the scant savings of the more competent and thrifty were exhausted, and the wolf was at the door. Some of them objected to working at other occupations than their own trades, or for less than union wages, for their pride as American workmen or as union members made them feel that it was degrading to do hard or disagreeable work for a smaller remuneration than they considered reasonable, and this doubtless caused destitution in some cases where a bare subsistence might have been obtained if they had been less squeamish.[2] But the hard fact remained that in the localities where industrial workers congregated there were many more applicants than jobs.

This situation during the first cheerless winter after

[1] "The Journal of the Knights of Labor" (Philadelphia), October 12, 1893, quotes Carrol D. Wright's report which gave the number as more than two million, and asserts that at the time of writing it was not less than three million, and again on January 4, 1894, it quotes the figures of Dunn's Business Agency which estimated the number at two million. Alfred S. Johnson (Ed.), "The Cyclopedic Review of Current History" (Buffalo, N. Y., 1894), Vol. IV, p. 139, quotes Bradstreet's estimate of 801,000 in 119 of the principal cities, and the more conservative total of something over a million. S. O. Preston, "Provision for or Treatment of the Unemployed", *Charities Review*, Vol. III, p. 218 (a paper read in December, 1893) estimated that fully twenty-five per cent. of the men ordinarily employed in manual labor were wholly or partially out of employment. The dependents of these men were variously estimated at from two to five times as many.

The distress was greatest in the manufacturing and mining centers and least in some of the New England cities and in the Old South. — See Report of Conference on the Relief of Unemployment, in *Journal of Social Science*, November, 1894, pp. 4 ff. "Cyclopedic Review of Current History", Vol. IV, p. 139.

[2] S. O. Preston, "Provision for or Treatment of the Unemployed", *Charities Review*, Vol. III, pp. 218, 219 (a paper read in December, 1893).

the panic strained the resources of charitable organizations to the breaking point. The New York *World* gave away more than a million loaves of bread, and the *Herald* distributed thousands of dollars worth of clothing.[1] Soup kitchens were established to help the poor keep body and soul together, but they attracted hordes of vagrants and they were objectionable as an encouragement to dependence. Municipalities in many cases provided work in the improvement of streets or parks at bare subsistence wages.[2] In Pittsburgh the funds collected by a relief committee were expended in employing as many as three to four thousand men on the improvements in Schenley and Highland parks at a dollar a day. Early in April, when the funds donated were exhausted, men continued to besiege the employment office after they were notified that no more of this work was to be had.[3] In Cincinnati only heads of families received a dollar a day; single men were permitted to work for meal and lodging tickets only. Denver maintained a municipal wood yard at which a destitute man might earn his meals and lodging by sawing wood for about three hours a day.[4] In San Francisco some of the unemployed were permitted to sweep streets for two half-days each week at a wage of a dollar and forty cents — enough to keep them alive for a week at the Salvation Army "Life Boat."[5] At Chicago, one bitter night in January, a thousand tramps, sheltered

[1] Henry Frank, "The Crusade of the Unemployed", *Arena*, Vol. X, p. 241 (July, 1894).

[2] *Journal of Social Science*, November, 1894, p. 6; Albert Shaw, "Relief for the Unemployed in American Cities", *Review of Reviews*, Vol. IX, pp. 29 *ff*. (January, 1894).

[3] Pittsburgh *Chronicle Telegraph*, January to April, 1894, *passim*.

[4] Albert Shaw, "Relief for the Unemployed in American Cities", *Review of Reviews*, Vol. IX, pp. 31–33.

[5] San Francisco *Chronicle*, November 8, 1893.

in the city hall, fought fiercely for the food brought in to them.[1]

Notwithstanding all these efforts at relief, the unemployment situation was still acute in the spring of 1894, and idle workingmen continued the search for a means of livelihood. Large numbers of them traveled long distances looking for an opportunity to earn wages. Many of them, even in better times, had probably never acquired the habit of paying railroad fares when they moved from place to place. They regarded this practice as an unnecessary extravagance, for there were always freight trains, with cars that had trucks and rods for the emergencies when the more sumptuous "side-door Pullman" accommodations proved impracticable, and passenger trains with "blind baggages" when speed was essential. These men were accustomed to utilize what facilities were offered by the good nature of train crews, sometimes smoothing over difficulties by small tips, or by their own skill at concealment. This method of travel involved discomfort and inconvenience, and a considerable element of danger, but no expense except for subsistence along the way, and to a great extent even this might be avoided if the workingman was not too proud to avail himself of the generosity of the general public in the form of "handouts."[2]

[1] Chicago *Tribune*, quoted in Pittsburgh *Chronicle Telegraph*, January 11, 1894.
On the unemployment situation in 1893 and 1894, see, in addition to the references already cited, Carlos C. Closson, Junior, "The Unemployed in American Cities", *Quarterly Journal of Economics*, Vol. VIII, pp. 168–217 (January; 1894); G. E. Hooker, "The Unemployed in Boston", *Independent*, Vol. XLVI, pp. 487, 488 (April, 1894); John J. McCook, "The Unemployed", *Charities Review*, Vol. III, pp. 236 *ff.* (March, 1894); "The Unemployed: A Symposium", *Arena*, Vol. X, pp. 701–720.

[2] For descriptions of some of these methods of travel, see Charmian London, "The Book of Jack London" (New York, 1921), Vol. I, pp. 153–156; Jack London, "A Jack London Diary: Tramping with Kelly through Iowa", *Palimpsest*, Vol. VIII, pp. 129–139 (May, 1926). See also the series of stories by Jack London in the

An honest workingman, travel-stained and grimy from his journey, making his surreptitious descent from a box car, lying in wait for the next freight, or coming out of the yards to see what the town afforded in the way of a job or a meal, might not always appear to the casual observer, or the policeman, to be distinguishable from a professional vagrant, for he was not dressed to put up at a good hotel without an argument; if he carried any hand luggage it was usually tied in a bundle; and he had no visible means of support. The itinerant laborer, however, was a distinctly different type from the habitual "knight of the road" who was permanently averse to work and frequently averse to water.

The tramp lived by his wits at the expense of society. He considered labor both degrading and unnecessary. He knew well how to "throw his feet" for a "handout" at a charitable back door, where, if he had good luck, he might obtain enough to share with the companions whom he had described to the sympathetic housewife as his motherless children. Better yet was a "set down" at the table in some hospitable kitchen, where he might avail himself of the best the farm could offer. Often the price of his meal was the entertainment of an audience that liked to hear a good story, to have its sympathies aroused, or to experience the satisfaction of having done a good deed. If he was an adept at his profession he was something of a practical psychologist who had had experience in reading character at sight; an artist at the extemporaneous manufacture of the

Cosmopolitan, May to December, 1907: "My Life in the Underworld", Vol. XLIII, pp. 17–22; "Holding Her Down", *ibid.*, pp. 142–150; "Pictures: Stray Memories of Life in the Underworld", *ibid.*, pp. 513–518; "The March of Kelly's Army", *ibid.*, pp. 643–648; "Hoboes that Pass in the Night", *ibid.*, Vol. XLIV, pp. 190–197. These articles are assembled in Jack London's book "The Road" (New York, 1907).

particular kind of heart-rending past that would appeal to the audience that appeared after he had knocked on the door; and a genius at explanation if he inadvertently failed to make his story cohere. He knew how to make himself comfortable in the open or in any shelter that was available without cost. In good weather it was a free, easy, and irresponsible life, with attractions for men who had learned it but who might have done better things. Such a man might be anything from a harmless wanderer to a hardened criminal.

Tramps who traveled by rail developed marvelous skill in ensconcing themselves upon the trucks of moving trains (which in those days were constructed more conveniently for this purpose than they are now), in tucking themselves away in empty ice compartments of refrigerator cars, and in other arts of concealed travel. It took a firm grip and a practiced eye to board a fast-moving train, and the men who had them despised the "walking bums" who lacked the skill and nerve to do as they did. Occasionally speed or distance was miscalculated, or a hold slipped when fingers were numbed by the cold. Rarely a heartless brakeman who had had bitter experience with brutal hoboes would try the only known method of getting a man out of the trucks without stopping the train—let down under the car on the end of a rope a heavy coupling pin that would bound viciously off the ties until the iron found its mark. Then a track walker would find mangled remains for an obscure burial.

The tramp was a familiar and picturesque character of the period. His number had been increasing rapidly since the seventies until, in the early nineties, it was estimated that there were from forty to sixty thousand

professional hoboes in the United States. These vagrants were not only a menace to hen roosts and a source
of anxiety to farmers' wives and railroads, but they
were a social problem of sufficient interest to be studied
and written about. In addition to the cartoons and
squibs that featured the tramp, and the ubiquity of the
species, the reading public was treated to enough serious dissertations upon the subject to be made fully
aware that there was a tramp problem.[1]

The extensive unemployment after the panic of 1893
caused more men to take to the road, and for longer
periods, than in normal times, and no doubt many who
had previously worked for a living discovered that it
was unnecessary, and stayed. Thus the line of de-
marcation between tramps and wandering workingmen
was vague, although the distinction between the types
is clear. The confusion in newspaper and other accounts which indiscriminately applied the term
"tramp" or "hobo" to itinerant or unemployed workmen often makes it difficult to distinguish the migra-
tions of the seekers for work from the movements of
those who were trying to avoid it, even after events
occurred that were striking enough to focus the public

---

[1] On the tramp problem, see Josiah Flynt, "What to do with the Tramp", *Century*, Vol. XLVIII, pp. 794–796 (September, 1894); C. S. Denny, "The Whipping Post for Tramps", *ibid.*, Vol. XLIX, p. 794 (March, 1895); E. Hofer, "The Tramp Problem", *Overland Monthly*, Vol. XXIII, pp. 628–632 (June, 1894); John J. Mc-Cook, "Tramps", *Charities Review*, Vol. III, pp. 57–69 (December, 1893); John J. McCook, "A Tramp Census and its Revelations", *Forum*, Vol. XV, pp. 753–766 (August, 1893); Carlos C. Closson, "The Tramp", *Arena*, Vol. X, pp. 709, 710 (October, 1894); Samuel Lane Loomis, "The Tramp Problem", *Chautauquan*, Vol. XIX, pp. 308–313 (June, 1894); *Review of Reviews*, Vol. XII, pp. 464–466 (October, 1895).

On tramp life during the nineties see Josiah Flynt, "Tramping with Tramps", *Century*, Vol. XLVII, pp. 99–108 (November, 1893); Jack London, "The Road" (New York, 1907), or the series of articles in the *Cosmopolitan* during 1907; Jack Black, "You Can't Win" (New York, 1927) — the story of a reformed "yegg."

attention upon the composition of the "industrial armies."

By the autumn of 1893 unemployed workingmen in the Far West were organizing to obtain free transportation. They traveled in bodies of from fifty to two or three hundred, with officers elected to conduct them to their destinations, and with a semi-military discipline. They put what money they had into a common fund, and each man received a ticket which entitled him to his share of anything that had been "begged or plundered." [1] Such gangs were too formidable to be withstood by train crews, and they forced the trains to carry them. When the railroads were complaisant, these men went where they wished without difficulty. The roads that objected refused to move the trains or sidetracked them, and sometimes called upon the local authorities to drive the intruders off.

The discipline and orderly appearance of these organizations frequently elicited favorable comment. A dispatch from San Bernardino, California, November 3, 1893, stated that three gangs of "tramps" aggregating three hundred fifty men had arrived at Colton on their way to New Orleans, where they expected to find work on the levees. They had started from San Francisco and had received many recruits on the way.

Many of them appear to be honest. They are well organized into companies, with captains and regular roll calls.

[1] San Francisco *Chronicle*, November 2, 3, 1893. "The Journal of the Knights of Labor", December 7, 1893, contained the following notice:

"Only a few Chinese have been deported from Los Angeles, Cal., while thousands of unemployed white men have rushed here in the vain hope of being able to earn a living. They come in armies of from 100 to 250, taking charge of whole trains. So L. A. 2405 takes this method of warning our brothers to give Los Angeles a wide berth until the People's Party can control national legislation."

The officers serve two meals each day, all sharing alike when they have anything to eat.

They secure food by sending delegations to the authorities of the cities through which they pass. Such a delegation visited this city and was given a hundred pounds of bacon, sacks of potatoes, beans, coffee, etc., which were conveyed to their camping grounds. Southern Pacific officials permit them to ride on freight cars.

Their appearance and orderly conduct enlists general sympathy, and their wants are being supplied. They made a stop here to secure provisions to carry them across the deserts of Arizona and New Mexico.[1]

The captain of a "tramp party" that traveled southward from Portland, Oregon, was reported to have made the statement:

We intend to go where we can get work. In our party are thirty-one loggers, fifteen miners, a railway ticket agent, two cooks, a waiter, and seven brakemen. Most of us came here from the Sound. We are honest men and want work. We can't get employment here and we do not want to impose on the good nature of the City Board of Charities any longer. Some of our party may be bad men, but I will promise that no one will violate the law. Most of our men are well educated, and I myself am a college graduate.

Either the leader of the party must have convinced

---

[1] A dispatch from Colton added that food had been given liberally by the citizens there, and that perfect order had been preserved. San Francisco *Chronicle*, November 4, 1893. For other similar cases of "tramp" traffic, see *ibid.*, November 23, 24, 25, December 2, 19, 1893. A band of forty on their way to work in the mines of Arizona carried their military organization to the point of posting guards to prevent any one from leaving camp without permission. Most of them were arrested by the sheriff for trying to ride on a train without payment of fares. "These men left Los Angeles three days ago in an organized body upon the representation that work could be had in the Prescott and Santa Fe, now building in Arizona. The agent of the contractors on that road wrote a letter to D. R. McDonell of the employment firm of Reed & Co. to send on forty men, and that the men could organize and beat their way over the railroads. In compliance with this letter forty men beat their way over the Southern Pacific to Colton, from which place they walked to San Bernardino. After fruitless attempts to catch a train in this city they tramped to Cajon." *Ibid.* November 25, 1894.

the chief of police at Portland that they were poor, honest men, or the chief must have seen advantages in allowing them to go elsewhere, for he obtained transportation for them across the Willamette so that they might catch a south-bound train.[1]

There were complaints that the tramp evil had become so serious that the Southern Pacific was about to take strenuous measures to check it, that the tramps used the trains as if they owned them, and that the railroad companies which put them off suffered loss through their malice. The San Francisco *Chronicle* asserted that the city of the Golden Gate was the objective of tramps from both north and south, the greater number coming from Oregon, where the people were giving every inducement to the vagrants to go to California, even praising the climate of the neighboring State to induce them to go thither.[2]

The semi-military organization of unemployed workingmen was not confined to these traveling contingents. In various cities the unemployed met and aired their grievances, sometimes under the auspices of radical leaders or parties, and sometimes more spontaneously.[3] Organization for mutual assistance naturally suggested itself, and armies of the unemployed were formed in cities where they were numerous. A document which contains what seem to be the minutes of two meetings at which one of these organizations was formed, throws much light upon the obscure origins of the industrial armies. The remarkably moderate tone of the speeches speaks well for the character of the men who promoted

[1] Portland *Oregonian*, quoted in San Francisco *Chronicle*, December 19, 1893.
[2] San Francisco *Chronicle*, December 19, 1893.
[3] For examples, see *Journal of the Knights of Labor*, September 14, October 12, 1893, January 18, 1894; "Cyclopedic Review of Current History", Vol. IV, p. 140.

this army, and their contents reflect the conditions that gave birth to the movement as well as the process by which the army came into being. It begins:[1]

A number of unemployed working men met in Miners Hall, on Thursday night, for the purpose of discussing matters pertaining to their interests.

One of the number named John, opened the meeting, saying, I have been out of work for more than six months and it is becoming a serious question with me if I will ever get work, my family and I have been economizing closely ever since I lost my situation, my children are to [sic] young to work even if they could get work to do; the question of economy is about played out as in a short time there will be nothing left to practice on. I have had pretty steady work all my life and never before suffered any serious inconvenience for want of it, but now in my enforced leisure and while going round looking for work I am pained and surprised to find many as bad, and many worse off than I am. The suffering from this cause is greater than I ever imagined it to be, and it is not confined to the time of idleness, but is continued long after work is obtained — continued in the endeavor to recover goods that have been parted with to procure present necessities and to again lay up some provision for the future. And now it seems to me, friends, that this is the fate of thousands upon thousands of working people; they work hard, live poor to save money, then comes a spell of idleness that eats up all their savings and when they get work again the same process is repeated. Some get discouraged get all broke up and take to drink — drink whenever and wherever they get the chance some take to stealing and after a while

[1] This manuscript is in the possession of the Wisconsin Historical Society. It is headed: "The Unemployed Army. Proceedings of Company A. First Regiment, Recorded by the faithful scribe Luke, Edited by Emgara." Above the title is written in a different hand, "By Adam Ramage", and the date, 1893. "Emgara" contains the letters of the name "Ramage", probably that of the editor who prepared the proceedings for printing. There is no indication of the place. The editor explains that for "obvious reasons the names here given are not given for the purpose of identifying the individual members, but simply to designate them", and he calls them John, James, Luke, etc.

are put in prison where they are a heap better off than to be on the streets out of work; but the worst of all is begging, when a man is reduced to the condition of a beggar he is low indeed. I can however sympathize with those who drink, steal and beg, now that I know myself what it is to be out of work and to see my means growing smaller every day and to see no prospect of bettering myself. Now friends that I have stated my case to you you have my reasons for asking you to meet me here tonight I sup[p]ose the right thing to do is to organize the meeting by the election of a chairman and a secretary.

A chairman being elected, he made a brief speech in which he expressed the belief "that all for whom there is work are at work now and that those who are idle are idle because under our present system there is no work for them and no way for them to get a living after they have used up their hard-earned savings except by begging or stealing", that something ought to be done, "grumbling or finding fault with others will avail us nothing", and he urged that some action be taken. A motion was made by one designated as Peter who said that he wished "to call attention to the fact that all industries are not controlled by a few individuals styled capitalists whose interests prompts [sic] them to employ the smallest possible number of workers and to exact the largest possible amount of labor from each worker." The result, he said, was that the army of the unemployed was growing and the burden on those who worked was increasing. He therefore asked for immediate action "to declare our rights and grievances and to demand that an opportunity be given us to earn our living." A committee was appointed to draw up the declaration, and the meeting was adjourned until a week later.

At the second meeting the declaration of rights and grievances was presented. A member of the committee that drafted it explained that "it will readily be seen that we have taken the Declaration of Independence and statement of grievances by the founders of our present government as the model and foundation of our work and indeed your committee is persuaded that the declaration is as true and just and the grievances are greater, flagrant, and harder — much harder to bear than any that ever were alleged against the tyranny of king George." The report of the committee was accepted with the understanding that it was to be discussed point by point in future meetings.[1]

The purpose of these two meetings was the same as that of the industrial armies which by the spring of 1894 were organized and drilling at Los Angeles and San Francisco and were forming elsewhere in the West. The earlier ones had probably formed independently of any impetus from the East — in fact, the idea of the march of the unemployed to the national capital seems to have been a western idea — but Jacob S. Coxey, of Massillon, Ohio, was the man who made it famous. The Ohio movement that bore his name affected the western armies to such an extent that they were generally known as "Coxey" armies, and, by some of them, at least, Coxey was considered the head of the whole affair.

[1] About half a page, containing the body of the declaration, has been cut out of the manuscript. At the end of the meeting it was voted that since the *Workmen's Advocate* of New York was "always ready to help along the cause of labor", the proceedings of the two meetings should be sent to it with the request to print them. This paper was the official organ of the Socialist Labor Party.

CHAPTER II

JACOB SECHLER COXEY AND HIS PROGRAM OF REFORM

Unemployment in the United States was an undoubted and an unpleasant fact, but the poor are always with us, and this fact might have been taken much more as a matter of course if it had not been for the unique advertising campaign instituted by Jacob Sechler Coxey. As an eminent journalist put it:

It seemed almost impossible to contrive any device by which this grim and worn-out topic could be served up in good saleable newspaper articles. But Coxey did the trick. Coxey compelled all the newspapers of the continent to devote from a column to six columns a day to reporting Coxeyism, that is to say, with echoing the inarticulate clamor for work for the workless. That was a great achievement. To have accomplished it shows that Coxey is not without genius. No millionaire in all America could, without ruining himself, have secured as much space for advertising his wares as Coxey commanded without the expenditure of a red cent by the unique device of his petition in boots.[1]

Taken literally, there were flaws in this statement. The stage was set when the chief actor appeared on it, for the conditions out of which Coxey's plan arose were too serious to be ignored. The movement was not entirely the work of any one man, but of many. Yet Coxey's enthusiasm, his ability to formulate a program, his financial means, and his instinct for advertising,

---

[1] W. T. Stead, "Coxeyism: A Character Sketch", *Review of Reviews*, Vol. X, p. 48.

led to the association of his name with the whole movement as that of its leader.

Coxey was an individual of local prominence before he became a character of national repute. He was born in Pennsylvania on Easter Sunday, April 16, 1854, at Selinsgrove, Snyder County. Five or six years later his parents moved to Danville. At the age of fifteen he quit school to go to work in the rolling mills, where, in the course of ten years, he acquired mechanical experience running a stationary engine.[1] Then, after a brief experiment as a dealer in scrap iron, he moved to Massillon, Ohio, where, in 1881, he founded the business that he still conducts. He purchased a sandstone quarry and prepared sand for steel and glass works. He also acquired extensive farming interests. On his stock farm in Kentucky he bred blooded horses and raced or sold them, which led unsympathetic critics to refer to him as a horse dealer of sporting propensities.[2] In 1894, therefore, Coxey was a successful, self-made business man who had accumulated a considerable fortune, being reputed among his neighbors to be worth $200,000; he had had experience both as an industrial laborer and as an employer; and he was in touch with the agricultural situation.[3]

Mr. Coxey's business career, however, was by no means his only major interest, for he was a congenital reformer, willing to spend both time and money to promote his plans for the betterment of the social order

[1] *Cause and Cure* (Coxey Good Roads and Non-Interest Bond Library), Vol. II, No. 2 (Massillon, Ohio, April, 1896), p. 15.
[2] New York *Nation*, Vol. LVIII, p. 264 (April 12, 1894); Chicago *Times*, May 4, 1894; Pittsburgh *Post*, March 28, 1894.
[3] This account is based upon Vincent, "Commonweal", p. 49; W. T. Stead, "Coxeyism", *Review of Reviews*, Vol. X, p. 52; and a brief autobiography dictated by Mr. Coxey for the writer on August 26, 1927, hereafter cited as "Coxey."

—and perhaps to satisfy his political aspirations. He had become interested in politics as a young man working in the rolling mills. The subject which especially interested him was the money question, then an important political issue. He inherited Democratic affiliations from his parents, at a time, according to his own statement, when the Democratic party believed "that the national banking system was wrong and that the government should not only coin money but issue it and get it direct to the people without the intervention of banks." In other words, he belonged to the greenback wing of the party. In 1876, when the Democratic Party departed from this faith and "sold out to Wall Street", he followed the principle rather than the party, and became a Greenbacker. In 1885 Coxey was a candidate for the State senate, basing his campaign upon the money-inflation issue. When the People's Party appeared, advocating free silver, paper money, and a long list of reforms, Coxey gave it his support, as most of the old Greenbackers and other money-inflationists did.[1]

In 1894, when every reader of a newspaper was having his attention turned to this interesting reformer and his fantastic project, Mr. Coxey had attained the age of forty. Representatives of the press, realizing the news value of personality, tried to let their readers know what manner of man he was. Business acquaintances in Pittsburgh, they said, described him as a shrewd business man with some hard sense in his head. He was also described as singularly tenacious of ideas upon which his mind was once set [2] — a diagnosis borne

[1] Coxey.

[2] Pittsburgh *Chronicle Telegraph*, March 22, 1894; Pittsburgh *Post*, March 25, 1894.

out by the fact that from 1894 to the present time he
has continued to advocate much the same ideas of reform.   In appearance he had the aspect of a "prosperous, sunburned farmer", not above medium size, well
dressed, with brown hair and a close-cropped mustache,
wearing rimless spectacles that gave him an air of quiet
respectability.   Voluble in speech, but not excitable,
he used argument rather than oratory to carry his point.
If he convinced his audience he did so apparently by
an air of quiet sincerity and by the plausibility of his
explanations rather than by any impressiveness of
manner or personal magnetism.[1]

No one can meet Mr. Coxey — wrote an unconvinced reporter — without being impressed with the wonderful ear-
nestness of the man.   While making the most astounding
statements his face does not betray the slightest indication
that he is announcing a surprising proposition; on the contrary he speaks as though it were a truth which should be
received as a matter of course.   He seems to be profoundly
impressed with the sufferings of mankind and with a belief
that there is a deep-laid plan of monopolists to crush the
poor to the earth.[2]

Coxey was a Greenbacker and a Populist, but he had
too much originality to follow a ready-made program
without offering suggestions of his own.   He was a firm
believer in the power of Congress to make irredeemable
paper money pass at its face value by endowing it with
legal-tender qualities.   Like his noted contemporary,
William Jennings Bryan, he felt that a more plentiful
currency would do much to relieve hard times and to
allay the misery that much of humanity was forced to

[1] Washington *Post*, April 23, 1894; Indianapolis *Journal*, April 23, 1894.
[2] Pittsburgh *Chronicle Telegraph*, March 22, 1894.

endure. Another aspect of his financial views appeared in his opposition to bondholders and national banks, and to "usury" in general — an attitude characteristic of Greenbackers and Populists and of various radical groups.

One dark and rainy night in December, 1891, when Mr. Coxey was driving home from Massillon, floundering in ruts and bottomless mud holes, he realized keenly the need of good roads. Suddenly the idea came to him that the only way to get a good road system was to have the Federal Government build it; and that Congress might exercise its constitutional right to issue money to pay for it. Combining his good-roads policy, his fiat-money ideas, and his desire to aid oppressed humanity by providing work for the unemployed, he developed his plan and embodied it in a bill which was introduced in Congress in 1892.[1]

The Good Roads Bill required the Secretary of the Treasury to issue five hundred million dollars in legal-tender notes to be expended upon the construction of good roads throughout the United States. The work was to be done under the direction of the Secretary of War, who was to spend the money at the rate of twenty million dollars per month, employing for this purpose all citizens of the United States who presented themselves, at a wage of a dollar and a half for an eight-hour day. This would give employment to all who needed it; it would put more money into circulation; and, incidentally, Coxey asserted, it would settle the eight-hour question then being agitated by labor organizations by bringing the Government into com-

---

[1] Coxey; Pittsburgh *Post*, March 25, 1894. *Cf.* "Coxey, His Own Story of the Commonweal" [1914], p. 45; Vincent, "Commonweal", p. 49.

petition with all employers who paid less or demanded longer hours.[1]

In order to promote his ideas Mr. Coxey organized the J. S. Coxey Good Roads Association of the United States, of which he became president.[2] In his correspondence with men interested in his plan, he began to receive complaints that while the Good Roads Bill was advantageous to the farmers, there was nothing in it for the cities. He had not thought of this, but he now set about to devise a remedy. The subject was on his mind when he went to bed on New Year's Eve, 1893. The solution came to him in a dream. He arose on New Year's morning, 1894, with a ready-made plan. "Browne," he exclaimed to the picturesque Westerner who was staying at his house, "I have it. I have solved the municipal improvement problem." He sat down and wrote it out. The result was the Non-interest-bearing Bond Bill.[3]

This second measure, more complicated than the first, provided another means of inflating the currency and of providing public improvements and employment. It was calculated to accomplish everything that was included in the first bill, and a great deal more. Coxey came to consider it the final solution of his problem, superseding the Good Roads Bill. It seems, however, that the Good Roads Bill received more public attention, partly, perhaps, because of its greater sim-

---

[1] *Cause and Cure*, Vol. II, No. 2, pp. 6, 10; Vincent, "Commonweal", pp. 51, 52; Osman C. Hooper, "The Coxey Movement in Ohio", *Ohio Archeological and Historical Society Publications*, Vol. IX, p. 160.

[2] Vincent, "Commonweal", p. 49; Stead, "Coxeyism", *Review of Reviews*, Vol. X, p. 52; Shirley Plumer Austen, "Coxey's Commonweal Army", *Chautauquan*, Vol. XIX, p. 332. The first bulletin of the association, giving the text of the Good Roads Bill, is dated December 7, 1893.—"Coxey, His Own Story", p. 45.

[3] Coxey.

plicity, and partly because it had appeared earlier, supported by the Good Roads Association. Coxey continued, throughout 1894, to push both measures, one with the emphasis on good roads, and the other with the emphasis on municipal improvements.

The Non-interest-bearing Bond Bill authorized any State, territory, county, township, or municipality which needed public improvements to issue non-interest-bearing bonds to the extent of half the assessed value of the property within its limits. These bonds might then be deposited with the Secretary of the Treasury as security for a loan of legal-tender notes to be issued by him for this purpose. This would furnish money for the construction of city streets, country roads, schools, courthouses, and other similar projects. The principal of the loan was to be repaid without interest in twenty-five annual installments of four per cent. each, to be raised by taxation, and as these installments came into the treasury, the money of which they consisted was to be cancelled and retired from circulation. At the end of the twenty-five year period, therefore, the bonds would be redeemed and the money for which they were a security would be retired. A provision similar to that in the Good Roads Bill required that the work on these public improvements must be paid for at a rate of not less than a dollar and a half for an eight-hour day, and that all idle men who offered to work must be employed on these terms.[1]

In a speech at Williamsport, Maryland, while his army was on the march to Washington, Coxey described the intended results of this measure as follows:

[1] For the text of this bill, see *Cause and Cure*, Vol. II, No. 2, pp. 5, 6; Vincent, "Commonweal", pp. 52, 53; Hooper, *Op. Cit.*, Vol. IX, pp. 161. 162.

This will enable the states, counties, townships, municipalities, towns or villages, to make all the public improvements that they will need for all time to come without paying one cent of tribute to any one in the shape of usury. They will be enabled to build their statehouses, their insane asylums, courthouses, infirmaries and schoolhouses. All municipalities can build their own market houses, public libraries, museums, enginehouses, schoolhouses, and public halls where people can come and discuss all questions that interest them; pave their own streets; own and build their own electric light plants, water works, street railroads, and other public improvements that are a convenience and comfort, and promote the advancement of the whole people.

After this system of public improvements is inaugurated it will settle the money question, as it will supply all the money needed for the public convenience, and to develop the resources of the country, and not one dollar can go into circulation without a service being rendered and the value credited to the government direct in the shape of public improvements, which will be beneficial to all.

This will supply actual money in place of confidence money. This will substitute a cash system for a credit or script system. The business of this country has been done on confidence money. Now that the confidence has vanished, business has also vanished.[1]

The last paragraph demands further explanation of Coxey's ideas of money and banking. The "confidence money" mentioned in this speech — or "credit money", as he described it elsewhere — consisted of commercial paper, the evidence of business transacted on credit. For example, he said, when a Pittsburgh steel manufacturer took notes from a purchaser in payment for his product, promising pay three or four months later, these notes served the purpose of money, because they had "exchanged the products from the steel manufac-

[1] Vincent, "Commonweal", pp. 53, 54.

turer to the jobber, or consumer, . . . just the same as though he had paid actual money for it." The manufacturer then discounted these notes at a bank, where he received credit, subject to check. Coxey estimated that in 1893 the banks had nine dollars of this credit money to every dollar of real money in their reserves. When confidence disappeared, and depositors demanded real money from the banks, of course there was not enough to pay them. Coxey was able to cite many specific cases of the impossibility of getting cash for credit at the banks during the business depression after the panic, and he gave examples of employers who were unable to pay wages because the banks refused to cash their checks.

This led Coxey to compare the uncertainties of credit money as a medium of exchange with the alleged advantages of a legal-tender currency plentiful enough to permit the transaction of all business on a cash basis. This, he said, would avoid disturbance of the medium of exchange by bankers' panics. The legal-tender notes which he demanded were to be paid out for work on public improvements of various kinds; this work, he asserted, would create value, and thus this money would represent value already in existence when the money began to circulate.[1]

Much of Coxey's scheme consisted of ideas that were more or less in the air at the time.[2] He assembled them

[1] Coxey gave a detailed explanation of his financial ideas at a hearing before a sub-committee of the Committee on Ways and Means of the House of Representatives, Jan. 8, 1895. W. J. Bryan was chairman of the sub-committee. Doubtless some of the details of his theories had been thought out since 1894, but the essentials remained the same. The official report of this hearing was reprinted by Coxey in *Cause and Cure*, Vol. II, No. 2, pp. 6-21.

[2] Letters from Albert A. Pope, of Boston, printed in the *Journal of the Knights of Labor*, Sept. 14 and Oct. 26, 1893, on the problem of unemployment, suggest that State legislatures and county and town authorities might put the unemployed to

into a system, and did what he could to advance them. The next step was to convert the public to his way of thinking — at first a discouraging task. The idea which enabled him to give his scheme nation-wide publicity seems to have been suggested by the picturesque Westerner who became Coxey's right-hand man.

At the silver convention held in Chicago in the summer of 1893, Coxey met Carl Browne, a man whose training and abilities fitted him well to agitate a set of radical reforms before rough-and-ready audiences. In the course of his varied past he had been printer, painter, cartoonist, editor, rancher, politician and labor agitator. He was born on July 4, 1849, at Newton, Iowa, where his father, a veteran of the Mexican and Civil wars, had been town marshal. Early in his career he developed ability as a clever cartoonist. He soon drifted to the Pacific coast, where he became an active member of the Workingmen's Party, participating in the demonstrations on the San Francisco "sand lots" against cheap Chinese labor. He became the private secretary of Dennis Kearny, the leader of the anti-Chinese disturbances. For a time he was editor and cartoonist of a weekly radical labor organ, *The Open Letter*.[1]

work on public works, especially highways, and that the irrigation of western lands by the Federal Government would help solve the problem. The last suggestion was included in the demands of some of the western industrial armies. At a large meeting of some of the unemployed at Chicago, it was demanded that the government issue circulating medium to the people, and employ idle men on roads and other

---

[1] An article in the *National Union Printer*, March 31, 1894, by a writer who claimed to have been a member of the executive committee of the Workingmen's Party at the time, asserted that Browne employed "rat" labor at less than union wages on this publication; that Browne and Kearney refused to remedy this condition; and that the resulting row broke up the Workingmen's Party. He also asserted that both Browne and Kearney were mixed up in another graft—soliciting funds for a labor temple that was never built. — Quoted in Pittsburgh *Chronicle Telegraph*, April 10, 1894. For General Charles T. Kelly's opinion of Browne, see below, p. 189, note 2.

Browne's picturesque appearance made him a conspicuous figure wherever he went. Tall, heavy, and bearded, his unkempt dark hair streaked with gray, he added to the effect by wearing an exaggerated Western costume. It consisted of a buckskin coat with fringes, and buttons made of Mexican silver half-dollars, high boots, a sombrero, a fur cloak when the weather permitted, and around his neck, instead of a collar, a string of amber beads, the gift of his dying wife. "It was such a costume," wrote a reporter, "as a bad actor would use in playing the rôle of a wild and woolly cowboy." [1] Closer inspection revealed the reason why his men called him "Old Greasy." It was suggested that he would have been a more pleasant companion if he had bathed oftener. One observer described him as a "great, big, strong fellow with a hearty bass voice, part fakir, part religionist, part Wild West cowboy, and withal a natural leader of men." [2] Samuel L. Gompers later wrote of him: "He was a man of parts, a big-hearted lover of men, a dreamer and an idealist." [3] He had a bluff, hearty manner that seemed to take well with the type of men he was soon to command. Altogether he seems to have been an

---

public improvements. *Ibid.*, Aug. 24, 1893. The sixteenth plank in the preamble of the Knights of Labor read: "That interest-bearing bonds, bills of credit, or notes, shall never be issued by the government, but that, when need arises, the emergency shall be met by issue of legal tender, non-interest bearing money." *Ibid.*, Dec. 28, Feb. 22, 1893. Officials of the Knights of Labor even went so far as to try to get a court order to make the Secretary of the Treasury show cause why he should not be restrained from making an issue of bonds. *Ibid.*, Jan. 26, Feb. 1, 1894. As General Howard pointed out, "the notion that those who occupy the seats of power can issue fiat money is . . . the doctrine of a large number of our citizens." Major-General O. O. Howard, "The Menace of Coxeyism. The Significance and Aims of the Movement", *North American Review*, Vol. CLVIII, p. 688.

[1] Pittsburgh *Press*, March 25, 1894.
[2] A. Cleveland Hall, "An Observer in Coxey's Camp", *Independent*, Vol. XLVI, p. 615 (May 17, 1894).
[3] Samuel L. Gompers, "Seventy Years of Life and Labor" (2 Vols., New York, 1925), Vol. II, p. 11.

individual of much native ability and force, and it was the opinion of some who knew or studied him that with proper training he might have advanced far in some more dignified career than that of radical agitator. It will soon appear that his personality and ideas were as bizarre as his appearance. Emotional and vituperative, he was an effective stump orator before the kind of crowd he delighted to address. Here was an excellent foil to the quiet and not undignified Coxey, whose appeal was to the intellect rather than to the emotions.[1]

The acquaintance of Browne and Coxey soon ripened into friendship. Coxey saw in the Westerner a man who had great possibilities as a popularizer of his reforms. He obtained Browne's services as a campaigner for the Good Roads Bill in the late summer and fall of '93. Browne went about with his "financial panorama", a series of cartoons illustrating the evils of the existing economic system and the good times that would be ushered in by the proposed legislation.[2] He attached it to a framework on the wagon in which it was carried from place to place, and lectured from it after the manner of a patent medicine salesman displaying and describing his wares. Coxey asked Browne to stay with him during the winter of 1893–1894, and the two men pondered plans for saving the country, and ways and means for popularizing their ideas.

The inspiration was not long lacking. According to

---

[1] On Browne's history and characteristics see: Vincent, "Commonweal", pp. 109 ff.; Austen, "Coxey's Commonweal Army", *Chautauquan*, Vol. XIX, pp. 332 ff.; Stead, "Coxeyism", *Review of Reviews*, Vol. X, p. 52; Washington *Post*, April 23, 1894; Chicago *Tribune*, May 6, 1894; Chicago *Times*, May 2, 1894; Colfax [Iowa] *Clipper*, quoted in Des Moines *Weekly Iowa State Register*, April 27, 1894; Pittsburgh *Press*, March 24, 1894; Vincent, "The Coxey Movement", *Official Souvenir of the People's Party Convention, 1896* (Milwaukee, 1896), p. 29.

[2] Coxey.

Coxey's statement, it came one day when he and Browne were driving to the sandstone quarry. They talked of methods of attracting national attention to the Good Roads Bill. Browne, in the course of the conversation, described the marches of the unemployed to demand relief in California. This suggested an idea to Coxey. "Browne," he said, "we will send a petition to Washington with boots on." [1] The idea of the "petition in boots", however, was commonly attributed to Browne alone, and according to newspaper reports he admitted that he was its sole author. The story ran that he had long cherished the notion of a march to the national Capitol, but that lack of funds prevented its execution. Coxey had the money to finance the venture, and Browne suggested that they join issues. [2]

At any rate, the decision was made to march an unemployed army to Washington — a living petition in favor of Coxey's scheme to provide fiat money, good roads, and work for the workless. The Good Roads Association, promoted during the last part of the year 1893, provided an organization that could play a useful part in spreading the reformers' propaganda. The plans matured quickly, and the time was set early in the spring of 1894.

[1] Coxey: cf. "Passing of Carl Browne", on last page of "Coxey, His Own Story"; Vincent, "Commonweal", p. 49. The origin of the phrase "petition in boots" led to various speculations. W. T. Stead attributed it to Professor Hourwitch of the University of Chicago, who compared the march of Coxey's army to the "petition in boots" of the Russian peasants, when they marched in bodies to present their grievances. — Stead, "Coxeyism", *Review of Reviews*, Vol. X, p. 48. Henry Vincent asserted that L. L. Polk, ex-President of the Farmer's Alliance and Industrial Union, had suggested the idea of a living petition to Congress, and that Polk on one occasion, deploring the inaction of Congress in regard to petitions, remarked: "We will send one with boots on," but Vincent doubts that Coxey ever heard of Polk's idea or his phrase. Vincent, "Commonweal", p. 16.

[2] Austen, "Coxey's Commonweal Army", *Chautauquan*, quoted in *Review of Reviews*, Vol. X, p. 64; Pittsburgh *Chronicle Telegraph*, April 17, 1894.

CHAPTER III

After Coxey had formulated his program and Browne and Coxey had between them hatched the idea of the march to Washington, the next step was to collect and organize an army of marchers.

At first it seems to have been Browne's intention that Chicago should be the starting point.[1] He was already known in that locality as a promoter of "Industrial Legions"—local organizations of a secret order of radical Populists formed after the election of 1892 to propagate the principles of the Omaha platform.[2] In August of 1893, at about the time when Browne and Coxey met at the Silver Convention, Browne began to address a series of open-air meetings in Lake Front Park, where he entertained the crowds with the aid of his "financial panorama."[3] In these Chicago speeches

[1] Vincent, "Commonweal", pp. 112, 113, 174; Pittsburgh *Post*, March 25, 1894.

[2] Browne had been working with the national commander of the Industrial Legion of the United States, Paul Vandervoort of Nebraska, a former commander in chief of the Grand Army of the Republic. The organization of the Industrial Legion was modeled closely upon that of the Grand Army. Another prominent member was H. E. Taubeneck of Illinois, chairman of the People's Party National Committee.—Fred E. Haynes, "Third Party Movements Since the Civil War, with Special Reference to Iowa" (Iowa City, 1916), pp. 270, 271.

[3] An account of a mass meeting on the Lake Front, printed in the *Journal of the Knights of Labor*, August 24, 1893, probably refers to one of the assemblages at which Browne held forth. The resolutions adopted suggest parts of the Coxey program, demanding, among other things, that Congress should issue a circulating medium direct to the people, that idle men should be employed on roads and other public improvements where convict labor had been used and that the hours of labor ought to be reduced until all could be employed. This meeting decided to parade through the streets, carrying the banners of various labor unions, and demanding work of the city.

Browne is said to have suggested a march of the unemployed to the capital. To him, also, is attributed a prominent part in obtaining for Chicago the national convention of the American Federation of Labor in December of 1893.[1] At this meeting he secured the American Federation's formal indorsement of the Good Roads Bill.[2]

Browne's work in Chicago was so effective that he was soon in hot water with the city authorities. Mayor Harrison prohibited the continuance of the meetings. When Browne and some of his supporters called upon the mayor to protest against his action, that dignitary made sport of the Westerner's leather coat and sombrero, receiving in reply a series of ready retorts as well as dissertations upon the constitutional rights of free assemblage and free speech. The upshot of the controversy was that Browne was banished from the city. The State Central Committee of the People's Party indorsed Browne as a national organizer of Industrial Legions, and appointed a committee to complain to the governor about the mayor's alleged violation of the right of free assembly, but the mayor was obdurate. Browne, however, soon found the means to return in

---

[1] Vincent, "Commonweal", p. 174. Vincent asserts that "the idea of the national meeting of the Federation of Labor convened in Chicago, December 12, 1893, may be placed to his [Browne's] credit."

[2] *Ibid.*, 112; *Cause and Cure*, Vol. II, No. 2, p. 23; *Cyclopedic Review of Current History*, Vol. IV, p. 310. The resolution adopted by the A. F. of L., December 15, 1893, reads that "Whereas, a bill is now before Congress intended to provide work for the idle, . . ." (Quoting Coxey's Good Roads Bill), and since a petition in its favor is being circulated throughout the United States for signature, it is resolved "That the American Federation of Labor declares in favor of the bill, not only as a relief for the unemployed, but a lasting good in providing good roads everywhere."— "Report of the Proceedings of the Thirteenth Annual Convention of the American Federation of Labor", 1893 (New York, 1894), pp. 45, 46. See also Edward W. Bemis, "The Convention of the American Federation of Labor", *Journal of Political Economy*, Vol. II, p. 299.

disguise, with a copy of Coxey's bill, but without his leather coat, to continue the agitation. He was befriended by a patent medicine fakir, one A. P. B. Bozarro. This shrewd worthy, doubtless aware of Browne's knack of attracting an audience that might part with money in the interest of health, permitted Browne to act as his assistant and to hold forth upon his favorite themes to the crowd assembled in a vacant lot to learn the virtues of the great Kickapoo Indian blood remedy.[1] Browne was now ready to organize an unemployed army in Chicago.

In the meantime Coxey decided that his home town of Massillon ought to have the honor of initiating the movement, and the base of operations was shifted to Ohio. Browne moved to Coxey's home, and during the winter of 1893–1894 they planned and made preparations. They held public meetings in Massillon and its neighborhood to disseminate their ideas, and they entered local politics, drawing up a platform and naming a ticket for the city election.[2] On January 23, 1894, the plan of campaign was published in a local paper. Coxey's bills were to be introduced in Congress in March, and the army of the unemployed was to leave Massillon on Easter Sunday, gather recruits along the way, and arrive in Washington in time for a great demonstration on the steps of the Capitol at noon of May 1. An extensive advertising campaign was commenced. Quantities of pamphlets and circulars were sent out; it was estimated that Coxey's printing bill before his army marched amounted to $2,000; and the very nov-

[1] S. P. Austen, "Coxey's Commonweal Army", *Chautauquan*, Vol. XIX, pp. 332, 333; Vincent, "Commonweal", pp. 112, 113, 174; Pittsburgh *Chronicle-Telegraph*, April 16, 1894.
[2] Vincent, "Commonweal", p. 50.

elty of the proposed expedition brought it plenty of free publicity.[1]

The announced purpose of the march was to secure the passage by Congress of the Good Roads Bill and the Non-interest-bearing Bond Bill, but there was another aspect of the affair that threatened almost to displace Coxey's cherished schemes. Browne had religious ideas more curious than his appearance or his past, which he called theosophy. They included a peculiar theory of reincarnation. He was aware of the fact that the human body is made up of chemical elements which, after death, return to earth in the form of inorganic compounds — return to "nature's reservoirs." By analogy he applied the idea to the spirit as well as the flesh. He taught that at death the human soul entered a reservoir "like a huge cauldron" which contained a mixture of all the souls that had gone before. When a child was born, it was provided from this reservoir with enough soul to serve the purpose. Each person, therefore, was a fractional reincarnation of the souls of all who had died before his birth. This included, of course, the soul of Christ. Now Browne discovered that in himself and Coxey there was reincarnated an exceptionally large quantity of Christ's soul, which, he said, accounted for the way in which they two had been brought together, for their brotherly affection for each other, and for the harmony in which they worked. He referred to Coxey as the "Cerebrum of Christ",[2] modestly retaining for himself the title "Cerebellum of Christ." He maintained, moreover,

---

[1] Austen, "Coxey's Commonweal Army", *Chautauquan*, Vol. XIX, p. 334.

[2] One of the reporters, better versed in Biblical lore than in physiology, got it "cherubim." Pittsburgh *Press*, March 25, 1894.

that the same force that had brought him and Coxey
together would cause others to flock to their standard,
and that when the "Army of Peace" arrived in Washington, so great a part of Christ's soul would by this
means be gathered together and brought to bear upon
Congress that it would be irresistible; in Browne's own
words, it would be a force "before which Hell, not to
mention the subservient tools of Wall Street" could
not stand. One of his bulletins explained that "if the
principles of Christianity were applied to affairs here
on this earth, it would bring Heaven here as He wished
it, 'on earth as is done in heaven' and not, as now applied, that believers must die, as by life insurance, to
win it." [1] Thus was Christ to come again, and bring
about the kingdom of heaven on earth, according to the
prophecy, ushering in "peace and plenty to take the
place of panic and poverty." [2]

Browne converted Coxey. By christening their organization "The Commonweal of Christ" they gave it
a religious tone that was taken more seriously by the
leaders of the army than by anybody else. On the
banner of the Commonweal, painted by Browne, was
a picture of the head of Christ which bore a strange
resemblance to the painter, who had trimmed his
whiskers, it was said, to resemble as nearly as possible
his favorite portrait of the Savior.[3] On the banner was

---

[1] Hooper, "Coxey Movement in Ohio", *Ohio Archeological and Historical Society Publications*, Vol. IX, p. 158.

[2] On Browne's "theosophy", see Austen, "Coxey's Commonweal Army", *Chautauquan*, Vol. XIX, p. 333; Hooper, "Coxey Movement in Ohio", *Ohio Archeological and Historical Society Publications*, Vol. IX, pp. 158, 159; Stead, "Coxeyism", *Review of Reviews*, Vol. X, p. 52; *Outlook*, Vol. XLIV, p. 824; Pittsburgh *Chronicle Telegraph*, March 19, 22, 1894.

[3] Hooper, "Coxey Movement in Ohio", *Ohio Archeological and Historical Society Publications*, Vol. IX, p. 159.

inscribed: "Peace on Earth Good Will to Men. He Hath Risen, but Death to Interest on Bonds." [1]

Among Greenbackers and Populists who were sympathetic towards paper money and the unemployed there were many who felt that the oldtime religion was good enough for them. A captain of the Salvation Army in Massillon urged her soldiers not to join Coxey's army, considering his utterances blasphemous.[2] All this talk and mummery that savored so strongly of sacrilege probably did the movement a great deal more harm than good,[3] — except, perhaps, for advertising purposes.

It was Browne's influence that forced this religious aspect of the affair into prominence. In fact, many people received the impression that Browne was the moving spirit of the enterprise, and that he had acquired a strange ascendency over Coxey, who merely served as the figurehead and supplied the funds. According to one writer on Coxeyism, Browne "made the plans, wrote the proclamations and bulletins, devised the organization, painted the banners, designed the badges, and conducted the correspondence." That Coxey "approved all the work and all the doctrine preached in his name by Browne, is not to be doubted, for no protest was heard from him and he played with evident satisfaction the rôle of presiding genius that was assigned to him by his more active associate." [4] In view

[1] Pittsburgh *Chronicle Telegraph*, March 22, 1894.

[2] Pittsburgh *Post*, March 25, 1894.

[3] *Ibid.;* Austen, "Coxey's Commonweal Army", *Chautauquan*, Vol. XIX, p. 334; Pittsburgh *Press*, April 2, 1894.

[4] Hooper, "Coxeyism in Ohio", *Ohio Archeological and Historical Society Publications*, Vol. IX, pp. 163, 164. *Cf.* Stead, "Coxeyism", *Review of Reviews*, Vol. X, pp. 48, 49; Austen, "Coxey's Commonweal Army", *Chautauquan*, Vol. XIX, p. 334; Pittsburgh *Press*, March 24, 1894.

of the sequel, however, there is reason to believe that Browne's influence over Coxey was exaggerated in statements of this kind. The explanation offered by Henry Vincent, the official historian of the Commonweal, was that Coxey's extensive business interests took up so much of his time that he turned the management of all the details over to Browne in order to facilitate the preparations for the expedition.[1]

Coxey was commonly described as general of the Commonweal army, and he was president of his Good Roads Association. Browne was marshal of the Commonweal and secretary of the Association. The leaders of the movement maintained that their organization was not an army, but a peaceable body of citizens bent on a peaceful errand, and that military titles were misleading, but the reporters and the public preferred the military momenclature, and it was as an army that the Commonweal was known to the world.[2]

On February 28, 1894, about a month after the announcement of the plan to the press, the Good Roads Association issued its Bulletin Number 3, describing its plan of organization of the Commonweal; the designs for badges to be worn by the members of the Commonweal to distinguish them from the populace; the route for the march; and notices of meetings along the way at which Coxey was to explain his bills, and Browne was to "lecture and exhibit his financial panorama and draw off hand cartoons on local and national subjects,

---

[1] Vincent, "Commonweal", p. 49.

[2] Austen, "Coxey's Commonweal Army", *Chautauquan*, Vol. XIX, p. 334; Hooper, "Coxeyism in Ohio", *Ohio Archeological and Historical Society Publications*, Vol. IX, p. 163; Vincent, "Commonweal", p. 77; Stead, "Coxeyism", *Review of Reviews*, Vol. X, pp. 48, 49; Pittsburgh *Post*, March 20, 22, 1894; Pittsburgh *Press*, March 26, 1894.

a la Thomas Nast." [1]   On March 19 Coxey's bills were introduced in Congress [2] by the Populist Senator Peffer of Kansas — he whom the more conservative young Theodore Roosevelt described as a "well-meaning, pin-headed, anarchistic crank, of hirsute and slab-sided aspect." [3]   The newspapers began to speculate on what would happen when Easter Sunday, March 24, arrived.

As the time approached there was bustle and activity on the Coxey farm and at Massillon. Browne was busy with his work as "chief of the literary bureau of the movement",[4] answering the flood of letters that appeared in response to the circulars sent out, pledging recruits, supplies and money. Many of them came from practical jokers who sent large checks, sometimes written in red ink, purporting to be signed by prominent financiers, upon which payment was promptly refused.[5] "Humble Carl," as Browne now called himself in one of his announcements,[6] engaged in the prosaic work of manufacturing banners and badges, as well as the more artistic occupation of painting the

---

[1] "Coxey, His Own Story of the Commonweal" (Massillon, 1914), p. 46; Pittsburgh *Chronicle Telegraph*, March 22, 1894; *Journal of the Knights of Labor*, March 15, 1894.

[2] Peffer, in introducing these bills (S. 1787 and S. 1788), explained that he did so by request and that he was not in sympathy with their objects, but that since they were respectful in tone he looked upon them much as he did upon petitions, and he asked that they be referred to the Committee on Education and Labor. Peffer said that he knew nothing about the Good Roads Association, but that he was personally acquainted with its representative, "a man of good character."— *Congressional Record*, 53rd Cong., 2d Sess., p. 3076.

[3] Joseph Bucklin Bishop, "Theodore Roosevelt and his Time" (New York, 1920), Vol. I, p. 56.

[4] Pittsburgh *Chronicle Telegraph*, March 22, 1894.

[5] Austen, "Coxey's Commonweal Army", *Chautauquan*, Vol. XIX, p. 334; Vincent, "Commonweal", p. 77; Pittsburgh *Post*, March 21, 1894; Pittsburgh *Press*, March 23, 1894.

[6] Pittsburgh *Press*, March 25, 1894.

banners. Browne "is no slouch as a sign painter", wrote one of the reporters. "He dashes off a work of art in no time, and he has a fairly good idea of color treatment. Carl's weak spelling shows in nearly every banner. In writing as well as speaking he invariably gets 'calvery' when he means 'cavalry'." [1]

Food was collected and three commissary wagons were provided to carry it in. There was a band wagon consisting of a covered dray with seats along the sides, otherwise described as bearing a close resemblance to the traveling conveyance of gypsies; and the panorama wagon, essential to Browne's lectures, was refitted and appropriately decorated. [2] The leaders held nightly meetings by way of continuing the "campaign of education" begun early in the winter. [3]

Coxey asserted optimistically that he would leave Massillon with a large body of marchers, and reach Washington with a hundred thousand men. [4] But as March 25 approached few of these men were in evidence; the small circus tent bought to house the Commonweal had few occupants when it was first raised on March 24, [5] and newspapers began to debate the question whether Coxey's Army was a bubble that had burst, "the greatest fake known to this generation", or whether it would consist entirely of reporters. [6] A cartoon on the morning the army started showed a cavalcade consisting of a goddess of peace, Coxey, and

---

[1] Pittsburgh *Post*, March 26, 1894.

[2] *Ibid.; Weekly Iowa State Register*, March 30, 1894.

[3] Pittsburgh *Chronicle Telegraph*, March 22, 1894.

[4] Stead, "Coxeyism", *Review of Reviews*, Vol. X, p. 49; Pittsburgh *Press*, March 22, 24, 1894.

[5] Pittsburgh *Press*, March 25, 1894.

[6] Pittsburgh *Chronicle Telegraph*, March 24, 1894; Pittsburgh *Press*, March 24, 1894.

Browne, followed by one soldier, a disreputable looking tramp, and a long column of reporters.[1]

Although recruits were slow in making their appearance in sufficient numbers to make up an army, various interesting characters began to appear in time to play their part in the performance. There was the Pittsburgh astrologer, "Cyclone" Kirtland, who foretold the success of Coxey's march from the stars [2] and prophesied that the army would be "invisible in war and invincible in peace." [3] There was the Indian half-breed, Honore Jaxon, arrayed in an Indian costume that rivalled Browne's Buffalo Bill attire — a white sombrero, leather breeches, a decorated belt, and a blanket, which, together with his handsome face and long hair, attracted much attention. He was reputed to have been a leading spirit in Riel's rebellion in Canada, where, it was said, he would have been hanged if he had been caught. Now he was under contract with the Chicago *Times* to make the trip half a day in advance of Coxey's army, sleeping in the open and living on oatmeal, at a total expense of not more than seventy cents.[4] He brought a letter from Mrs. Lease of Kansas in which she sent Coxey her best wishes and a word of encouragement.[5] There was Douglas McCallum of Chicago, the "best dressed man in the mob", sporting a plug hat and a fur-lined overcoat. He was noted as the author of a curious pamphlet entitled "Dogs and Fleas, by one of the Dogs." He traveled over the route of the army, stopping at hotels

[1] Pittsburgh *Post*, March 25, 1894.
[2] *Ibid.*, March 26, 1894; Pittsburgh *Press*, March 24, 1894.
[3] Pittsburgh *Press*, April 1, 1894.
[4] *Ibid.*, March 23, 25, 1894; Pittsburgh *Chronicle Telegraph*, March 30, April 2, 1894; Pittsburgh *Post*, March 31, 1894.
[5] Pittsburgh *Press*, March 22, 1894.

where he signed on the registers "Dogs and Fleas, Chicago, Ill.," and then proceeded to try to sell his publication to the guests. "Whether he is an anarchist, a fool, or a Coxeyite would be hard to say" wrote a representative of the press. He seemed to enjoy the confidence of the leaders of the army, but he ridiculed the march in the presence of the newspapermen.[1] A real cowboy, "Oklahoma Sam" Pfrimmer appeared in time to start the journey. He joined, he said, to see the fun and because his father was an "original Green-backer." He seems to have acted as courier and trick rider to the expedition.[2] "Weary" Bill Iler, chief commissary and driver of the panorama wagon, gained his name from his apparent disinclination to do anything more strenuous than hold the reins.[3]

Shortly before Easter Sunday, there appeared in the Coxey camp a mysterious stranger, a "big, hand-some, well-dressed man" who went by the name of Louis Smith. He refused to disclose his identity, but offered his services, and he was promptly appointed assistant marshal. He was a born leader and a strict disciplinarian, who had evidently had military experi-ence. He disciplined the recruits, made them salute the officers, and drilled them until they could go through a few simple military movements in a very creditable manner.[4] He rode and walked like a cavalryman,[5] and his dictatorial manner led to the rumor that he had

---

[1] Pittsburgh *Press*, March 25, 1894; Pittsburgh *Chronicle Telegraph*, April 5, 1894.

[2] Chicago *Tribune*, May 6, 1894; Pittsburgh *Chronicle-Telegraph*, April 5, 1894; Pittsburgh *Post*, March 26, 1894.

[3] Pittsburgh *Chronicle Telegraph*, March 31, 1894; Washington *Post*, April 19, 1894.

[4] Chicago *Tribune*, May 6, 1894; San Francisco *Chronicle*, March 25, 1894.

[5] Mathew F. Griffin, "Secret Service Memories", *Flynn's Weekly*, Vol. XIII, p. 924 (March 13, 1926).

been an officer in some foreign army. A correspondent described him as the best informed man in the Commonweal — one who in conversation on general subjects talked and acted like a gentleman. The reporters, unable to find out who he was, dubbed him "the great unknown." [1]

On March 22, three days before Easter Sunday, there was no army in Massillon, but the leaders were sanguine.[2] Then a few recruits straggled in. On Saturday the streets of Massillon were thronged with more than the usual Saturday crowd; seventy-five men had enlisted, and every freight brought more. Twenty iron workers arrived from Cleveland, and a telegram from Henry Vincent, the Chicago reformer, announced that a large body would come from his city in time to start. There was no longer any doubt that there would be an army and it was predicted that five hundred men would march.[3] On Sunday, however, the weather changed for the worse, with flurries of snow, doubtless discouraging all but the hardiest, and the Commonweal got under way with only a scant hundred in the ranks.

The crowds of spectators who braved the biting wind of that raw and chilly Easter observed a spectacle unique in its significance, but nevertheless with a certain air of familiarity, for it was described as having a close resemblance to an old-fashioned country circus.

[1] Pittsburgh *Press*, March 29, 1894. The *Press* correspondent remarked that the "unknown's" manner "would lead one to believe that he was honest, and the fact that he had successfully concealed his identity from over a score of the brightest newspaper men in the country acquits him of being a fanatic seeking notoriety."— *Ibid*. A Secret Service man who marched with the army was likewise unable to find out who he was.—Mathew F. Griffin, "Secret Service Memories", *Flynn's Weekly*, Vol. XIII, p. 924.

[2] Pittsburgh *Chronicle Telegraph*, March 22, 1894.

[3] Pittsburgh *Post*, March 25, 1894; Pittsburgh *Press*, March 25, 1894; San Francisco *Chronicle*, March 25, 1894.

A few minutes before noon the Commonweal procession swung down Main Street. First marched Jaspar Johnson, the Negro color bearer, with the Stars and Stripes. After him rode Marshal Carl Browne in his boots and buckskins, mounted upon one of Coxey's superb stallions.[1] He was followed by several mounted aides, among them Jesse Coxey, the General's sixteen-year-old son, in a military uniform with blue coat and gray trousers, typifying the union of the two combatants in the Civil War;[2] and the trumpeter, "Windy" Oliver. Then came General Coxey in his phaeton, followed by a carriage containing Mrs. Coxey and their infant son, Legal Tender Coxey,[3] with other members of the family. Somewhere along the line rode the cowboy, Oklahoma Sam. At the head of the column of the unemployed came another color bearer who carried the banner of the Commonweal of Christ, with its ambiguous portrait and its reference to resurrection and bonds; then Assistant Marshal Smith, the great unknown, mounted on another of Coxey's steeds, in immediate charge of the marchers. The hundred industrials were a ragged, unkempt lot, most of them with the appearance of professional hoboes. Warmly dressed spectators shivered in the piercing wind, but not more than half a dozen of the marchers had overcoats or gloves. There were the three commissary wagons, and the band

---

[1] Coxey's horses taken on the expedition were estimated to be worth $40,000. Washington *Post*, April 30, 1894.

[2] Pittsburgh *Press*, March 26, 1894.

[3] Coxey's explanation of the reasons for giving the boy this name was "that in after years as he grows up people will naturally inquire 'What is the meaning of that name? What do you mean?' and questions of like import. It will ever be a pertinent reminder of the sovereign right of the government to use its own full legal tender as money, and that nothing else is money."—Vincent, "Commonweal", p. 50. See also Washington *Post*, May 1, 1894.

wagon with the panorama wagon, driven by "Weary" Bill Iler, bringing up the rear. After the procession proper followed the reporters, half as numerous as the army.[1] The principal omission from the program as it had been planned was due to the absence of a goddess of peace at the head of the procession because Coxey's divorced wife refused to permit their daughter to accompany the expedition in that capacity.[2]

Curious spectators crowded the streets, gazing sympathetically at the scantily clad men of the Commonweal or cracking jokes at their expense. Rigs following the procession out of town lengthened the column to a mile or more, and the Canton-Massillon electric railway, running parallel to the road, did a thriving business.[3]

The representatives of the press included forty-three special correspondents, four telegraph operators, and two linemen. Sixteen of the reporters who started from Massillon marched all the way to Washington.[4] Coxey's army was now furnishing the newspapers with so much copy that they were willing and eager to get for themselves that further expenditures for advertising were superfluous. The papers featured the march of the Commonweal in daily dispatches which made the most of the humorous elements in the affair. They described the general, with his air of a mild but enthusiastic farmer-reformer; they noted the squint of his inquiring eye, and his well-dressed appearance with

[1] Pittsburgh *Post*, March 26, 1894; Pittsburgh *Press*, March 25, 1894; Pittsburgh *Chronicle Telegraph*, March 26, 1894; *Weekly Iowa State Register*, March 30, 1894; Stead, "Coxeyism", *Review of Reviews*, Vol. X, pp. 52, 53; Hooper, "Coxeyism in Ohio", *Ohio Archeological and Historical Society Publications*, Vol. IX, pp. 164–168.

[2] On the "goddess of peace" controversy, see Pittsburgh *Post*, March 22, 26, 1894; Pittsburgh *Chronicle Telegraph*, March 22, 24, 1894.

[3] Pittsburgh *Post*, March 26, 1894.

[4] Chicago *Tribune*, May 6, 1894.

an inveterate crease in his trousers which led some to assert that at heart he was a dude. They described the antics and the exploits (most of which, no doubt, actually happened) of Browne, Smith, the astrologer, Oklahoma Sam, and the other curiosities; how several prominent members received dishonorable discharges because they had exhibited themselves in a Pittsburgh dime museum; how an old man dropped dead and a young man had an epileptic fit after a sight of the army;[1] how "the veiled lady", reputed to be the "unknown's" wife, and suspected of being a Chicago anarchist, kept in touch with the expedition;[2] how the "unknown" quarreled with Browne and stole his army from him;[3] and other things in a similar vein. The press thus treated the public to a great deal of amusement at the expense of the Commonweal; and indeed, it would have neglected the possibilities of the subject if it had done otherwise, for, aside from the strangeness of the whole idea of the expedition, there was a certain element of truth in the statement that from "start to finish the army of the Commonweal of Christ has been the objective point of every fakir in the land."[4]

But such as it was, the "petition in boots" was on its way to Washington with a serious purpose.

[1] Pittsburgh *Press*, March 30, April 3, 1894.

[2] *Ibid.*, March 31, 1894; Pittsburgh *Post*, March 31, 1894; Pittsburgh *Chronicle Telegraph*, April 6, 1894. A reporter for the Pittsburgh *Press*, March 29, 1894, mentioned "a fake sprung by the New York and Chicago papers" to the effect that Smith's wife was to join the Commonweal. He doubtless referred to the veiled lady.

[3] See below, *ff*. p. 97.

[4] Chicago *Tribune*, May 6, 1894.

CHAPTER IV

THE PETITION IN BOOTS

Hark, hark! Hear the dogs bark!
Coxey is coming to town.
In his ranks are scamps
And growler fed tramps
On all of whom working men frown.

This doggerel appeared under a cartoon in the Pittsburgh *Press* of Palm Sunday, showing a single workingman and a pack of dogs protecting the Capitol from a horde of tramps led by Coxey on a white horse. It represented a preconceived estimate of the composition of Coxey's army that was neither uncommon nor accurate. Many who were interested in the movement raised the question: were these trampers tramps, or were they the unemployed workingmen they pretended to be?

It was the expressed aim of the sponsors of the movement to limit the membership in the Commonweal to the respectable unemployed. Only citizens of the United States were admitted. "We want no thieves or anarchists — boodlers or bankers — to join us," one of Browne's bulletins ran. "We want patriots, not bummers," and he expressed the thrifty hope that none in ill health would join.[1] Massillon, however, was not an auspicious place for the enlistment of such an army, for it had no spontaneous organization of the unem-

---

[1] Hooper, "Coxeyism in Ohio", *Ohio Archeological and Historical Society Publications*, Vol. IX, p. 163.

ployed, nor, it seems, any large number of unemployed ready to join an organization like Coxey's. Commentators more discriminating than those who referred habitually to Coxey's men as "hoboes" agreed that the Commonweal, when it started from Massillon, was hardly a body of representative workingmen. One described the column of marchers as consisting of "one hundred of the toughest-looking bums that ever graced a station house or a box car." [1]

It was principally the good fortune of bad weather, bad roads, and poor food during the first few days' march that saved the army from continuing to be what its enemies said it was. Most of the professional vagrants, who had joined in the hope of a comfortable jaunt with gratuitous square meals, dropped out before the end of the first week of marching, and their places were taken by workingmen who had been forced to take to the road. [2] One reporter was led to revise his estimate of the men by an occurrence that showed both a laudable ambition and the difficulties in the way of its fulfilment, and he wrote:

That the class of men now in the army is a great improvement over the gang of "hoboes" who left Massillon a week ago was shown this morning about daylight when nearly 100 men went to the brook that flows through the fair

[1] Pittsburgh *Post*, March 26, 27, 1894. The reporter for the *Post*, who marched with the army from Massillon to Washington, was Shirley Plumer Austen, whose articles in the *Chautauquan* are cited elsewhere.

[2] Austen, "Coxey's Commonweal Army", *Chautauquan*, Vol. XIX, p. 334. After three days' marching the Pittsburgh *Post* reporter estimated that there remained about 25 "bums"; the rest appeared to be real workingmen, many of whom had union cards — March 28, 1894. See also *ibid.*, March 31. The correspondent of the Pittsburgh *Chronicle Telegraph*, March 30, 1894, described the Commonweal at Columbiana, Ohio, as consisting of two companies; the "Chicago Commune" of 100 men which started from Massillon, made up largely of tramps who got the best food and did the least work; and the "Coxeyana Commune" of 40 men, consisting of unemployed workingmen.

grounds and at least made an excuse at a toilet. Some of them did it thoroughly, using old newspapers for towels and soft clay for soap. Not a few had pocket combs, and succeeded in making themselves look quite respectable.

He added that the "Unknown", surprised at this attempt at cleanliness, issued soap from the commissary wagon.[1] The average respectability of the marching column was further increased when Browne gave the remaining tramp element permission to ride on trains. Every morning after breakfast the members of the "flying squadron" made their way out of camp to steal rides on freights, and showed up in time for dinner at the next stopping place.[2]

The impression of several observers of the army who were not inclined to dismiss the subject with a sneer, and who saw it on the latter part of the march or at Washington, was that the majority of the men were of the more shiftless and incompetent type of workingmen, naturally the first to be out of employment, and now, for the time being, tramps by force of circumstances. A reporter at Hancock, Maryland, described them as follows:

It is a mistake that has been encouraged by many papers to look on Coxey's army as an aggregation of "bums", deadbeats, and professional "hoboes." It is true there are many regular tramps with the army, but the rank and file is made up of regular workingmen, some of whom are simply mechanic's helpers, and still others with no trades at all. . . . It is not the best class of men who first get out of work in hard times. . . .

But the most of them are honest, as honesty goes in their class, and they are earnest, in a dumb, helpless sort of way,

---

[1] Pittsburgh *Press*, April 1, 1894.

[2] Austen, "Coxey's Commonweal Army", *Chautauquan*, Vol. XIX, p. 334; Vincent, "Commonweal", p. 63; Pittsburgh *Post*, April 2, 1894.

that is, willing to be led by whoever will take the trouble to lead them and make fair promises. It is true the majority of the army has a very vague notion of its ultimate destiny, and when it comes to talking about the upset prices of bonds, nationalistic tendencies, unearned increment, and kindred socialistic topics, they are totally at sea. But to say, as has been said, that the Commonwealers do not know what they want in Washington is nonsense.

They cannot have listened to Carl Browne's harangues night and day for three weeks without imbibing many of his ideas, and they are distinctly of the opinion that Congress, if it will, can print money just as it prints agricultural reports, and that the money will be as good as any made.[1]

A visitor in the camp at Rockville, Maryland, who had come out from Johns Hopkins University to study the army before it arrived in Washington, reached similar conclusions. He entered the camp, he said, with the impression gained from newspapers "that Coxey's army consisted of tramps and bums", but he came away with an entirely different notion. "These men," he wrote, "are not tramps, but for the most part unskilled, uneducated workmen; men just above the tramp class, who are the first to suffer during times of financial depression and the last to regain employment." Most of them were young, many mere boys. They showed no sign of physical degeneracy; on the contrary "many of them seemed like men whom a recruiting sergeant would be glad to enlist in the regular army." He observed them doing things that he thought tramps would do only under compulsion — shaving each other and washing themselves and their clothes. "Any tramp with the least skill in his profession would have fared

[1] Washington *Post*, April 19, 1894.

better alone by begging, than did these men united and with a definite object." The most important phase of the Commonweal movement, he thought, was its educational aspect — or, to use a more recently developed term, the effect of its propaganda. The men had joined the Commonweal with a vague idea that times were bad, without understanding why; now they thought they knew, and their newly acquired ideas, rapidly becoming fixed in their minds, were "unfortunately, fast grounded on socialism." [1]

There was some difference of opinion among students of the Commonweal as to the attitude of its members toward Coxey's program. Several seemed to feel that the men had "blindly followed the commissary wagon and a fanatical leader",[2] actuated merely by a natural desire to improve their condition after months of unemployment, and hoping vaguely that their "petition in boots" would result in legislation that would bring better times and more money.[3] Others thought that the men understood the Good Roads Bill and believed that it would pass Congress and thereby relieve their distress.[4] "All the men in my company," wrote the detective already mentioned, "were unfortunates out of work, penniless, but sincere believers in Coxey's visionary scheme." [5]

Aside from the leaders and the freaks there were a few of a somewhat higher type, who had joined because of conviction or necessity. These superior persons, not

[1] Hall, "An Observer in Coxey's Camp", *Independent*, Vol. XLVI, pp. 615, 616.
[2] Chicago *Tribune*, May 3, 1894.
[3] Austen, "Coxey's Commonweal Army", *Chautauquan*, Vol. XIX, p. 334; Austen, "The Downfall of Coxeyism", *ibid.*, p. 450; *Outlook*, Vol. XLIX, p. 824.
[4] Tracy, "A Mission to Coxey's Army", *Catholic World*, Vol. LIX, p. 678.
[5] Matthew F. Griffin, "Secret Service Memories", *Flynn's*, Vol. XIII, p. 919 (March 13, 1926).

more than a dozen or fifteen in number, ate at the headquarters tent and appeared to have little in common
with the rest of the men. The stories told by several
of them to a newspaper man throw some interesting
sidelights upon the movement and its causes.[1]

The man who looked most like a representative workingman was A. H. Blum of Canton, Ohio, president of
the Canton Iron Molder's Union, and ex-president of
the Canton Trades Assembly. He was well dressed, and
he had "an intelligent face and manly bearing", and
money enough to stop at hotels. He explained that
he had joined the Commonweal because the movement
was indorsed by his union and by the American Federation of Labor. It was his belief that something ought
to be done to relieve the condition of the workingman,
and that the Coxey movement was a step in the right
direction. He had been idle for some time because he
would not do the work of a skilled mechanic for the
wage of a common laborer. Many of his friends, he
said, had "expressed surprise at his joining the Commonweal, which was looked upon as an aggregation of
good-for-naughts." He was in charge of the commissary
wagons on the march, but he had little to do with Coxey
or Browne, and he had no use for "theosophy." [2]

Marshal John Shrum, "a tall, gaunt man with a face
made striking by the loss of one eye", had the appearance "of a man who had had a long and unsuccessful
struggle to keep the wolf from the door." He was a
naturalized German, forty-three years old, a member of
a labor organization, and a Populist. In Iowa, where
he had left his wife and infant dependent upon charity,

---

[1] Austen, "The Downfall of Coxeyism", *Chautauquan*, Vol. XIX, pp. 448, 450.
[2] *Ibid.*, p. 449.

he had mined coal and had edited a small paper, *The Mystic Messenger*, for which he acted as a correspondent while with the Commonweal. He had joined, along with five other miners, to avoid starvation. His opinions were suggestive of the name of his paper. "Universal coöperation between man and man," he said, "in my estimation would lay aside all petty grievances between labor and capital. Let the people own all the property in common and the big industries that are now in the hands of the plutocrats. I don't exactly understand Mr. Browne's reincarnation, but I certainly do agree with him in the inefficacy of prayer. . . . I am a free thinker, and believe that religion is detrimental to the human race." Schrum thought that the churches were upheld by the rich.[1]

The secretary of the Commonweal, Frank Ball, was a hotel or steamboat steward by trade and a socialist by conviction. He was twenty-eight years old, prepossessing in appearance, and he seemed fairly well supplied with money. He had been much impressed by Browne's arguments when he had heard that redoubtable orator hold forth at the Chicago World Fair, and when, after ten weeks of idleness, he heard of the Commonweal, he decided to become a member. "I joined entirely from principle," he said, "for I think it will be productive of good. I am going to stay with it till the thing is settled, and don't believe Congress can hold out against us very long." [2]

During the last two weeks of the march the army was accompanied by Edward A. Moore of Chicago, a repre-

---

[1] Austen, "Downfall of Coxeyism", *Chautauquan*, Vol. XIX, pp. 448, 449; Pittsburgh *Chronicle Telegraph*, April 5, 1894. The quotations are from Austen's article.

[2] Austen, "Downfall of Coxeyism", *Chautauquan*, Vol. XIX, p. 449.

sentative of the "'unsubsidized' press in the form of a
rabid Populist organ", who distributed his newspaper
liberally among the men. According to his story he had
been an anti-Chinese agitator; in the election of 1888
he had been chairman of the County Central Committee
of the Union Labor Party of Cowley County, Kansas;
in 1890 he had been the People's Party candidate for
the office of Secretary of State in Colorado; and he
had been a business partner of Mrs. Lease. He said:
"I most certainly believe in the Coxey movement and
you will see the plutocrats down on their knees before
we are through with them. Congress has got to recog-
nize us or there will be trouble." [1]

There were others who failed to take themselves and
the Commonweal as seriously as those just described.
A race track "swiper" accounted for his presence as
follows: "I have only myself to look after and am having lots of sport on this trip. I was 'on the hog' when
the circus started, and as they were to furnish grub I
joined. I don't know nothing about Coxey's bills or
'Old Greasy's' religious stuff. I am having a whale of a
time with the outfit." [2] Another explained to a correspondent that he was not interested in politics, but
that he wanted to see Washington. He said that he
made enough selling a labor book along the way to pay
his way back to Ohio. [3]

No systematic attempt seems to have been made to
compile statistics on the occupations, religious and
political affiliations, and other similar information
about the men of Coxey's army, as was done in the

[1] Austen, "Downfall of Coxeyism", *Chautauquan*, Vol. XIX, p. 449.
[2] *Ibid.*, p. 450.
Outlook, Vol. XLIX, p. 824.

case of two armies from the West. One of the Catholic priests who conducted a mission to the army after its arrival at Washington stated that "some are iron-molders, some brass workers, some railroaders, some miners", and there was at least one printer, with "a sprinkling of tramps"; there were few "sullen, desperate characters." [1] Griffin, the detective, discovered two veterans of the Union Army and one ex-Confederate. He found only one dangerous agitator, who recommended blowing up the Capitol, but this "red" seemed to have little support among the men, being hissed from the platform when he tried to speak at a meeting.[2]

It was hardly to be expected that all the men of such a miscellaneous collection of humanity as Coxey's army should be altogether exemplary in their conduct. But on the whole their behavior seems to have been better than might have been expected. There were more disturbances while the hobo element predominated than later; at Louisville, Ohio, after the second day's march, the press reported a row in a saloon between a Coxeyite and a local man in which the local man lost his watch; and there were several drunks and fights in the camp. Several similar disturbances were reported during the next few days, but it was noted that Browne and Smith always discharged the culprits from the army, with a chastening effect upon those who had not yet offended. Perhaps, after all, these disturbances were not altogether the fault of the members of the army. A dispatch from New Gallilee, Ohio, where the army's conduct left a very good impression, stated that the town

[1] Tracy, "A Mission to Coxey's Army", *Catholic World*, Vol. LIX, p. 678.
[2] Matthew F. Griffin, "Secret Service Memories", *Flynn's*, Vol. XIII, pp. 920, 921, 926 (March 13, 1926).

marshal admitted that the Coxeyites behaved better
than the townspeople.[1] Moreover, as the army progressed, much of the temptation was removed by local
authorities who had learned some of the lessons of recent
history. Detective Griffin, who joined the army at
Pittsburgh, wrote in his reminiscences:

Whenever we entered a town which boasted saloons, the
grog shops were closed tighter than drums, even the local
patrons being denied their usual tipple while we were among
them. And if ever there was an army which did its marching
on water — for drinking — it was Coxey's motley throng.[2]

But although the conduct of the men may not have
been exemplary with respect to the consumption of
available intoxicants, it was noted that it committed
no depredations of the kind expected of a tramp army.
A visitor noted that chickens and turkeys wandered
unmolested about the camp.[3] "'You cannot find so
much as a chicken feather among my men,' Coxey
boasted, when he led his men to Washington past hen-
coops innumerable." [4]

The organization of the Commonweal was outlined
in a bulletin issued by Browne at Massillon. The
smallest unit was a "group" of five men, in charge of
a "group marshal" who drew the rations for himself
and his four men, and supervised their conduct on the

---

[1] Pittsburgh *Post*, March 27, 28, 31, April 1, 1894.
[2] Griffin, "Secret Service Memories", *Flynn's*, Vol. XIII, p. 923 (March 13,
1926). See also Pittsburgh *Chronicle Telegraph*, March 31, 1894. There seem to
have been exceptions, however. The New York *Times* of April 19, 1894, describing
the army at Hancock, Md., ran the headline: "Coxey's Tramps Rushed for Saloons." See also Washington *Post*, April 18, 1894; Austen, "Coxey's Commonweal
Army", *Chautauquan*, Vol. XLIX, p. 336; Pittsburgh *Chronicle Telegraph*, April
26, 1894.
[3] Hall, "An Observer in Coxey's Camp", *Independent*, Vol. XLVI, p. 615.
[4] Stead, "Coxeyism", *Review of Reviews*, Vol. X, p. 49.

march and in camp. Groups were to be combined into companies or "communes" of from thirty to one hundred five men, each with its marshal and its banner. Communes might be federated into regiments or "communities" containing from 215 to 1055 men. Two or more communities might be combined into a "canton." [1] The bulletin added that "all labor unions, Farmers' Alliances, or other organizations desiring to join may do so without organizing as above, and will be given the right of line." Browne also devised an elaborate system of badges indicating each man's rank and his place in the organization.[2]

The organization was Browne's, but the discipline was Smith's. It was the "Unknown" who drilled the men, made them salute their officers, and kept them in line on the march. S. P. Austen wrote in regard to the excellent order of the marchers:

Carl Browne saw in this the spirit of the reincarnated Christ abroad in the army, but to mere mortals it appeared to be due to the military organization of the Commonweal and to the strict discipline enforced by the next in rank to Browne, the Chicago Indian medicine vender, who gained much notoriety as "the Great Unknown." [3]

The army marched, on an average, about fifteen miles a day, usually starting at about half-past ten in the morning and arriving at its scheduled destination

[1] Hooper, "Coxey Movement in Ohio", *Ohio Archeological and Historical Society Publications*, Vol. IX, pp. 162, 163; Vincent, "Commonweal", p. 76; Austen, "Coxey's Commonweal Army", *Chautauquan*, Vol. IX, p. 335. There are some discrepancies as to the details of this table of organization in these accounts, but the outline is the same in all.

[2] Hooper, *Op. Cit.*, p. 163.

[3] *Chautauquan*, Vol. XIX, p. 335. The Pittsburgh *Chronicle Telegraph*, April 2, 1894, attributes the increasingly effective discipline on the march and in camp to the "Unknown's" iron discipline.

late in the afternoon.[1] The pace often maintained by the men confirmed the impression that they were by no means inferior physical specimens. On the third day's march the army was reported to be marching at the rate of four miles per hour.[2] On the fourth day the army covered twelve miles in four hours despite the fact that the roads were described as "fearful in places"; the marchers making fast time on the good stretches.[3] One reporter asserted that on a forced march toward the summit of the Cumberland Mountains, going up hill through snow a foot deep, the army made eighteen miles in four hours.[4] Many were soon footsore. Even in cold weather they welcomed an opportunity to bathe their feet in a roadside stream,[5] and while resting in camp they were commonly to be seen with their shoes off.[6] During much of the journey the number of men in the column varied between two and three hundred; Austen describes it at an average "war footing" as consisting of five "communes" of about forty-five men each.[7] It was asserted that there was a constant shifting of the personnel, but the enlistments somewhat more than made up for the desertions.[8]

[1] Austen, "Coxey's Commonweal Army", *Chautauquan*, Vol. XIX, p. 335.

[2] Pittsburgh *Press*, March 27, 1894. On the marching ability of the army, see also *ibid.*, April 8, 1894; Pittsburgh *Chronicle Telegraph*, April 14, 1894.

[3] Pittsburgh *Post*, March 28, 1894.

[4] Chicago *Tribune*, May 6, 1894.

[5] Matthew F. Griffin, "Secret Service Memories", *Flynn's*, Vol. XIII, p. 920; Pittsburgh *Press*, April 1, 1894.

[6] Chicago *Tribune*, May 6, 1894.

[7] Austen, "Coxey's Commonweal Army", *Chautauquan*, Vol. IX, p. 334.

[8] Austen states that before the army reached the Cumberland Mountains fully 2000 names had been enrolled by the recruiting officers, but that of about 200 men. who climbed the mountains, only nine had marched all the way from Massillon.—*Ibid* A dispatch in the Chicago *Times*, May 2, 1894, states that of the 400 then in Washington, only 19 had started from Massillon. Vincent, on the other hand, states that the army was permanent in character, and that it suffered little from desertions, crossing the mountains with scarcely a name stricken from the muster rolls, and

The recruiting of the army was not left entirely to the chance of finding men ready to enlist in the cities through which it passed. In many other places efforts were made to collect bodies of men to join the Commonweal at some convenient point. In Philadelphia, as early as March 18, a week before the army marched from Massillon, one J. M. Byrnes of Los Angeles, California, appeared with credentials as a recruiting officer of Frye's army, which proposed to march to Washington to coöperate with Coxey,[1] and on Easter Sunday there was a well attended meeting to collect Coxey recruits.[2] Populists at Harrisburgh, Pennsylvania, having received copies of Coxey's bulletin describing his route to Washington, set to work earnestly to organize a party to join his army at Hagerstown, Maryland, and issued a thousand circulars to be distributed among the unemployed of that locality.[3] Smaller towns also sent their delegations. At Alliance, Ohio, appeared ten men from Milfort and Crystal Springs, well equipped with blankets and gum boots, bringing letters certifying that they were members in good standing of the Crystal Springs People's Party Club.[4]

Populists and labor organizations exerted themselves not only to provide men, but also to furnish supplies. The army lived upon the country. Before leaving

he prints a roster.— "Commonweal", p. 104. Vincent, however, had left the army at McKeesport, Pa., and had returned to Chicago.— Pittsburgh *Press*, April 8, 1894.

[1] Pittsburg *Post*, March 19, 1894.

[2] *Ibid.*, March 26, 1894.

[3] The circulars read: "Join Coxey's army. All loyal citizens who believe that Congress, now in session at Washington, D. D. [sic] should pass some laws in the interest of the unemployed, with a view of providing employment, so that those willing to work need not beg, are invited to meet at the Kelker street market house, Sunday afternoon, April 8, 1894, 1:30 o'clock. Everybody invited to attend."— Pittsburgh *Press*, April 1, 1894. See also Pittsburgh *Post*, April 1, 1894.

[4] Pittsburgh *Press*, March 28, 1894.

Massillon, Coxey had explained that he had already
been at much expense in launching the movement, and
that if the downtrodden farmers did not rise to the
emergency, his men would have to go hungry.[1] On
another occasion he said that he expected the people to
feed the army along the way, and that if they did not,
his men would do as Christ did when he pulled the ears
of corn: the people of the United States, living presumably according to Christ's teaching, ought not to
object.[2] Coxey's prominence among Ohio Populists
was doubtless a factor in obtaining support in that
quarter, and Browne, who was a member of several
secret industrial organizations, appealed to them for
aid. Where Populism and organized labor were strong,
elaborate preparations were often made for the Commonweal's entertainment. At Beaver Falls, Pennsylvania, for example, on March 19, a joint meeting of the
Trades Council and the Beaver Falls Economy Literary
Club adopted resolutions indorsing the Coxey movement, and appointed committees to solicit food.[3] A
week later a Coxey club was organized, described as
"composed of solid business men and industrious mechanics", and a representative of the trades council
and other organizations prepared to meet the army at
Salem to see what it needed.[4] For two or three days
before the army arrived wagons went about town, collecting great quantities of provisions.[5]

The arrangements for sheltering and feeding the army

[1] Pittsburgh *Post*, March 19, 1894.
[2] Pittsburgh *Press*, March 22, 1894.
[3] Pittsburgh *Post*, March 28, 1894; Pittsburgh *Chronicle Telegraph*, March 21, 1894.
[4] Pittsburgh *Post*, March 28, 1894. For the step taken by the Canton, Ohio, Populists to assist Coxey, see *ibid.*, March 24, 1894.
[5] Pittsburgh *Press*, April 1, 1894.

were quite in keeping with character of the expedition. The Commonweal carried a small circus tent, sixty feet in diameter, in which the men slept on straw, with no more covering than what each man brought with him. The open fires by which the tent was heated filled it with smoke, and often thawed the frozen ground into mud.[1] Frequently less uncomfortable quarters were provided by local authorities or philanthropists to shelter the men from severe weather. At Canton, Ohio, about two thirds of the men were permitted to sleep in the jail,[2] and at Louisville, Ohio, seventy-five of them spent the night in the city hall.[3] Besides the circus tent there was a "headquarters tent" in which the officers, the teamsters, and a select group of others slept and messed.[4] Coxey, Browne, and a few others who could afford it lodged at hotels, which led to no little criticism of the leaders, and to some questioning of their sincerity.[5]

During the early part of the march quantities of food were donated—often more than the commissary wagons could carry, and Coxey shipped part of the

---

[1] Pittsburgh *Press*, March 26, 1894; Stead, "Coxeyism", *Review of Reviews*, Vol. X, p. 53.

[2] *Weekly Iowa State Register*, March 30, 1894.

[3] Pittsburgh *Post*, March 28, 1894.

[4] Austen, "The Downfall of Coxeyism", *Chautauquan*, Vol. XIX, p. 448.

[5] Washington *Post*, April 20, 1894. "A few weeks ago," wrote Hall after the army was in Washington, "it looked as if 60,000 men would be marching to Washington. . . . Mr. Coxey made a great mistake in announcing himself as a candidate for Congress and also in lodging at fine hotels instead of remaining with his men. He probably would have had a large following of the working classes could they have trusted him, but from the first they shrewdly suspected that his zeal for their cause was founded on desire for self-advancement."—"An Observer in Coxey's Camp", *Independent*, Vol. XLVI, p. 616. Vincent defended Coxey, stating that every night it was General Coxey's custom to see that the needs of the men were provided for before he left the camp. He says that it was the practice of rival hotel keepers to race out to meet the army and offer to the general and his staff the courtesies of their respective hostelries.—"Commonweal", pp. 81, 82.

provisions to points where it was most likely to be needed. But although there seems to have been plenty of good food available during the early part of the march, the fare furnished the men was anything but sumptuous; at times they received a ration consisting only of a chunk of bread or cold boiled potatoes, and "alleged coffee." Carping critics wondered what became of the remainder, and attacked the commissary department, asserting that the pie and other delicacies never got beyond the officers' mess in the headquarters tent.[1] The stories of the use of the only camp kettle for laundry as well as culinary purposes were most unedifying. It was asserted that more desertions were due to poor food than to any of the other hardships of the march.[2]

In addition to the donations of food made on account of sympathy for the men or the movement, or to keep the army from overrunning the town,[3] there were other sources of income. At each camping place a meeting was held at which a collection was taken up. During the latter part of the march, the Commonweal encamped whenever it was possible in an inclosure of some kind, and charged an admission fee. The men also sold souvenirs and pamphlets to add to the income from other sources.[4]

---

[1] Pittsburgh *Press*, March 28, 30, April 2, 1894; Pittsburgh *Post*, March 28, April 1, 1894; Pittsburgh *Chronicle Telegraph*, March 29, 1894.

[2] Chicago *Tribune*, May 6, 1894; Austen, "Coxey's Commonweal Army", *Chautauquan*, Vol. XLIX, pp. 334–336.

[3] For example, at Cumberland, Md., it was reported that food was given plentifully, "with a good grace" but that it was the price paid for keeping the men out of the town.— Washington *Post*, April 18, 1894.

[4] *Outlook*, Vol. XLIX, p. 824; Vincent, "Commonweal", pp. 94, 98, 100; Hall "An Observer in Coxey's Camp", *Independent*, Vol. XLVI, p. 615. The income from the collections at the meetings does not seem, as a rule, to have been large. At Alliance, Ohio, a meeting at which about 200 people were present contributed

The march of the Commonweal into a town was an event like the annual circus parade. Every one had heard of Coxey's Army, and the public was interested. Sometimes, as the column approached its daily destination late in the afternoon, crowds of enthusiasts or curiosity seekers went out to meet it — with a brass band, if one was available. Sometimes a body of college students on a lark marched along, singing college songs and giving their college yells.[1] The automobile had not yet arrived, but the nineties were the period of bicycle clubs, whose members not infrequently turned out to hail Coxey as the champion of good roads.[2] Curious spectators lined the streets and followed the procession to the vacant lot assigned as a camping place. There the men gathered in a circle; the chief marshal advanced to the center with the color bearer and set up the flag, and orders were given to those who carried banners to advance and plant them near it. Then the marshals of the communes came forward to receive their instructions; some were ordered to unload the tent and to distribute and drive the stakes; and the commissary marshal ordered his men to gather wood, kindle fires, and prepare the provisions. All was bustle and activity until the tent was pitched.[3] If time remained, the men not engaged in special occupations removed their shoes, and rested on their blankets, shaved each other in improvised barber's chairs, or

$13.—Pittsburgh *Post*, March 28, 1894. At Beaver Falls, Pa., where the army received a "generous reception", the proceeds of the afternoon meeting amounted to $48, and of the evening meeting to $39.73.—*Ibid.*, April 2, 1894. At one of the Pittsburgh meetings $67.57 was collected.—*Ibid.*, April 5, 1894.

[1] Pittsburgh *Press*, March 30, 31, 1894; Pittsburgh *Chronicle Telegraph*, April 2, 1894.

[2] Vincent, "Commonweal", p. 69.

[3] *Ibid.*, p. 76.

engaged in other domestic activities.[1] Members of the "flying squadron", usually about fifty in number, slipped in before it was too late. Rations were issued to each group of five, and the supper was dispatched.

Then came the meeting to which the public was invited.[2] The ceremonies opened with songs.[3] Hymn singing emphasized the religious aspect of the movement. The Commonweal, however, did not believe in prayer.[4] One Sunday, when the camp was pitched near a sectarian college, a member of the faculty offered

[1] Griffin states that the army had "regimental farriers, barbers, cobblers, tailors, and of course a band", and that all the men who had not grown beards were required to shave every day.— "Secret Service Memories", *Flynn's*, Vol. XIII, pp. 917, 919, 921.

[2] See Hall, "An Observer in Coxey's Camp", *Independent*, Vol. XLVI, p. 615; Stead, "Coxeyism", *Review of Reviews*, Vol. X, pp. 53, 54; Chicago *Tribune*, May 6, 1894. Sometimes the meeting was held in the local "opera house" instead of in the camp.

[3] The following, written by Carl Browne, was printed in the Pittsburgh *Post*, March 26, 1894. It was entitled "After the Commonweal March is Over", and was sung to the tune of "After the Ball is Over", a popular song of that time:

Chorus:

After the march is over
After the first of May
After these bills are passed, child
Then we will have fair play.

Many a heart will be happy
As to their homes we'll away
For we will have no interest on bonds
After the first of May.

It was reported that Charles K. Harris, of "After the Ball" fame, offered to print 10,000 copies of this parody and give one to each soldier on condition that this be made the army's official song.—*Ibid.*, March 27, 1894.

[4] In one of his sermons Browne said: "There are instances of people praying to heaven, where they believe God is, and thought themselves helped. But there was never a prayer sent up to heaven that changed a law of nature."—Pittsburgh *Post*, March 26, 1894. A reporter, describing the reception of the army at Beaver Falls, Pa., where workingmen sympathized with Coxey's economic reforms, wrote that "almost to a man they are ready to attack and do violence to the unprincipled wretches who have dragged the religion of Christ into the dust and made mockery of all that they hold most dear. No matter how low a workingman has sunk by lack of employment none care to hear such a greasy ruffian as Carl Browne claim that the little prayers their mothers taught them in happy days long since, never reached the ears of a Deity."—Pittsburgh *Press*, April 2, 1894.

A NIGHTLY ENCAMPMENT

A *DE LUXE* BARBER SHOP *EN ROUTE*

to send a minister to officiate at the army's services. Browne declined the offer with thanks. "Tell your professor," he said to the messenger, "that our motto is 'God helps those who help themselves,' and that we are going to Washington to get what we want." [1]

After the singing Coxey mounted the panorama wagon to speak. He explained his bills and their intended effect, urging the necessity of their enactment to solve the labor problem, to remedy unemployment, to bring the eight-hour day to the wage earner, and to create general prosperity by furnishing a plentiful currency. Pinning his faith to these two bills as the only remedy for economic ills, he drew a gloomy picture of the times to come if they should fail, concluding one of his speeches with the statement:

There is little hope for the future in a business sense unless the two measures mentioned are passed. These would bring immediate relief to the unemployed in making public improvements and substitute actual money in the place of confidence money that has already vanished, thus taking away all possibility of panics and hard times in the future and make it an impossibility for a man to seek work without finding it. [2]

The tone of his speech was moderate, and he advanced his ideas in a clear, straightforward manner that impressed many of his hearers favorably. [3]

Then came Browne's performance. At the beginning of his harangue he usually interested his auditors and put them in a good humor by telling parables to illus-

---

[1] Vincent, "Commonweal", p. 70. *Cf.* Pittsburgh *Press*, April 2, 1894.

[2] Speech at Williamsport, Md., Vincent, "Commonweal", p. 55.

[3] Hall, "An Observer in Coxey's Camp", *Independent*, Vol. XLVI, p. 615; Stead, "Coxeyism", *Review of Reviews*, Vol. X, p. 54; Austen, "Coxey's Commonweal Army", *Chautauquan*, Vol. XLIX, p. 336.

trate the aims and objects of the Commonweal.[1] Sometimes he rose and addressed the audience as "fellow
dogs", and then explained as follows:

Mr. McCullom, of Chicago, who is here with us, has
written a book, entitled the "Dogs and Fleas", in which he
anticipates the march of Brother Coxey and myself in our
march to Washington. He tells how in Kihidrom there
dwelt a colony of dogs which are bitten to death by fleas
and not one of the canines could tell why they were in such
straits. One day a crank dog came along and nudging one
of the flea-ridden brutes called out "fleas", and then passing
into various groups of the insect-pestered animals, cried
viciously, "fleas, ye fools, fleas", until finally the distressed
dogs were induced to stop scratching and look in the right
direction, being made to see that all their troubles came from
fleas.

Then Browne applied the story and pointed out the
moral: the people were the dogs, and the fleas were the
bankers, bondholders, and monopolists who were accustomed to "suck the life blood out of their victims";
and he told what he and Coxey proposed to do about
it:

On one occasion when the troubles of the dogs had become
almost unbearable, a number of them were assembled discussing the situation when a big dog appeared on the scene
with the light of a big idea and the others accepted him as
their leader. Under his direction they came to a place where
a lot of timber had been cut and each one of the canines
seized in his mouth a chip and trotted away with it into the
banks of a river into which they slowly plunged. Everyone
knows how much a flea dislikes water and the result was
that as the several bodies of the animals became submerged
the fleas crept forward until they were driven upon the chips,
when the enlightened dogs let go the chips, which went float-

ing down stream carrying a dense mass of howling, disappointed bloodsuckers. Now, we are the dogs, and Brother Coxey is giving us the chips in the shape of his two bills before Congress, and we are going to Washington to get rid of the fleas.[1]

After this preliminary discourse Browne displayed and explained his financial panorama, with its striking pictorial contrasts between the evil times then prevailing and the prosperity and comfort that might be brought about by a realization of the Commonweal's program. He also drew offhand cartoons as he spoke, and discussed them in a style resembling that of a dime museum orator. The language with which he advocated paper money or condemned plutocracy, national banks, and interest-bearing bonds, in his "disjointed tirade against government in general and the existing financial system in particular" [2] was often striking and original. The religious aspects of the Commonweal were by no means neglected. W. T. Stead described Browne's Sunday sermons as "a strange mixture of prophecy and politics, of theology and finance",[3] in which he quoted scripture and mixed metaphors with equal recklessness. One of his texts was Revelations XIII: 1: "And I stood upon the sand of the sea, and saw a beast rise up out of the sea, having seven heads and ten horns, and upon his horns ten crowns, and upon his heads the name blasphemy." He compared the sands upon which the apostle stood to New York City, and the beast which rose from the sea was the money power. Its seven heads

[1] Vincent, "Commonweal", pp. 19, 20. *Cf.* Pittsburgh *Chronicle Telegraph*, April 4, 1894.
[2] Austen, "Coxey's Commonweal Army", *Chautauquan*, Vol. XLIX, p. 336; Pittsburgh *Post*, March 26, 1894.
[3] Stead, "Coxeyism", *Review of Reviews*, Vol. X, p. 54.

were the seven great monopolies conspiring against the people's money — the Standard Oil Company, the combined railroads, the iron producers, the newspapers, the national banks, the speculators in grain, and the gold-mining concerns. The horns were the money bills passed by Congress.[1] Browne also described another beast representing the money power, with only two horns—the hypocritical church and the politicians,—"both of which worship this beast and kill people who do not worship it." Consequently, he concluded, it was no wonder "that people criticise Mr. Coxey and that the subsidized newspapers all over the land are calling him a lunatic, for so it is prophesied by St. John." [2] A fragment from one of Browne's general orders gives a further idea of his style in composition:

The deputy sheriffs have taken to the woods, but tomorrow they may put in an appearance to earn their per diem. Be not disrespectful to them, or to anyone else for that matter. We are fast undermining the structure of monopoly in the hearts of the people. Like Cyrus of old we are turning aside "the boodler's" Euphrates and will soon be able to march under the walls of the second Babylon, and its mysteries too. The infernal, bloodsucking bond system will be overthrown for "the handwriting is on the wall." [3]

At the conclusion of Browne's speech the collection was taken up. The visitors left, and the men who had not yet retired turned into their uncomfortable sleeping quarters. The guards were posted, with a re-

[1] Stead, "Coxeyism", *Review of Reviews*, Vol. X, p. 54; Pittsburgh *Post*, March 26, 1894; Pittsburgh *Press*, March 26, 1894. There seems to have been some confusion in the reports as to whether the monopolies were heads or horns. The list here given is from the Pittsburgh *Press*.
[2] Pittsburgh *Post*, March 26, 1894.
[3] Vincent, "Commonweal", p. 108. A part of this quotation is given with minor variations in Stead, "Coxeyism", *Review of Reviews*, Vol. X, p. 54.

lief every two hours,[1] and the camp settled down for the night.

[1] Austen, "Coxey's Commonweal Army", *Chautauquan*, Vol. XLIX, p. 336; The Pittsburgh *Press*, March 30, 1894, reported that two sentinels, instructed by Browne to keep correspondents out of the camp, had assaulted two of the reporters who tried to enter late at night. The sentinels, however, "were in a few minutes extremely sorry that they had run foul of two men who a few months ago wore long hair and played football" — which suggests changes of styles in football as well as in ladies' adornment since 1894.

CHAPTER V

THE MARCH TO THE CAPITAL

On Easter Sunday Coxey's army marched through falling snow over the eight miles of road between Massillon and Canton. As it advanced upon Canton other marchers besides the original hundred joined the ranks. At Reedurban the column halted while sandwiches were served. It was still snowing, and bitter cold. Arriving at its destination at four o'clock in the afternoon, the Commonweal, now two hundred strong, marched through a large crowd to its camping place in a pasture near the fair grounds, and the tents were pitched for the first cheerless night. The meeting that evening was called off because of the inclement weather, and most of the men sought the jail or other suitable shelter. A number of enlisted tramps, having had their fill of winter marching, deserted before morning.[1]

The next morning, while the army prepared its meager breakfast, General Coxey read the papers at his hotel. Among the news items he discovered an open letter addressed to him by Senator William S. Stewart of Nevada. The departure of the Commonweal was delayed by two hours while the General concocted a suitable reply, which he gave to the press.

Senator Stewart had called attention to the ballot as the proper means by which the sovereign people of the United States could retain their right to life, liberty and the pursuit of happiness. Formerly, he said, the

[1] Pittsburgh *Post*, March 26, 1894. Of 235 men given shelter in the circus tent, only 80 remained.

ballot had been used to elect Washingtons, Jeffersons, Jacksons, and Lincolns, which "sent terror and dismay to tyrants, despots, and plundering oligarchies throughout the world", but for two decades its use had brought no such results; now a "soulless despot of alien origin", whose name was Money, was "monarch of the commercial world", and administrative and legislative bodies were his servants. Nevertheless, the ballot box was the only place "where the forces of liberty and equality can meet and overthrow the enemy of human rights", and in November there would be an opportunity for the voters to overthrow the old parties which had "surrendered the rights of the people to the rule of concentrated capital." Any attempt by a starving multitude to march to Washington might give the Government an excuse to use force to maintain law and order on the ground that it was merely suppressing anarchy and insurrection. Therefore he urged Coxey to abandon "the folly of marching an unarmed multitude against the modern appliances of war under the control of a soulless money trust", and to organize his army only to win victory at the polls.

In his reply to the senator's communication, Coxey remained firm in his defense of the Petition in Boots and of paper money. He denied that his peaceful procession was an army or that he was a general, "no matter how much a subsidized press, at the dictation of the money power, tries to make this appear." The Commonweal would march on peaceably, he said, depending upon a peaceful public to defend it "from Pinkerton's policemen, military, soldiers, or petty politicians." After complimenting Stewart upon his past leadership of the silver forces in the Senate against gold and bonds, Coxey insisted that the time had now come when "he who is not for us is against us." If the silver men, by slighting the Commonweal movement, became the allies of gold against legal tender, then "the Rubicon is crossed by the silver forces and we cannot falter. The fiat must now go forth—demonetization of gold as well as silver." [1]

After the General had disposed of the senator, the army continued its march through Ohio. In most of the towns through which it passed, Populists and labor organizations mustered enough strength to give it a rousing welcome. At Alliance the enthusiastic reception by the citizens was augmented by a hundred students from Mount Union College who visited the camp and cheered for the "soldiers", and seventy-five recruits more than replaced the deserting hoboes. [2] Leetonia, where the Commonweal made a noonday halt, was a good Coxey town, said a newspaper dispatch, because the miners in Cherry valley had been on strike for a month against a twenty per cent. wage reduction. Although they "had little themselves, they had a warm meal prepared for the men in an old rail mill." The reporter complained that Browne refused to let the men eat in peace, insisting upon making a speech. [3] At New Waterford, a celebration had been arranged by "a relic of the old Greenback party who has a fixed income, but would like to see the Coxey bills pass." [4] The houses were decorated for the occasion when the population, the Mount Hope College

---

[1] Vincent, "Commonweal", pp. 58–61; Pittsburgh *Post*, March 26, 27, 1894; Pittsburgh *Press*, March 26, 1894. Browne also wrote a reply.

[2] Pittsburgh *Press*, March 28, 1894.

[3] Pittsburgh *Chronicle Telegraph*, March 30, 1894.

[4] Pittsburgh *Press*, March 31, 1894.

students, and the band escorted the Commonweal into the town.[1]

There were exceptions, however, to this warm hospitality. The chilly reception at East Palestine was attributed to the fact that there were only two Populists in the village, one of whom had the mumps.[2] The indifference of New Galilee to the Commonweal was said to have been caused by an absorbing conflict between the churches and the secret orders over the licensing of saloons, and to the church people's opposition to "theosophy."[3]

The "Unknown" divulged his reasons for joining the Commonweal and his ideas of reform while the army was at East Palestine. He proposed a system of publicly owned farms on which the unemployed might work under military discipline for the benefit of the state.[4] At Columbiana, where the army avoided the necessity of pitching the tent by encamping in a deserted foundry, some one recognized "Unknown" Smith as the ringmaster of a small circus that had visited the town three years before.[5]

During the Commonweal's sojourn there, Columbiana became the birthplace of a new organization. Browne, in one of his outbursts of righteous indignation at the way in which the newspapers poked fun at him and the army, referred to the reporters as "argus-eyed demons of Hell." A score of the correspondents promptly organized under that name, and appeared the

---

[1] Pittsburgh *Press*, March 31, 1894; Pittsburgh *Post*, March 31, 1894.
[2] Pittsburgh *Press*, March 31, 1894; Pittsburgh *Post*, March 31, 1894.
[3] *Ibid.*, April 1, 1894.
[4] Pittsburgh *Chronicle Telegraph*, March 31, 1894.
[5] *Ibid.*, March 30, 1894. Coxey, who had been attending a horse sale in Chicago, rejoined his men at this point. *Ibid;* Pittsburgh *Press*, March 28, 1894.

next day wearing badges on which were printed the letters A. E. D. H. The membership of this exclusive group was limited to those who actually marched with the army from camp to camp. J. R. Caldwell of the New York *Herald* was elected Arch Demon Number 1, with unlimited authority to act for the organization during the continuance of the Coxey expedition.[1] Browne's resentment against the unkind slurs of the press led to his order excluding all newspaper men from the camp at night, and to the consequent discomfiture of the camp guards when they tried to eject two reporters who had recently played football.[2]

On the last day of March, while the army was crossing the Pennsylvania line, a delegation of more than a hundred striking potters was making its way out of New Liverpool, Ohio, marching to join Coxey. A large proportion of them were Germans, many of them middle-aged men. They were skilled workmen, comfortably dressed and well equipped for the march — a striking contrast to the "hundred vagabonds" who had left Massillon five days earlier.[3]

It was at Beaver Falls, Pennsylvania, that the army received its most generous ovation, for reasons diagnosed by a reporter as follows:

[1] Pittsburgh *Press*, March 30, 1894; Vincent, "Commonweal", p. 64. The charter members enumerated in the Pittsburgh *Press* were: J. A. Mackay, Associated Press; S. P. Austen, Pittsburgh *Post;* Walter Robinson, Cleveland *Plain Dealer;* Jacob Waldeck, Cleveland *Leader;* Wilbur Miller, Cincinnati *Enquirer;* Clifton Sparks, Chicago *Tribune;* W. H. McLain, St. Louis *Chronicle;* R. P. Skinner, New York *Recorder;* C. S. Seymour, Chicago *Herald;* W. J. Christy, Austin Beach, Pittsburgh *Times;* Harry S. Calvert, Pittsburgh *Leader;* Ray Baker, Chicago *Record;* W. P. Babcock, New York *World;* B. E. Way, Canton *News Democrat;* James W. Faulkner, Cincinnati *Enquirer;* I. D. Marshall, New York *Press;* Andrew Bloomer, Chicago *Inter-Ocean;* and the Pittsburgh *Press* staff correspondent (who signed his articles "Little").

[2] Pittsburgh *Press*, March 30, 1894.

[3] Pittsburgh *Post*, April 1, 1894.

There is existing between workingmen an affinity that on such occasions as this makes them all of a kin. The men in the army with the exception of less than a dozen in the Chicago commune, had been hard-working, industrious men, and by being out of employment for some months have thought it better to join Coxey's army than to run up board bills on poor boarding-house keepers. Trades unions have always been strong in Beaver Falls and the surrounding towns, and the great preparations that had been made was [sic] entirely due to the fact that many of the working men here had an honest desire to give to their kind.[1]

April 1, when the army arrived, was Sunday, and thousands of visitors thronged to add to the enthusiasm. When the marchers reached their camping grounds they found a crowd of six thousand or more people assembled. About one hundred thirty recruits — many of them potters from East Liverpool — enlisted, and a new commune was formed. The wagons that had been engaged for two days in gathering supplies had collected four tons of provisions, most of which were shipped to Uniontown in preparation for the crossing of the mountains. Students from the neighboring college came to the camp, gave their yells, and listened to the speakers.[2] The leaders discussed economic reform and "theosophy" at meetings in both afternoon and night, taking up collections totalling nearly ninety dollars.[3]

The next day's march of eighteen miles from Beaver Falls to Sewickley was the longest yet undertaken. Until it was nearly ended it was a continuous ovation. As the column made its way out of Beaver Falls, factories and mills were closed to give the workers an op-

[1] Pittsburgh *Press*, April 2, 1894.
[2] Pittsburgh *Post*, April 2, 1894; Pittsburgh *Press*, April 2, 3, 1894; Pittsburgh *Chronicle Telegraph*, April 2, 1894.
[3] See above, p. 64, note 4.

portunity to see Coxey; the school children were given a recess, as on circus day; and every one seemed to be taking a day off to celebrate the occasion. Having shipped most of the surplus provisions to Uniontown, the army was traveling light, for it was expected that at Economy much food and clothing would be donated. There were between two hundred fifty and three hundred men in line, for few wanted to ride freights past this hospitable village. It was reported that when word was passed along the line that a number of Pittsburgh detectives had joined the army, some twoscore of the marchers suddenly disappeared from the ranks; nevertheless more than two hundred reached Economy, where a square meal had been prepared under the direction of one of the trustees of the village.[1]

It was not until the Commonweal reached Sewickley that this enthusiasm abated, but in that aristocratic suburb of Pittsburgh a chilly reception awaited. A vacant lot was procured for the camp, but no provisions were forthcoming. Many of the residences were guarded by special officers, and the chief of police issued orders that no one be permitted to leave the camp. Perhaps it was in retaliation for this order that the "Unknown" ordered that all visitors be kept out of the camp, with the result that the sentries ejected President Judge Stowe off the premises in a manner unbecoming the dignity of the bench.[2] In spite of this untoward incident, however, Sewickley seems to have

---

[1] Pittsburgh *Press*, April 3, 1894. The number of men marching on this day is given as stated in this paper and the Pittsburgh *Chronicle Telegraph*. The *Post* gives a smaller number.

[2] Pittsburgh *Post*, April 3, 1894; Pittsburgh *Press*, April 3, 1894; Vincent, "Commonweal", p. 71. On the next day Coxey called upon the judge to apologize, but finding him in court, did not intrude upon him. — Pittsburgh *Press*, April 4, 1894.

discovered over night that Coxey's army, instead of
being composed of dangerous characters, was a harmless
body of unfortunates kept under reasonably strict discipline; the town thawed and the men were given a
good breakfast.[1] The next stop was Allegheny, in the
heart of the industrial district.

In Pittsburgh and its suburbs Coxey sympathizers
had been perfecting their organization long before the
Commonweal arrived. At Homestead, where the bitter
taste left by the strike in the Carnegie steel works two
years before was not yet forgotten, preparations were
under way by the middle of March, ten days before
Coxey's army left Massillon. The leading spirit there
was Elmer E. Bales, a former employee of the Carnegie
Company, who reported on March 16 that nearly a
hundred unemployed steel workers had already signed
an agreement to join the Commonweal, with the understanding that they would leave the ranks at the first sign
of disorder.[2] In Wood's Run and Lower Allegheny,
where many mill workers were unemployed because of
strikes or lockouts, and where Populists were numerous,
there was great enthusiasm, and elaborate preparations
were made to welcome Coxey. The leader was James
Shipman, described as "an old-time Greenbacker", who
agreed that if Alderman Harkins of the eleventh ward
would raise a company of one hundred men to join
Coxey, he and his friends would furnish rations and

---

[1] Vincent, "Commonweal", p. 72.

[2] Pittsburgh *Chronicle Telegraph*, March 16, 17, 1894. When the army was at
Beaver Falls "Coxeyites and Populists" at Homestead held a meeting for those who
intended to join the Commonweal, where they listened to Bales, to one Jean Sullivan, a Populist, and to a sensational address by William Foy, a man who had been
shot by a Pinkerton detective in the Carnegie strike. Bales reported that several
business men had contributed bread and meat to supply the expedition. — Pittsburgh *Press*, April 2, 1894.

supplies for ten days' march.[1] In Pittsburgh it was reported that Alderman McNierney was an officer in a Coxey contingent, that Constable Rogers was to be a lieutenant, and that Coxey meetings were being held in the alderman's office at 5419 Butler Street.[2] C. A. Burrows, chairman of the People's Party county committee, and A. M. Schwartz, president of the carpenter's brotherhood, were among those who were active in circulating petitions in favor of Coxey's bills.[3] These and other similar efforts [4] made it seem probable that the Commonweal would have a prosperous time in the Pittsburgh district — if the authorities would permit it. General Coxey had been in Pittsburgh before his army left Massillon, to make arrangements for the care of the Commonweal, obtaining the aid of Mr. Henry B. Rea, a commission merchant with whom he had had business dealings.[5] On March 31 he made another brief visit to complete his preparations, spending much of the time in conference with Populist leaders.[6]

It was evident that the attitude of the Allegheny and Pittsburgh police would be none too friendly, if not positively hostile. There were reasons why the authorities should view with anything but complacency all attempts to stir up the vast number of unemployed in these cities and their environs, especially at this particular time. Neither the authorities nor the workingmen had forgotten the bloodshed of the Homestead strike. On April 3 it was announced that the relief

[1] Pittsburgh *Press*, March 28, April 2, 1894.
[2] Pittsburgh *Post*, March 25, 26, 1894.
[3] Pittsburgh *Chronicle Telegraph*, March 17, 1894.
[4] Pittsburgh *Post*, March 31, 1894; Pittsburgh *Press*, April 2, 3, 1894.
[5] *Ibid.*, March 22, 1894; Pittsburgh *Chronicle Telegraph*, March 23, 1894.
[6] *Ibid.*, March 31, 1894.

fund was exhausted, and that Pittsburgh could no longer employ needy men in the parks.[1] In the coke districts to the southward, near Connelsville and Uniontown, thousands of lawless strikers, most of them foreigners, were marching from place to place and creating a reign of terror. The front page of the Pittsburgh *Post* of April 4, with its four columns of description of the arrival of Coxey's army in Allegheny, carried in the column at the opposite side of the page the headlines: "Ready for Raid"; "Five Thousand Strikers Will Invade the Southern Coke Districts"; "Men Will Be Driven From Work"; "Three Hundred Determined Deputies Now Are on Guard." The next day's dispatches from Uniontown reported double this number of marching strikers. Half a dozen men had been shot to death and as many more desperately wounded. The "Huns" had killed the chief engineer of a mine by hurling him from a tipple.[2] Might not Coxey's army precipitate violent acts on the part of the suffering unemployed in Pittsburgh?

Doubtless the authorities raised this question. Considering the circumstances the policy they adopted was a moderate one. They permitted the Commonweal to pass through, but they kept it under strict surveillance. Coxey received assurance from the director of public safety at Allegheny that his army might enter the city if it remained orderly,[3] but preparations were made to meet it at the city limits with a large force of police and detectives, and to see that none of the soldiers left the ranks.[4]

---

[1] Pittsburgh *Post*, April 3, 1894.
[2] *Ibid.*, April 4, 5, 1894.
[3] Pittsburgh *Press*, March 31, 1894.
[4] Pittsburgh *Post*, April 3, 1894. Several days before the Commonweal arrived

On April 3, when the Commonweal was to arrive at Allegheny, the police authorities of Allegheny and Pittsburgh had all the men they could muster stationed at strategic points along the line of march and parties of deputy sheriffs were also in evidence. So far as the Commonweal was concerned, however, this large force was unnecessary, for the appearance of a police inspector and three detectives on the preceding day seems to have scared all the crooks out of the army.[1]

The police, however, were not the only ones who made preparations. The Coxey sympathizers laid elaborate plans to meet the procession with a large escort. The Coxey headquarters in Pittsburgh, at the office of Stevenson and Burrows, patent attorneys, were thronged with Populists and Coxeyites, among them Douglas McCallum, author of "Dogs and Fleas", and Henry Vincent of the Chicago *Express*. Honorary Marshal Burrows appointed J. H. Stevenson marshal of the Pittsburgh escort. A fine banner was ready for presentation to Coxey, with the inscription: "Pittsburgh and Allegheny. Laws for Americans. More Money, Less Misery. Good Roads. No Interest-Bearing Bonds." In the South Side about sixty volunteers from the 27th Ward organized a company to join Coxey, enrolling their names in a book in Alderman Hartman's office.[2] In Allegheny the labor organizations met in their respective halls — the molders, the patternmakers with a drum corps, and the boilermakers and bakers with a brass band. At Wood's Run a large body of unemployed work-

it was observed that there was an unusually large number of tramps in Pittsburgh, presumably attracted by the approach of Coxey's army. Chief of Police Roger O'Mara proposed to lock up all vagrants until the army had passed on. — Pittsburgh *Chronicle Telegraph*, March 30, 1894.

[1] Pittsburgh *Press*, April 3, 1894; Pittsburgh *Post*, April 4, 1894.
[2] Pittsburgh *Press*, April 3, 1894.

men led by Marshal James Shipman had another brass band. At Homestead, where Elmer Bales had reduced his estimate of the number who would march to Washington to thirty men, handbills were distributed stating the provisions of Coxey's bills.

Throughout the morning small squads of men were to be seen moving in the direction of Wood's Run, where the Commonweal was to enter the urban district. The street cars were filled, and before noon the streets were lined with spectators. At Exposition Park, where the army was to go into camp, the crowd began to assemble early in the afternoon. Windows commanding a view of the street or the park were packed. A squad of policemen was on the job to maintain order. Groups of men were seen lounging about the neighboring streets, some with bundles, evidently intending to enlist. Early in the day a load of donated provisions had been brought to the gate, but the driver was refused admittance until the army arrived. The only visible preparation for the entertainment of the Commonweal was made by a dozen men and boys who crawled through a hole in the fence and started a roaring fire.[1]

As the Commonweal tramped out of Sewickley that morning it was reported that the streets were thoroughly cleaned of cigar stubs.[2] The opening of the public schools had been postponed until ten o'clock in honor of the occasion, and the streets were full of fascinated small boys who followed the column to the outskirts. It was a pleasant spring day, with dust lying heavily upon the roads, ready to be kicked up by the footsore marchers. The route was a picturesque one,

[1] Pittsburgh *Press*, April 3, 1894.
[2] Pittsburgh *Post*, April 4, 1894.

commanding views of the broad bends of the Ohio with its bordering hills, and the comments of the trampers showed that many of them were by no means oblivious to the beauties of the scene. Appreciation of the beauties of nature, however, did not prevent a pathetic assertion of their sense of the practical. Near Dixmont men broke from the ranks in a rush for a pile of old shoes in a roadside dumping ground.

Carriages and men with bicycles lined the road, and there was a crowd at every crossroad. The spectators appeared like those at a circus parade, but instead of hundreds there were thousands. At Emsworth the school children were lined up to watch the parade. Before reaching Bellevue the principal police officials of Allegheny and Pittsburgh, with a number of detectives, joined the procession. Not finding any criminals in the Commonweal, they contented themselves with following the column into Allegheny. At Bellevue a body of bicyclers met the army and acted as an escort to Jack's Run. There the column halted at one o'clock, threw out a picket line to hold back the crowd, and dispatched a light lunch, each man receiving two slices of bread, and a piece of cold pork which many of the hungry trampers rejected as inedible.[1] Proceeding slowly, for the dense mass of spectators impeded its progress, the army soon met the Wood's Run escort — two hundred workmen with a fife and drum corps. Other escorts joined the column until they aggregated several times the strength of the army, now reduced to somewhere between one hundred fifty and two hundred marchers.

[1] This description of the march from Sewickley is taken from the Pittsburgh *Post*, April 4, 1894 and the Pittsburgh *Press*, April 3, 1894.

By this time the column was complete for its entrance into the city. It was led by a squad of dusty policemen. After them rode James Shipman on a white horse, at the head of a body of Populists and a hundred members of Iron Molders' Union Number 14. Next came a hundred wheelmen, and a brass band headed the Wood's Run escort and five hundred bakers, boilermakers, and patternmakers. A row of carriages bore prominent police and fire department officials and deputy sheriffs; then more wheelmen, and a body of students from the Western University, vociferating a variety of "shopworn college yells in which Coxey's name was mixed." Then the Commonweal. In the lead rode Marshal Carl Browne, Oklahoma Sam, and Jesse Coxey. The bugler tried to compete with the band until, as a reporter remarked, "Things took on the air of a political demonstration." General Coxey, in his phaeton, was stopped frequently by enthusiasts who wanted to shake his hand or to snap a camera at him. He was followed by a group of "argus-eyed demons", and by the army itself, with its wagons ready to receive the donations of food expected on the way to the camp.[1]

In entering Wood's Run the Commonweal and its escort had their first difficulty with the police. The route through Wood's Run and Allegheny selected by the Coxey sympathizers was now packed by crowds that showed an enthusiasm quite alarming to the authorities. The Allegheny police, therefore, decided that there would be less danger of a disturbance if the army was conducted to its camp by the back streets. The escort at the head of the parade encountered a cordon of police drawn across the street, and the column was

[1] Pittsburgh *Post*, April 4, 1894.

ordered to march around by the Brighton road. Some of the ironworkers were for forcing their way through the officers of the law, but their leader, James Shipman, "the old warhorse of the Greenback Labor party", persuaded them to comply with the police orders. Several thousand people who had waited along McClure and Beaver avenues failed to see the parade, and provisions that were to have been loaded into the commissary wagons had to be hauled to the camp the next morning. Great was the anger aroused, and an indignation meeting denounced the Allegheny police authorities with much bitterness. When others attacked Shipman for his unprotesting compliance with the order, he explained that there were men in his following who were ready to fight the officers, and that if he had not used his influence to prevent trouble, lives might have been lost.[1]

Arriving at the camp in Exposition Park, the Commonwealers found that they were to be held virtually as prisoners until they left the city. When they and their escort protested, they discovered that the police had been told not to be afraid to use their clubs.[2] The manager of the Palace Theatre had invited Coxey to bring his army to the performance that night, but the police objected and the invitation was withdrawn. In spite of these annoyances, Browne issued an order exulting over the reception by the populace, which commenced:

[1] Pittsburgh *Chronicle Telegraph*, April 4, 1894; Pittsburgh *Post*, April 4, 1894; Pittsburgh *Press*, April 4, 1894.

[2] Pittsburgh *Post*, April 5, 1894. Superintendent of Police Muth was quoted as saying: "The iron workers of the Wood's Run district set up to run things yesterday, and that is why the army came in by the Brighton road. At the park the same men tried to raise trouble but the officers used their clubs. We had too many brass buttons for them." — *Ibid.*, April 4, 1894.

Comrades —
> "Peace hath her victories
> No less renowned than war."

Your victory to-day over the combined forces of plutocracy and church hypocrisy was most signal. No Norman king, or Roman legion, or Grecian phalanx, loaded down with trophies of a conquered province or principality, ever received the ovation like you received at the hands of the good people clean from Sewickley through "Robbers' Roost" to lovely Allegheny City. The responsive throbs of human hearts in unison with yours was so manifest that like electricity for [sic] a static battery even the flashes were visible to the naked eye. The oppressed people greeted your dust-stained columns as the people of Washington, or rather those of the Union, did brave General Tecumseh Sherman and his boys in blue when they marched up Pennsylvania avenue over a quarter of a century ago for freeing the African slave.

He went on to explain that the Commonweal was gradually killing off the enslavers of the whites, and exhorted his men to be of good cheer because the people of Pittsburgh were awaiting the opportunity to give them food and shoes.[1]

That night a meeting was held in a vacant lot near Exposition Park. By eight o'clock so many people had gathered there that when Coxey mounted the panorama wagon to speak the late comers were unable to get within range of his voice. After a few remarks about the subsidized press and the four million unemployed, Coxey explained his bills and the purposes of the Commonweal. He was followed by Browne and "Unknown" Smith. Browne, in the process of explaining his financial panorama, blamed both Democratic and Republican politicians for the condition of the workingman,

---

[1] Pittsburgh *Post*, April 4, 1894.

and made bitter charges against Cleveland, John Sherman, the Rothschilds, Carnegie, and other notables. At one point he roused his auditors to such a high pitch of enthusiasm that the crowd surged forward and almost upset the wagon. The police made ineffectual efforts to break up the jam. "I tell you, Browne," shouted an influential and demonstrative Populist, "the bankers have paid these men to do this. The police are also hired to break up these meetings." He was promptly arrested, and the meeting passed off without further disturbance.[1]

The men confined in the park were given a good supper, and since the tent was pitched on dry ground they were fairly comfortable near the log fires. Some twoscore Coxeyites, however — either stragglers or men who had escaped from the park — sought shelter in the Allegheny police station, where they were promptly locked up. About a dozen, who looked like workingmen rather than tramps, or who were vouched for by a "war correspondent", were released, and the rest were sent to the workhouse for twenty days. This led to further accusations of "police persecution", but the impression of the reporters seems to have been that it purged the army of its remaining quota of toughs and professional vagrants. Browne said he was glad they had been arrested, since they had violated his orders to stay in camp, and the next day he published an order announcing that all members of the Commonweal who asked for food or lodging outside of the camp would be promptly discharged.[2]

---

[1] Fittsburgh *Post*, April 4, 1894. Coxey estimated the crowd at 15,000.
[2] Pittsburgh *Press*, April 4, 1894; Pittsburgh *Chronicle Telegraph*, April 4, 1894; Pittsburgh *Post*, April 5, 6, 1894.

The Commonweal remained in camp during the day and night of April 4, obtaining a needed rest and plenty of food. A large force of policemen and plain clothes men remained to supervise the army, and the day was filled by a series of tilts between the officers of the law and the Commonweal leaders. A parade through the streets of Allegheny was called off because the route mapped out by the police differed essentially from that planned by the Coxeyites. Although the arrangements at the park made recruiting difficult, there were thirty-eight enlistments.[1] The police had orders to arrest any of Coxey's men found outside of the camp, and a second crop of arrests and workhouse sentences resulted.[2] The bitterness of the Commonwealers at the police restrictions was matched by the resentment of their sympathizers. J. H. Stevenson, the Pittsburgh Populist leader, said that the Populists were indignant over the treatment of the army, and asserted that the arrests were made not for good cause, but because the men were Commonwealers.[3] James R. Sovereign, Grand Master Workman of the Knights of Labor, condemned the vagrancy laws which made it possible to arrest an unemployed workman merely because he had no money.[4]

Meanwhile two meetings were held in Pittsburgh. In the afternoon some ten or twelve thousand people gathered on the Monongahela Wharf. When Coxey drove up without his army the crowd closed in upon

[1] Pittsburgh *Post*, April 5, 1894.
[2] *Ibid*. The *Post* stated that about 40 were locked up before six o'clock — all of whom were orderly and perfectly sober. A dispatch dated Pittsburgh, April 5, in the *Weekly Iowa State Register*, April 13, 1894, stated that "Sixty-seven members of the army were arrested on the streets of Allegheny last night, and at today's hearing thirty-five were discharged and twenty-two sent to the workhouse."
[3] Pittsburgh *Chronicle Telegraph*, April 5, 1894; Pittsburgh *Post*, April 6, 1894.
[4] *Journal of the Knights of Labor*, April 12, 1894.

him until a wheel of his phaeton was smashed. The "Unknown" was there on his horse. "Dogs and Fleas" McCallum and other literary salesmen plied their trade. Coxey and Browne spoke, although, to the disappointment of many, the strong wind prevented the setting up of the panorama. The evening meeting in the old city hall was packed to the doors, and Browne, held an overflow meeting on the wharf, where he drew almost as large a crowd as had been there in the afternoon. Indoors, when Chairman J. H. Stevenson introduced General Coxey, he was "greeted with enthusiasm that knew no bounds" by an audience described as consisting mainly of intelligent members of the laboring classes, "with a sprinkling of aristocracy." When Coxey concluded his speech the crowd called for the "Great Unknown", who spoke until Browne appeared to display his panorama. The chairman, on behalf of the citizens of Pittsburgh and Allegheny, presented the General with the banner prepared for the occasion, asking him to take it to the steps of the Capitol. The meeting adopted resolutions thanking Superintendent Roger O'Mara of the Pittsburgh police for his courteous treatment, and by way of contrast Browne's order was read condemning Superintendent Muth of Allegheny for his scurrilous treatment of the army.[1] Doubtless the General had good reason to believe that his appearance had been a great success.

Before leaving Allegheny the army was deprived of three members who now figured even more prominently in the press dispatches than before. Harry Davis, proprietor of the Eden Musée, a Pittsburgh dime museum, had made unsuccessful attempts to induce Gen-

[1] Pittsburgh *Post*, April 5, 1894.

eral Coxey to place himself on exhibition at Davis'
establishment.[1] Davis now obtained a contract for a
week's engagement at the museum with Astrologer
Kirtland, "Weary" Bill Iler, Jasper Johnson, the Negro
color bearer, and his mascot, Bunker Hill, "the dog
that never deserts the flag" (being chained to the flagstaff). Coxey promptly dismissed all four from the
Commonweal. "We will have no dime museum freaks
in this aggregation," he said.[2]

On the morning of April 5, Coxey's army, after its
day of rest and persecution, packed up to leave Allegheny. The fifty policemen and the 207 Commonwealers were met at the gates of Exposition Park by an escort of about five hundred men, with band and drum
corps. The police marched them to the Union bridge,
which was not the one they wanted to cross, and turned
them over to Pittsburgh. The men left Allegheny with
a feeling of relief and a grudge against the police. Beyond the bridge were more vast crowds, much enthusiasm, and more policemen, but no arrests or disorder.
Up Fifth Avenue, past the offices of the "subsidized
press" and the Eden Musée, where the lately discharged
members watched them pass by, past the Jones and
Laughlin steel works, where the workmen were lined
up to see the spectacle, the progress of the Commonweal
march was cheered to the outskirts of the city. "The
Commonweal had its own way in Pittsburgh," wrote
the official historian of the expedition, "and every request or desire made known on the part of the leaders

[1] Coxey was reported to have had offers from at least three dime museum propri-
etors before he left Massillon. — Pittsburgh *Press*, March 25, 1894; Pittsburgh
Post, March 31, 1894.
[2] Pittsburgh *Post*, April 4, 1894; Pittsburgh *Press*, April 4, 1894; Pittsburgh
Chronicle Telegraph, April 5, 1894.

was immediately granted." [1] Kaufman's store donated three hundred pairs of shoes and as many vests, a merchant gave five hundred pairs of socks, and provisions were given in abundance.[2] Half a mile beyond the city limits the column was met by the Homestead escort, led by Elmer Bales and marching to the music of the Homestead Steel Workers' Band.[3]

The population of Homestead was out in force to give the marchers a hearty welcome. Their escort led them through the streets to their camp in Fred Schuchman's ice house, which was presently overcrowded by the influx of recruits. Here, at the home of the Carnegie Steel Company, the army attained its greatest numerical strength. Newspapers estimated it at five or six hundred, and Browne claimed to have seven hundred names enrolled. Many of the newcomers were foreigners — Poles, Hungarians, or Slavs — who spoke little English. A new commune — the "Pittsburgh Commune" — was organized, bringing the number of these units up to five. While the recruiting officers did a thriving business, the hardened campaigners bathed and washed their clothes in the chilly Monongahela. The "Unknown" complained of police restrictions similar to those in Allegheny, but no arrests were reported. The usual meeting was held in the Opera House. Homestead contributed, in addition to three wagonloads of provisions, some much-needed blankets, shoes, and other supplies.[4] The new commissary officer appointed

[1] Vincent, "Commonweal", p. 77.

[2] *Ibid.*, p. 79.

[3] For descriptions of the march through Pittsburgh, see Pittsburgh *Chronicle Telegraph*, April 5, 1894; Pittsburgh *Post*, April 6, 1894; Pittsburgh *Press*, April 5, 1894; *Weekly Iowa State Register*, April 13, 1894.

[4] Pittsburgh *Press*, April 6, 1894; Pittsburgh *Chronicle Telegraph*, April 6, 1894; New York *Times*, April 6, 1894.

at this time, Alexander Childs, was a nephew of H. C. Frick of the Carnegie Company.[1]

As the army marched up the valley of the Monongahela, the "Unknown" was identified by a Chicago traveling man as Captain Livingstone, late of the British army, whom he had met at a Chicago hotel during the World's Columbian Exposition. He was said to have served in several foreign armies in various parts of the world. There was a rumor that this mysterious individual was one of Uncle Sam's cleverest secret service men. He was also identified as Major William Packard Clarke, the best drillmaster in the Colorado National Guard, and the grandson of ex-Governor William Packer of Pennsylvania. A facetious editor wondered if he could be Governor Waite in disguise.[2]

Bad weather and bad roads made the march up the valley difficult, and reduced the number of marchers, but the men pushed on pluckily, putting their shoulders to the wheels and helping the wagons out of the mud holes when necessary. At Duquesne, McKeesport, and Monongahela City the enthusiasm of the populace was unabated.[3] The "Unknown" was identified again — this time as a patent medicine fakir.[4] At Brownesville, where the old national road crossed the river, the army arrived with two hundred sixty-eight men. Good weather and a good meal prevented more desertions during the night. The army was now approaching the most difficult part of the journey, through sparsely

---

[1] New York *Times*, April 6, 1894; Griffin, "Secret Service Memories", *Flynn's*, Vol. XIII, p. 920.

[2] Pittsburgh *Chronicle Telegraph*, April 6, 1894; Pittsburgh *Post*, April 6, 1894.

[3] Pittsburgh *Chronicle Telegraph*, April 6, 7, 1894; Pittsburgh *Press*, April 6, 8, 1894.

[4] Pittsburgh *Chronicle Telegraph*, April 7, 1894.

settled and mountainous country, where little aid
could be expected of the inhabitants. Browne announced that the fare on the march across the mountains would consist of hardtack and coffee, with ham
for supper.[1]

The next stop was at Uniontown, where the mountains loomed ahead. An April blizzard, with heavy rain
turning to sleet and snow, enveloped the country, and
the army remained snowbound for a day, resting for
the ordeal to come. Fortunately a better shelter was
provided than the tent, which could hardly have been
raised in the face of the heavy wind. The canny superintendent of the street-car line that ran to the fair
buildings not only tendered the use of the buildings and
provided straw to sleep on, but he offered to feed the
men so long as they remained on exhibition.

Here the "Cyclone trio", who had followed the army
after the expiration of their week's engagement at the
Pittsburgh dime museum, appeared and desired re-
instatement. They were greeted enthusiastically by
the men, and the "Unknown" favored their readmis-
sion, but Browne held firmly to Coxey's decision that
there should be no museum freaks in the Commonweal.
This was not the last clash of authority between Browne
and Smith. The freaks were court-martialled and were
forced to leave the camp. At Uniontown the "Unknown" was identified as Jensen, a Swede employed
by the Pinkerton detective agency, who in the pursuit
of his calling had toured the country with most of the
big circuses. Commissary Marshal Blum reported that
he had four days' rations on hand for the crossing of

[1] Pittsburgh *Chronicle Telegraph*, April 9, 1894.

the mountains. Browne advised all who feared the journey to drop out before it was too late.[1]

The Commonweal marched out of Uniontown an hour before noon on April 11, in a driving snowstorm, through mud ankle deep, which soon changed to slush, and before the column was halfway to Laurel Summit the snow was several inches deep, and falling so fast that it was impossible to see more than fifty yards ahead. There were two hundred fifteen men on foot, with about thirty others mounted or acting as teamsters. The horses suffered more severely than most of the men, and frequently the marchers had to push the wagons up the slopes. The Commonweal camped in a barn that night. The mountaineers of Laurel Ridge turned out to see the army, in no friendly spirit. Some of them, full of moonshine, galloped about the camp, making the stormy night more hideous with their shouts and howls.[2]

After this hostile demonstration, the army may have been more pleased than annoyed by the party that joined the march on the next day. At Addison, when Coxey and Browne were making the usual speeches, a body of armed men were observed to be edging their way toward the speakers' platform. When Browne concluded his harangue a man wearing two army revolvers mounted the platform. He introduced himself as the sheriff of Somerset County.

"Three cheers for the sheriff of Somerset County", cried a derisive voice.

The cheers were followed by several minutes of hoot-

[1] Pittsburgh *Chronicle Telegraph*, April 10, 11, 1894; Pittsburgh *Press*, April 10, 11, 1894; New York *Times*, April 11, 1894; *Weekly Iowa State Register*, April 13, 1894.
[2] Pittsburgh *Press*, April 13, 1894.

ing, which the sheriff took with a smile. When the noise subsided, he continued:

"My mission is one of peace and good will. I have a posse of twenty-five deputy sheriffs with me, and we will escort you across our little county until you reach the Maryland line. Thank you all for your kind attention."

Now there was genuine applause, for the sheriff's good nature had won over the men completely. The next morning the army started its march through six inches of snow, accompanied by the sheriff and his deputies, together with a band which played, in honor of the occasion, "Hail to the Chief." [1]

For the first time the Commonweal was behind schedule, and Browne forced it on as rapidly as he could. This was the most difficult part of the journey. After the army had crossed the Maryland line, where the sheriff's party left it, a reporter wrote:

The trip of the last three days has been a test of physical endurance of man and beast. While the men have borne up bravely, even attempting to keep up their spirits with song and jest while wading in snow and mud with the wind penetrating their rags with ease, the horses have been the greatest sufferers. [2]

Only one hundred forty men remained in the ranks when the summit of the Alleghenies was attained. [3] There, in the camp in an old deserted mansion, Browne issued General Order Number 17, in eulogy of those who remained steadfast:

[1] Griffin, "Secret Service Memories", *Flynn's*, Vol. XIII, pp. 922, 923; Pittsburgh *Chronicle Telegraph*, April 14, 1894.
[2] Pittsburgh *Chronicle Telegraph*, April 14, 1894.
[3] Chicago *Tribune*, May 6, 1894.

Today you have not only won the respect of every admirer of the heroic, but you have demonstrated in still more forcible manner the fact that you are not the lazy and vicious class that some of the newspapers brand you. . . . You need fear nothing more severe than you have experienced today on the rest of the journey, and when you reach the other side of the mountains your names will go on the scroll of fame. Like Henry V. said to his men after the battle of Agincourt, your names will be as familiar as household words.[1]

Each of these faithful few received later a "Souvenir for heroic conduct in crossing the Cumberland Mountains in the face of snow and ice, and despite police persecution and dissention breeders." It was a printed card signed by J. S. Coxey and Carl Browne. The "persecution" doubtless referred to the experiences in Allegheny. The "dissention breeder" was Smith, who, during the last day's march over the mountains, temporarily stole the army from his superior.[2]

Relations between the chief marshal and his assistant had been strained for some time before the final outbreak. Newspaper reports had indicated friction between the leaders during Coxey's absence on a journey to Pittsburgh and Massillon while the army crossed the mountains. The "Unknown" had openly cursed Browne.[3] This was the result of something more than a mere personal quarrel. Before the Commonweal had left Homestead a member of the Pittsburgh Commune had explained to Detective Griffin: "Somebody is going to give that Colonel Brown fellow what's coming to him if he doesn't change his tune. . . . He's

[1] Vincent, "Commonweal", pp. 91, 92.
[2] Chicago *Tribune*, May 6, 1894.
[3] Pittsburgh *Press*, April 13, 14, 1894.

too bossy for the job. . . . He thinks he's everything."

The detective found that the men had been complaining to Jesse Coxey, the General's popular son, of the chief marshal's domineering attitude. Soon Griffin heard talk of a mutiny, and learned that the "Unknown" and Jesse Coxey were supposed to be on the side of the mutineers. On the day when the Commonweal crossed the Mason and Dixon Line Griffin's friend, the Civil War veteran, remarked cryptically that something was likely to happen on Friday, the thirteenth. Nothing happened on that day except that some of Browne's officious orders were openly derided by the men. The next morning the word was passed along the line and when Browne gave the command "Forward, March", not a man moved. The malcontents were now sure of their strength. On a repetition of the command, all stepped forward. It was understood that the "Unknown", who had recently suffered many humiliations at Browne's hands, was to be the leader.

Near Grantville, Maryland, the "Unknown" and the chief marshal fell into a dispute over orders. Presently Browne was heard to denounce Smith as a paid troublemaker.

"You're a Pinkerton spy," he shouted.

"Take that back this instant or I'll shove your detestable false face into the back of your head," the "Unknown" threatened.

Browne apologized and retracted his statement. The "Unknown" turned to the army. He said that he could endure Browne's sneers no longer, and inquired whether the men wished to follow him or "this leather coated skunk." He then suggested that it was time to move on.

"The army will remain here until I give the order to march," announced Browne pompously.

The "Unknown" snapped out the command: "Forward, March."

The army stepped out.

"Halt," bellowed Browne, but the army marched on.

The mutineers' victory was complete for the time being. Browne jumped into a buggy and drove rapidly to Frostburg to wire his troubles to Coxey. The "Unknown" remained in command for one day. Coxey returned posthaste, deposed and dismissed the "Unknown", and reinstated Browne. Jesse Coxey also left the army for a time. The General controlled the commissary, and there was no attempt to dispute his authority. Browne was doubtless wiser for this experience, and there was no cause for further mutiny.[1]

The "Unknown" now identified himself as A. P. B. Bozarro (or Pizzaro), manufacturer of a blood medicine at 801 South Peoria Street, Chicago, Illinois. Browne confirmed this identification. Bozarro was none other than the Indian patent-medicine salesman who had befriended Browne after his expulsion from Chicago by Mayor Harrison. Browne explained that shortly after leaving Pittsburgh he had found it necessary to reorganize the army because Bozarro "had inculcated a military idea contrary to the original plan" of the Commonweal. He advanced the theory that the "Unknown" was the reincarnation of a good spirit and a

---

[1] Griffin, "Secret Service Memories", *Flynn's*, Vol. XIII, pp. 921–926; Pittsburgh *Press*, April 15, 1894; Pittsburgh *Chronicle Telegraph*, April 16, 1894. The dialogue is quoted from Griffin. The Pittsburgh *Press* dispatch stated that Browne was as drunk as a boiled owl and that the men were disgusted with him.

bad spirit in the same man; when the evil spirit predominated, Bozarro was a man to be shunned.[1]

Bozarro and "Cheek" Childs presently appeared at
Hancock, Maryland, a day in advance of the army and
collected money for it, after which they decamped. The
General and the restored marshal, in great wrath, issued
a warning against these impostors and tried to have them
arrested for obtaining money under false pretenses.[2]

The depleted ranks of the Commonweal were partially
refilled between the mountains and Washington, but
the number did not again reach five hundred before the
army arrived in the District of Columbia. At Cumberland, Maryland, Coxey loaded his men, horses, and
supplies into two coal barges as twenty-six tons of
freight, each soldier at an estimated net weight of one
hundred fifty pounds. In this manner they traveled
ninety miles in two days at a cost of $85. The men
were packed upon a layer of straw placed on the bot-
toms of the barges. In the lead was the *Good Roads*,
commanded by Marshal Browne. Next came the *J. S.
Coxey*, commanded by Jesse Coxey, who was now restored to his position of chief of staff. These vessels
were followed by the *Argus* or *Flying Demon*, which
carried the A. E. D. H. Browne in a general order now
compared the march of the Commonweal to the voyage
of Cleopatra to meet Anthony.[3]

[1] Pittsburgh *Chronicle Telegraph*, April 16, 17, 1894. This identification seems
to have been the correct one. The "Unknown" is referred to as a Chicago Indian patent-medicine man in the Chicago *Tribune*, May 6, 1894, and in Austen,
"Coxey's Commonweal Army", *Chautauquan*, Vol. XIX, p. 335.

[2] Pittsburgh *Chronicle Telegraph*, April 19, 1894; Washington *Post*, April 18,
1894; *Weekly Iowa State Register*, April 20, 1894.

[3] Pittsburgh *Chronicle Telegraph*, April 17, 18, 1894; Washington *Post*, April 18,
1894; New York *Times*, April 18, 1894; Stead, "Coxeyism", *Review of Reviews*,
Vol. X, p. 55.

At Hagerstown, where the army rested three days before resuming the journey on foot, it was learned that the late "Unknown" now had an army of his own consisting of twenty-three men. Coxey was absent on a trip to New York, where he attended a horse show to dispose of some of his own animals, and addressed a large audience at the People's Party headquarters, telling about his army and his plans.[1] There was a rumor that the officers, fearing the influence of Bozarro over the men, hesitated to march until the General's return, for the soldiers respected Coxey and he could restrain them from any overt act.[2]

The Commonweal marched out of Hagerstown, however, before the General's return, with three hundred ten men in line. At Frederick the sheriff and a body of mounted deputies met the army to escort it across Frederick County.[3] Since the population of Maryland seemed for the most part unfriendly,[4] Browne had the presence of mind to provide each of his men with a flagstaff, announcing in a general order — the one already quoted in which he referred to the deputy sheriffs and the walls of Babylon — that the loss of a "staff of peace" was equivalent to a discharge from the army. These stout oaken staves, four feet long, were doubtless intended for use in teaching good manners to unfriendly dogs, and in other emergencies.[5]

At Frederick the camp was thrown into great excitement when Browne read two telegrams sent to the army. One, from Henry Vincent of Chicago, announced

[1] New York *Times*, April 22, 24, 1894.
[2] Pittsburgh *Chronicle Telegraph*, April 21, 28, 1894.
[3] *Ibid.*, April 24, 1894.
[4] Vincent, "Commonweal", pp. 95 *ff.*, *passim*.
[5] Pittsburgh *Press*, April 28, 1894; Vincent, "Commonweal", pp. 107, 108.

that a thousand striking iron-molders had arranged for railroad transportation, and that they would meet the Commonweal at Rockville. The other, stating that the Iowa militia had fired upon the men of Kelly's army, killing six, brought forth shouts of anger.[1] The belligerent feelings thus aroused found expression that night. Browne, it seems, had issued an order in which he advised his followers that bad whiskey was dangerous, but that good liquor was useful in moderation. Some of the Coxeyites succeeded in practicing all these precepts except for the item relating to moderation. The result was a riot in which blood was shed. The mayor refused to permit the Commonweal to parade through the town.[2]

At Rockville, where the army went into camp at the fair grounds, "Bozarro's bummers" sat on the fence and scoffed at the Commonweal, but the irritation caused by these jeers was forgotten when the Philadelphia division of about fifty men, all carrying flags, appeared to join the main body. This army had been recruited in eastern Pennsylvania by Marshal Christopher Columbus Jones, a diminutive reformer fifty-nine years of age, who wore a silk hat and a long gray beard, who could "quote poetry by the yard and talk until doomsday." He believed in reincarnation and Coxey's bills. His secretary, Henry G. Clinton, was a young man, formerly a carpenter by trade, who also "sustained a plug hat with impressive dignity."[3] Jones' men were "a sleek, well-fed looking crowd of young men", who seemed to be of the better

---

[1] New York *Times*, April 26, 1894; *Weekly Iowa State Register*, April 27, 1894.

[2] Pittsburgh *Chronicle Telegraph*, April 26, 1894.

[3] Washington *Post*, April 30, 1894; Pittsburgh *Post*, April 29, 1894; Pittsburgh *Press*, April 28, 1894.

CARL BROWNE, CHRISTOPHER COLUMBUS JONES AND
GENERAL COXEY

class of workmen, all claiming to be workers at skilled trades.[1]

Recruiting activity for this contingent had begun early in March, and for a time Jones seemed to have a large following. Vincent states that among those who flocked to Jones' standard were one hundred students and two professors from Lehigh University, who believed that the Coxey movement would further the speedy realization of the principles of freedom and equality.[2]

Jones, however, when he left Philadelphia on March 12, had not more than a hundred men in his whole army. A detective in disguise carried his banner, and about fifty newspaper men followed the parade through the city.[3] At Wilmington, Delaware, they were jailed as vagrants and were notified that they must move promptly out of the State to escape punishment. Moving on by easy stages through New Jersey and Maryland, they lived on the fat of the land and arrived at Rockville in time to enter the District of Columbia with Coxey's main body.[4]

Ten thousand people turned out to see the army march into Brightwood Park, on the outskirts of the District of Columbia. On the last day of April the army rested in Camp George Washington, having made the journey on schedule time, prepared to make the great attempt of May day.[5]

---

[1] Austen, "Downfall of Coxeyism", *Chautauquan*, Vol. XIX, pp. 450, 451; Hall, "An Observer in Coxey's Camp", *Independent*, Vol. XLVI, p. 616.
[2] Vincent, "Commonweal", p. 206.
[3] *Ibid.*, p. 206; Pittsburgh *Press*, April 12, 1894.
[4] Vincent, "Commonweal", p. 207; *Weekly Iowa State Register*, April 20, 1894; Washington *Post*, April 20, 1894.
[5] *Review of Reviews*, Vol. X, p. 57; Pittsburgh *Chronicle Telegraph*, April 30, 1894.

CHAPTER VI

While the Commonweal was making its way toward the nation's capital city, the public wondered what was going to happen when it arrived. Coxey had predicted that he would have a hundred thousand men on May first. His army had never exceeded a few hundred but there were other companies. As Coxey approached the District of Columbia, Kelly with some fifteen hundred was marching across Iowa. In Ohio the militia was called out to eject Galvin's men from a train, and Fry's army was at Indianapolis. Randall's men were prepared to start from Chicago. In the Pacific Northwest several thousand men were trying to make their way eastward over the railroads. How many of the unemployed would join these armies on their way? It was feared that an ominously large number might appear in Washington. If thousands of hungry and desperate workingmen assembled there, with criminals and tramps in their wake, how could they be prevented from making depredations, even if there was no serious uprising?

Among those most interested in these questions were the people of Washington. Nervous or timid persons were apprehensive of dire results if the city should be invaded by a hostile mob of desperate men such as these armies were reputed to contain. "Coxey's Army is no longer a joke," said one newspaper. "The growth and progress of this horde of dangerous characters are most serious matters for Washington to contemplate. It is time for Washingtonians to consider what can be done to avert the threatened invasion of the district by this swarm of human locusts." [1] Washingtonians and others were assured, however, that proper police and military preparations were being made to meet all contingencies that might arise.

The Government secret service had taken the Coxey movement seriously from the beginning, sending out its operatives to enlist in the Commonweal at Massillon and at other points along the route; and to keep the authorities informed. As Matthew F. Griffin, the operative already quoted, explained in his reminiscences, the two chief duties of the secret service were "to guard the President and to protect the integrity and safety of the country's currency." In addition to the fear that the President and other high officials might be in danger, therefore, he describes another reason for apprehension:

Apart from the danger to the lives of the nation's leaders, there was in the United States Treasury, with its vast stores of gold and silver and paper money, millions and millions of dollars housed in strong steel vaults. But no vault could withstand a determined man with drill and nitroglycerine. And what could an army of one hundred thousand desperate and determined men do?

What a city to loot! There was reason for alarm. [2]

There seems to be no evidence showing that any such ideas as these ever entered the heads of the Coxeyites, and Coxey was opposed to acts of violence, but the authorities were taking no chances. Military and

---

[1] Washington *News*, quoted in *Public Opinion*, Vol. XVII, p. 24 (April 5, 1894).
[2] Matthew F. Griffin, "Secret Service Memories", *Flynn's*, Vol. XIII, p. 917 (March 13, 1926). See also *ibid.*, p. 915; Pittsburgh *Press*, March 25, 1894.

naval officers were reported to be in conference over
the defense of the capital. In due time Brigadier General Ordway reported that he had fifteen hundred men
in Washington, and that several thousand more could
be rushed in from Philadelphia, New York, and Annapolis within a few hours. Sharpshooters reinforced the
usual guards at the treasury. The National Guard was
ready. Two hundred special policemen were sworn in,
and on April 30 a double force of officers was placed on
duty in the capitol building.[1]

Long before May 1 advance parties of unemployed
began to appear. On April 7 Captain George W. Primrose and forty men, nearly half of whom had started
from Texas in March, arrived in Washington.[2] They
were promptly arrested for vagrancy, but they were
discharged (for lack of evidence, it was said) on condition that they leave the city unless they could obtain
immediate employment; the judge had decided "that
Captain Primrose and his men were tramps, that they

[1] On the military and police preparations see Pittsburgh *Post*, March 22, 1894;
San Francisco *Chronicle*, March 24, April 12, 1894; New York *Times*, April 20, 25,
27, 28, 1894; Washington *Post*, April 29, 1894; Chicago *Tribune*, May 1, 1894;
Griffin, "Secret Service Memories", *Flynn's*, Vol. XIII, pp. 916, 917 (March 13,
1926); Vol. XIV, pp. 86, 87 (March 20, 1926).

[2] The Primrose band had organized in San Antonio, Texas, about March 20.
They had made their way eastward by rail, arriving in St. Louis on March 30 and
at Cincinnati by April 4. A Cincinnati dispatch of April 4 stated that these men
did not beg, but depended upon voluntary contributions, and that, as their rules
required, they were "a clean-faced lot." One was the son of a wealthy New York
real estate dealer, and another the son of a well-known Brooklyn divine, — both
well educated, but unable to get work. The minister's son was found so weak from
lack of food that he was taken to a hospital. The leaders disclaimed any connection
with either Coxey or Fry. Primrose was reported to have said at Cincinnati that
from all parts of the west and south (meaning probably the southwest) "groups of
men in fives and fifties, by some occult impulse, are marching to Washington. They
are not tramps and beggars, but men who want work. They are not going because
Coxey started, but there is vast unrest among the people, and Captain Primrose says
that they will see a crowd such as the world rarely saw." — Pittsburgh *Post*, April
1, 5, 6, 8, 1894.

had been guilty of tramping, and he then rather inconsistently sentenced them to tramp." [1]

On April 23 the commissioners of the District of Columbia issued a proclamation which warned the army of the uselessness of its mission, explaining that there was no employment in Washington, that the District already had difficulty in caring for its own poor, and that the laws would be strictly enforced. [2]

Coxey's Good Roads Bill was reported unfavorably to the Senate by the Committee on Education and Labor while the army was in Pennsylvania. [3] On April 14 Senator Peffer, of Kansas, who had introduced this bill, offered a resolution for the appointment of a "committee on communications" of nine senators, to receive all written, printed, or oral communications from citizens or bodies of citizens visiting Washington to petition or remonstrate, in order that these petitioners "shall have full and respectful hearing, and that proceedings attending their communications with the Senate shall be orderly and not subject to interruption by the transaction of other business." [4] Peffer thought that this would do much to overcome the feeling that the Senate was an "American House of Lords", out of touch with the people. Senator Allen, of Nebraska, although he did not indorse the Coxey movement or the other attempts to present petitions in person, claimed that American citizens had a right to present petitions in this way. Both of these Populist senators

---

[1] M. M. Trumbull, "Current Topics", *Open Court*, Vol. VIII, p. 453; *Public Opinion*, Vol. XVII, p. 43 (April 12, 1894).

[2] Vincent, "Commonweal", pp. 102, 103; *Weekly Iowa State Register*, April 27, 1894.

[3] *Congressional Record*, 53rd Cong., 2d Sess., p. 3606 (April 10, 1894).

[4] 53rd Cong., 2d Sess., *Senate Miscellaneous Document No. 151.*

complained of the newspaper accounts of General Ordway's military preparations, and of the intentions expressed to stop the Coxeyites at the borders of the District of Columbia by force.

Allen made an attack upon lobbyists, containing comparisons that must have been by no means pleasing to some of his colleagues.

> Sir — he said — many of them are met almost with hats off; they are met almost with outstretched arms and words of welcome, and yet they are doing the country more damage and more injury than all of the Coxey armies; . . . and yet here is the threat . . . that honest workingmen who are out of employment, every one of whom perhaps is as good as any Senator in this chamber . . . are to be met with a military force because they come here to place their grievances before Congress in person.[1]

All this was good Populist doctrine, appropriate to the senators from Kansas and Nebraska. On the next day Senator Hawley of Connecticut replied, asserting that Allen's speech "would have been received with tumultuous applause in a meeting of anarchists", and that it contained "the bacteria and bacilli of anarchy."[2] After a discussion which was described as "much the warmest in which Senators have engaged for some time", the Senate refused to consider Peffer's resolution on April 21, but not by a very large majority.[3]

The appearance in Washington of a delegation of

---

[1] *Congressional Record*, 53rd Cong., 2d Sess., pp. 3842, 3843 (April 19, 1894.)

[2] *Ibid.*, 53rd Cong., 2d Sess., p. 3884; *Public Opinion*, Vol. XVII, p. 95; Indianapolis *Journal*, April 21, 1894.

[3] New York *Times*, April 20, 1894. The vote was 26 (Dem. 21, Rep. 5) to 17 (Rep. 12, Pop. 4, Dem. 1).—*Public Opinion*, Vol. XVII, p. 95. The *National Watchman* (a Populist organ in Washington, D. C.), April 27, 1894, suggested: "Every laboring man in the nation should cut out this vote and preserve it. Only one Democrat in the Senate voted for it."

more than a thousand Philadelphia workmen to protest against the passage of the Wilson Tariff Bill gave rise to comparisons which varied with the point of view from which they were written. The editor of a western Republican paper, under the heading, "A Real Army of Labor", announced that while no one had any faith in the Commonweal army, this great labor convention at Washington on April 20 would not be "an army of cranks, but of peaceable, intelligent men who have suffered hardships and deprivations on account of the tariff tinkerers." [1] *The Journal of the Knights of Labor* observed:

One thousand comfortably employed workmen of the protected industries go to Washington in Palace coaches and are received by Senators with open arms and escorted to the galleries, while the petitions are read. Ten thousand unemployed men march, foot-sore and tired, over the mountains, to Washington, to petition for work, and they are threatened with the police and military. See the difference! [2]

Before the Peffer resolution was disposed of by the Senate, symptoms of Populist sympathy for the Coxey movement appeared in the House. Representative Haldor E. Boen, of Minnesota, introduced a resolution which instructed the Secretary of War to provide camping grounds and tents for all organized bodies of laborers that came into the district. John R. Davis, of Kansas, went still further when he introduced a bill which directed the Secretary of War immediately to enlist half a million men in a volunteer industrial army, to serve for one year, to be clothed, paid, and fed as

[1] *Weekly Iowa State Register*, April 6, 1894; see also Washington *Post*, April 21, 22, 1894; Indianapolis *Journal*, April 23, 1894.
[2] Quoted in *Public Opinion*, Vol. XVII, p. 116.

regular soldiers, and to be employed on public works. The cost was to be defrayed by an issue of treasury notes. This contained the essential features of Coxey's original bills — money inflation, public improvements, and work for the workless.[1]

On April 25 a caucus was held at the Populist headquarters in Washington to determine what attitude the party should take toward the approaching Commonweal, and to take steps toward avoiding conflict and possible bloodshed, for grave fears for the result were expressed if the police should take too decisive action to exclude the army. Coxey's bills were not indorsed; it was said that they were not a part of the party's program. No formal resolutions were adopted, but it was agreed that the Coxeyites ought to be protected in the exercise of the rights of free speech, petition, and peaceable assemblage. The resolution which had been introduced by Senator Allen earlier in the day was approved as an expression of the Populist attitude toward the movement.[2] This resolution read as follows:

Whereas it is currently reported that unarmed, lawabiding and peaceably disposed but unemployed citizens of the United States of America are about "to peaceably assemble" in the city of Washington and "to petition the government for a redress of their grievances;" and

[1] *Congressional Record*, 53rd Cong., 2d Sess., p. 3935; *National Watchman*, April 27, 1894; Indianapolis *Journal*, April 21, 1894. Senator Peffer, on April 25, introduced another bill to provide work for the unemployed in the District of Columbia, proposing to appropriate $1,000,000 to be expended for the improving of public grounds, paying $1.50 for an eight-hour day. *Ibid.*, April 26, 1894; *Congressional Record*, 53rd Cong., 2d Sess., pp. 4059, 4060.

[2] Senators Stewart of Nevada and Allen of Nebraska, Representatives Pence and Bell of Colorado, Baker and Harris of Kansas, Boen of Minnesota, Keim and McKeigan of Nebraska, and Chairman Taubeneck of the People's Party National Committee, were present. *Weekly Iowa State Register*, April 27, 1894; Indianapolis *Journal*, April 26, 1894.

Whereas threats of arresting such persons have been made upon their entering the District of Columbia and the City of Washington: Therefore be it

Resolved, That under the Constitution of the United States of America citizens of the United States, regardless of their rank or station in life, have an undoubted and unquestionable right to peaceably assemble and petition the Government for a redress of their grievances at any place within the United States where they do not create a breach of the peace, menace or endanger persons or property, or disturb the transaction of public business or the free use of streets and highways by the public.

Second, That such persons have as undoubted a right to visit and assemble in the city of Washington . . . as in other portions of the territory . . . of the United States.

Third, That such persons have a right to enter upon the Capitol grounds . . . and into the Capitol building itself, as fully and to as great an extent as other citizens or persons . . .; and any threat of violence to such persons under such circumstances would be a clear violation of their constitutional and inalienable rights.

Fourth, That we commend the prompt enforcement of all just and constitutional laws looking to the preservation of the public peace and the prevention and punishment of crime, but under the pretense of preserving the public peace and the prevention and punishment of crime, peaceable and lawabiding citizens must not be disturbed in the full and free exercise of their constitutional rights.[1]

Senators raised objections to these resolutions on the grounds that nobody had denied the doctrines there set forth, that they intimated a deplorable want of confidence in our institutions and in the execution of the laws, and that there had been no threats of violence against the Coxeyites. In defence of his action Allen

---

[1] 53rd Cong., 2d Sess., *Senate Miscellaneous Document No. 163; Congressional Record,* 53rd Cong., 2d Sess., p. 4060.

quoted newspapers at considerable length on General Ordway's alleged military preparations for the reception of Coxey, and the danger of a revolution "caused by usury and monopoly." [1] He was met by several law-and-order speeches, notably one by Senator Wolcott of Colorado, to the effect that although the resolutions changed no existing law, when taken in connection with the preamble they seemed "to extend a cringing invitation to some thousands of people calling themselves unemployed laborers" to invade Washington; that the only inducement to such an invasion had been the utterances of men in high places, some of them in the Senate, who had spoken of "a servile police force and a paid soldiery", not to mention the Populist governors of his own and several other States; and that it was time for men in public life "to cultivate more regard for the perpetuity of republican institutions and to pander less to that miscalled portion of the labor vote whose labor is with their throats, and never with their hands." It was time, he said, that "we had courage to stand together against socialism and populism and paternalism run riot." He thought that any one who wanted a job could get one. [2]

The Coxey affair was getting more attention in Congress than most of the congressmen and senators seemed to desire. As the time for the proposed meeting on the Capitol steps approached, there were reports that the leaders of the House were taking precautions to prevent

---

[1] *Congressional Record*, 53rd Cong., 2d Sess., pp. 4060, 4106 *ff*.

[2] *Ibid.*, p. 4107 (April 26); *cf*. New York *Times*, April 26, 1894. Two days later the local assembly of the Knights of Labor in Denver resolved "That Senator Wolcott, in attacking the Coxey movement and in his denunciations of Governor Waite, does not express the sentiment of the majority of our citizens, but the desires of the monopolies he represents." *Weekly Iowa State Register*, May 7, 1894.

Coxey talk in the House at the time of the demonstration, and arranging that all resolutions or other references to the subject should be promptly referred to committees without debate.[1]

When Coxey arrived at Washington, he obtained at the office of the commissioners of the District of Columbia a permit for his parade, as was required by law. The Chief of Police called his attention to the statute which prohibited the passage of processions or the carrying of banners through the Capitol grounds, and the holding of mass meetings or the making of speeches there, and warned him that he would be arrested if he attempted any of these things.[2] The General, however, announced his intention to make the attempt. He held, as Senator Allen did, that the constitutional guarantees of freedom of petition and free speech protected him and his followers in their right to meet at the Capitol regardless of any local regulations that seemed to forbid it, to air their grievances, and to urge the passage of his bills. He said that if he were arrested he would carry the matter to the courts and obtain a decision there "as to the rights of the people under the constitution in this regard."[3]

Coxey tried to induce the Speaker of the House and the Vice President to suspend the regulations, and he succeeded in getting an interview with Speaker Crisp. Coxey asserted that he represented the American

---

[1] Chicago *Times*, May 1, 1894; *Weekly Iowa State Register*, May 4, 1894; Pittsburgh *Post*, April 30, 1894.

[2] The Philadelphia workmen, mentioned above, had broken up their procession when they approached the Capitol grounds, and had entered in the capacity of individual citizens. The exclusion by the police of a procession of Odd Fellows on April 26 was regarded as a precedent for the case of Coxey's army. — Vincent, "Commonweal", p. 329.

[3] Chicago *Times*, May 1, 1894; Chicago *Tribune*, May 1, 1894; New York *Times*, May 1, 1894.

people. Mr. Crisp inquired by what authority he
represented sixty-five million people; the people's representatives, said the Speaker, were the three hundred
fifty-six congressmen, and the remedy was the ballot
box. Coxey said that Congress did not represent the
people; that the ballot box was too slow, for relief must
be had at once; that Congress never paid much attention to written petitions, and he thought his method
would compel consideration; and that he believed it was
duty of Congress to appropriate money for the relief the
of the unemployed. The Speaker replied that Coxey
was trying to intimidate Congress, and that he would
not grant the request even if he had the authority.
"The chief representative of the Democratic Party in
Congress," said Coxey, "has refused to grant the rights
of the American people." [1]

On May Day morning the forces of the Commonweal
were marshalled for the fray — and so were the officers
of the law. Early in the day a squadron of mounted
police swung into position before the east front of the
Capitol. Then others appeared, mounted or on foot,
until there were two hundred in addition to the regular
force. Thirty were stationed in the rotunda, and others
elsewhere in the building. All avenues of approach
were guarded by mounted men.

Meanwhile, at the Coxey camp, Browne drilled the
army, addressed the audience, and had his men in line
long before the start at ten o'clock. Then the column
wended its way along a mile of woodland road, and on
into Washington. The order of the procession was similar to that of Easter Sunday, with certain additions.
It was led by a platoon of nine policemen. Mrs. Anna

[1] Indianapolis *Journal*, May 1, 2, 1894; *cf. Public Opinion*, Vol. XVII, p. 136.

L. Diggs, a Populist agitator from Kansas, rode in one of the carriages. The Commonweal band of six pieces, "mostly bass drum and cymbals", was "pounding determinedly in an attempt at 'Marching through Georgia'." [1] This time there was a goddess of peace — two of them, in fact. Miss Mamie Coxey, the seventeen-year-old daughter of the general, had run away with her brother Jesse and had come to Washington for the occasion. She was a most attractive young lady, with flowing golden hair, and as she rode near the head of the procession in a becoming white riding habit, shading her face with a tiny parasol, her horse prancing to the music of the band, she impressed the crowds — and the reporters — so favorably, that newspapers told how the spectators broke into spontaneous cheers at the sight of her.

A shriek of bagpipes heralded the coming of the Philadelphians who brought up the rear. At their head was another goddess of peace — "a good-looking, plump, red-cheeked maiden of 18, draped in the Stars and Stripes with not inartistic effect, a gilt star flashing from her blue turban, and dark hair streaming down her back", mounted upon an ambling plough horse evidently selected for his docility. She was escorted by the wizened and diminutive Christopher Columbus Jones, with his long gray beard and high beaver hat, upon a spirited black stallion "to which he clung desperately with terror imaged in his face." [2] There were five hundred or more of the unemployed, marching silently and in good order. The Commonwealers carried on their four-foot staves the banners with the

[1] Pittsburgh *Chronicle Telegraph*, May 1, 1894.
[2] *Ibid.*

strange device — "Peace on earth, good will toward men, but death to interest on bonds."

When Pennsylvania Avenue was reached, it was lined with spectators. Policemen were everywhere. "There were enough on duty," wrote one witness, "to take every single Coxeyite into custody, and many seemed anxious to do so. The Washington authorities were undoubtedly very badly scared, and held a large body of police and military in reserve for emergencies." [1] The great concourse of people that gathered near the Capitol was variously estimated at from fifteen to thirty thousand — a greater crowd, it was said, than had been seen at any inauguration. "That which was most significant in the parade . . ." said the correspondent of the *Outlook*, "was not the character of the five hundred recruits who made up the Coxey army, but the sympathy shown for them by the greater part of the fifteen or twenty thousand people who crowded the streets and lined the walks and terraces of Capitol Hill." [2]

Up the Avenue the Commonweal marched, amidst cheers, toward the Capitol. But barring the way, at the end of the Avenue, a solid phalanx of police extended from curb to curb. The decisive moment had arrived. The army turned aside, as if to march by, and then halted on B Street. Coxey, Browne, and Jones, after a hurried conference, walked alone toward the Capitol. They were discovered and the mounted police galloped after them. The three Commonweal leaders went over the low stone paling that surrounded the grounds and disappeared in the shrubbery; the

[1] Hall, "An Observer in Coxey's Camp", *Independent*, Vol. XLVI, p. 616.
[2] *Outlook*, Vol. XLIX, p. 823.

police jumped their horses over and followed, and the crowd surged after them. Browne, conspicuous in his buckskins and sombrero, had almost reached the foot of the steps when two policemen threw themselves upon him. "I am an American citizen," he shouted, "I stand on my constitutional rights." He was handled roughly and hustled away. Coxey succeeded in reaching the steps, where he was recognized and surrounded. He asked to be allowed to speak, but that was forbidden. He then drew from his pocket a written protest which he had prepared for this contingency, but he was led away without being permitted to read it. As he passed a group of reporters he tossed his protest toward them, saying, "That is for the press." Jones was also taken into custody. The crowd about the foot of the steps shouted angrily. As Coxey, who had been thrust through the dense mass of humanity by the police, climbed into the carriage where Mrs. Coxey with little Legal Tender awaited him, a "fierce cheer went up", and the police, who seem to have lost their heads completely, began to use their clubs; the mounted police charged, and fifty or more people were beaten or trampled.[1]

[1] This description of the events of May 1 is based upon Hall, "An Observer in Coxey's Camp", *Independent*, Vol. XLVI, p. 616; Washington *Post*, May 2, 1894; Pittsburgh *Chronicle Telegraph*, May 1, 1894; Chicago *Tribune*, May 2, 1894; Indianapolis *Journal*, May 2, 1894; *Weekly Iowa State Register*, May 4, 1894; *Outlook*, Vol. XLIX, pp. 823, 824.

For newspaper criticisms of the conduct of the police, and accusations of unnecessary brutality, see Chicago *Times*, May 2, 3, 1894; *National Watchman*, May 11, 1894; Washington *Times*, quoted in Pittsburgh *Press*, May 2, 1894; *Journal of the Knights of Labor*, May 3, 1894. A Chicago *Times* editorial of May 3, entitled "A Blunder at Washington", said: "More exact information from Washington strengthens the conviction that the police treatment of Coxey and his followers was vicious and brutal. The desire of the district authorities seems to have been less to enforce the law than to slaughter Coxeyites. It is entirely evident that nothing except the peacefulness of the industrials averted bloody work and that the

During all this excitement the army had stood passively in line where its leaders had left it. It was led back to the camp by Jesse Coxey and his sister, "followed by hundreds of poorly dressed men and women, who cheered it all the way without intermission." [1] Although Coxey was released by the officers after he had been led away from the Capitol steps, Browne and Jones were taken to jail, but they were soon bailed out. That evening Browne, considerably battered, returned to camp, made a speech, and issued "Special Order Number 1", in which, with references to the Rothschilds, Belshazzar of old, good roads, and the "damp, dark dungeon" in which he had been confined for nearly five hours, he announced:

Liberty lies weltering in her own blood in the Nation's Capital City to-night, stabbed in the home of friends and supposed guardians. Free speech has been suppressed and police clubs have taken the place of the scales of justice. . . . Brothers, we have entered upon the beginning of the end. [2]

The end, however, was a protracted affair. The army was in camp, and was to remain near Washington for some time to come. Perhaps it was true, as the *Nation* said, that some of the glamour had been taken away from the movement "by the very prosaic treatment" of the Commonweal and its leaders, [3] but Coxey had found the martyrdom which he had been accused of seeking.

mounted ruffians of the district police did not wait for resistance before plying their clubs and spurring their horses upon Coxeyites and innocent spectators." If Coxey had been allowed to speak, it was asserted, the excitement would have died away, but this had made a martyr of him. It concluded that "The best way to keep order is to permit the maximum of personal liberty."

[1] *Weekly Iowa State Register*, May 4, 1894.
[2] Washington *Post*, May 2, 1894.
[3] *Nation*, Vol. LVIII, p. 337.

There were inquiries as to why, when so many people had trampled on the grass, only Coxey, Browne, and Jones had been arrested for it.[1] There were men who had no intention of indorsing the Commonweal movement, and possibly some who agreed with the suggestion that Carl Browne was a reincarnation of Balaam's ass,[2] who believed that these petitioners, no matter how mistaken, had a right to be heard, that the law under which the arrests were made was unconstitutional, or at least a bad law, and that at any rate the brutality of the police in their treatment of these inoffensive offenders and of spectators alike was unnecessary and reprehensible.[3]

To persons of Populist sympathy, obvious comparisons were suggested between the manner in which Congress treated Coxey, the representative of the poor, and the way in which it treated lobbyists employed by corporations. Coxey's speech, prepared for delivery from the Capitol steps, made an appeal to this sort of sentiment. After citing the constitutional guarantees of the right to assemble and petition, and of free speech, he continued:

We stand here today to test these guarantees of our Constitution. We choose this place of assemblage because it is the property of the people, and if it be true that the right of the people to peaceably assemble on their own premises and utter their petitions has been abridged by the passage of laws in direct violation of the Constitution, we are here to draw the eyes of the entire nation to this shameful fact. . . .

Upon these steps where we stand has been spread a carpet for the royal feet of a foreign princess, the cost of whose

[1] *National Watchman*, May 11, 1894.
[2] Chicago *Tribune*, May 2, 1894.
[3] See Hall, "An Observer in Coxey's Camp", *Independent*, Vol. XLVI, p. 616.

entertainment was taken from the public treasury without the approval or consent of the people. Up these steps the lobbyists of trusts and corporations have passed unchallenged on their way to the committee rooms, access to which we, the representatives of the toiling wealth producers, have been denied. We stand here today in behalf of millions of toilers whose petitions have been buried in committee rooms, whose prayers have been unresponded to, and whose opportunities for honest, remunerative, productive labor have been taken away from them by unjust legislation, which protects idlers, speculators, and gamblers.[1]

Other outpourings of Populist feeling voiced similar sentiments.[2] Conservatives, on the other hand, quoted the opinion handed down by Judge Cooley to the law students at the University of Michigan. The United States, he said, is not a democracy, but has a republican form of government, under which it is the duty of citizens to elect representatives. These representatives can not be coerced after they are elected, but the people

[1] The "Brief History of the Commonweal", at the end of *Cause and Cure* (Coxey Good Roads and Non-Interest Bond Library), Vol. III, No. 22, Dec., 1897 (pages not numbered), states that "Coxey reached the steps only to be confronted by a lieutenant of police who forbade him to speak from the Capitol steps. Anticipating such a possibility, Mr. Coxey then gave to the press the following protest: "Washington, D. C., May 1. — The following is what Coxey intended to say today."

Mr. Coxey recently told the writer that he had no set speech written out for delivery, and that this document was his "protest." It doubtless represents, however, the content of what he intended to say. It is also described in "Coxey, His Own Story" (April, 1914), p. 48, as "The Speech He Had Intended to Deliver at the Door of Congress." The text, in addition to these places, is to be found in later numbers of *Cause and Cure*, in the *Congressional Record*, 53rd Cong., 2d Sess., p. 4512; in the New York *Times*, May 2, 1894, and in other newspapers.

[2] According to the *National Watchman* of April 27, 1894, "Petitioning Congress is about as senseless as baying at the moon, and if those who send them [petitions] should witness the treatment they receive, this kind of folly would cease. . . . Moral: don't send paper petitions, send live ones."

The Washington *Times* said: "The sacred right of petition has for the first time in the history of our country been not only denied, but denied by a policeman. This act will be received with loud acclaim by the privileged classes, who have been and are fattening upon the misery and privation of the great body of the people. It is a temporary victory for might over right." Quoted in *Public Opinion*, Vol. XVII, p. 136.

may petition them. "The notion that petitions may be presented in person," he said, "is preposterous. If the right existed all legislation might be stopped by previous arrangement to present petitions for the purpose." [1]

A number of congressmen had been spectators of the May Day demonstration, among them Tom L. Johnson of Ohio. On the next day Johnson created something of a sensation in the House when he presented a resolution calling for an investigation of the affair of the Capitol steps.[2] He maintained that, the Capitol grounds being in charge of the two houses of Congress, the "policemen who beat and bullied a lot of defenceless men were acting as our guardians", a matter that affected the dignity of the House, and he wanted the resolution passed as a question of privilege. He explained that he did not believe in Coxey's propositions, although he sympathized with the suffering and destitution of which they were a misguided expression.

But . . . — he said, — that the representatives of this nation should have no better reception for a peaceful body of poor, unemployed men, no matter how erroneous their economic views, than to meet them with the upraised clubs of police, is, in my opinion, a disgrace. It is politically a blunder, and morally a crime, and it cannot but stir up feelings of bitterness which a proper course would have allayed.

[1] Chicago *Tribune*, May 4, 1894; New York *World*, May 3, quoted in *Public Opinion*, Vol. XVII, p. 138.

[2] "Whereas it is well known that the Capitol grounds were, on May the 1st, overrun by a large assemblage of people, including a considerable number of the regular and special police of this district; and

"Whereas it is publicly stated that the safety of the members of this House has been endangered, thereby making it necessary for the House to rely upon the clubs of policemen for protection:

"Resolved, That the Committee on Buildings and Grounds be instructed to inquire into the question as to whether unnecessary force was used, whether unoffending citizens were cruelly beaten, and whether the dignity of the House has been violated. . . ." *Congressional Record*, 53rd Cong., 2d Sess., p. 4334.

When the opponents of Johnson's course discovered that he not only wanted to have the resolution referred, but that he actually wanted to pass it, he was squelched. The Speaker could see no question of privilege; he said that if there had been a violation of law, the law could take charge of it. The resolution was referred to the Committee on Public Buildings and Grounds, and it was done for.[1]

The commander of the Commonweal made plans for a long siege of Congress and announced that he expected thousands of the unemployed to join his camp. But when the police had escorted him away from the scene of the disturbance and had allowed him to go free, the law was not done with him. All three of the leaders were haled into court to answer the charge that they had violated the Capitol Grounds Act. The formal complaint against them alleged, in the quaint and archaic language of the courts, that

" one Jacob S. Coxey, one Carl Browne, and one Christopher C. Jones, . . . with force and arms . . . did then and there unlawfully enter upon the grounds of the United States Capitol, and did then and there display a certain flag and banner designated and adapted to bring into public notice a certain organization and movement known and described as to wit: 'J. S. Coxey's Good Roads Association of the United States and Commonweal of Christ,' and moreover, that the said Coxey, the said Browne, and the said Jones, likewise with force and arms, "did then and there step upon certain plants, shrubs, and turf then and there being and growing"; in both cases "against the form of the statute in such case made

---

[1] *Congressional Record*, 53rd Cong., 2d Sess., pp. 4335, 4361; Chicago *Tribune*, May 3, 1894; Chicago *Times*, May 3, 1894.

The speech of Congressman Johnson, the millionaire manufacturer from Cleveland, "regarding to needless clubbing Coxey's followers by the police, has given to the matter a publicity which fully makes amends for its glossing over by most of the daily press." *Outlook*, Vol. XLIX, p. 824.

and provided, and against the peace and Government of the United States of America." [1]

The defendants denied that they had done these things.

The police court was honored by an array of distinguished personages such as was seldom seen there as counsel. District Attorney Birney,[2] contrary to his usual custom in police court cases, appeared in person to lead the prosecution. Besides the regular attorneys for the defence, Senator Allen and half a dozen Populist congressmen were present. The defence raised the question of the constitutionality of the law, and Senator Allen argued the point, but it was overruled by the court. On May 8, Coxey, Browne, and Jones were found guilty of carrying banners, and Coxey and Browne of walking on the grass.[3] On May 21 they were given twenty days for the former, and five dollars fine for the latter offence.[4] On the day after his con-

---

[1] *Congressional Record*, 53rd Cong., 2d Sess., pp. 4513, 4514.

[2] A grandson of the Abolitionist candidate for the presidency. — Pittsburgh *Chronicle Telegraph*, May 8, 1894.

[3] Chicago *Times*, May 5, 1894; Chicago *Tribune*, May 9, 1894; *Weekly Iowa State Register*, May 11, 1894; *Public Opinion*, Vol. XVII, p. 161; New York *Times*, May 5, 1894; Pittsburgh *Press*, May 4, 1894.

[4] *Weekly Iowa State Register*, May 25, 1894. The three men, after conviction, were released on bail pending a motion for a new trial. But it was discovered that through an error or an oversight in a recent law reorganizing the courts of the district, there was no court to which a police court case could be appealed. Chicago *Times*, May 9, 1894.

For attacks upon the "farce trial" and conviction, see editorial on "Russianized America", *National Watchman*, May 25, 1894; *Journal of the Knights of Labor*, May 10, 1894; Chicago *Times*, May 5, 1894.

According to a Washington dispatch of May 5, Representative Pence created a sensation in the courtroom by asserting that the court was trying "to help the prosecuting officers out of a hole from which they had shown absolute incapacity to lift themselves." Pence examined a policeman who was recorded as complainant in the case, and showed that this officer had not entered any complaint, and could not explain how the charge of disorderly conduct against Browne had been entered. This charge was withdrawn. The judge denied that Browne had received rough treatment. — Pittsburgh *Chronicle Telegraph*, May 6, 1894.

viction Coxey appeared before the House Committee
on Labor and asked for a hearing for himself and Browne
on his two bills, but the committee was not disposed to
listen.[1] His troubles were aggravated by the report
that the first Mrs. Coxey was taking steps to sue him
for the abduction of his daughter, the goddess of
peace [2] and on the day he was sentenced he went to
jail, from which he was to emerge as a Populist politician of national prominence.

Before the trial was concluded the Capitol steps affair received more ventilation in the Senate. The day
before the conviction Senator Allen introduced another
resolution, which asserted that Coxey, Browne and
Jones had been assaulted by police in the service of the
United States, arrested, and imprisoned, while peacefully entering the Capitol grounds "in a quiet and
orderly manner to join others there on the said grounds
by lawful right", and which provided for a committee
of five senators, not more than two to be of the same
party, to report the facts, "with such recommendations
. . . as may be necessary to prevent the repetition of
such outrages on the rights of American citizens hereafter." [3] Allen explained that he had never heard of
Coxey until he was called into consultation with some
of the Populist congressmen about the arrest and prosecution of the Commonweal leaders, and that he had no
sympathy for Coxey's aims; he was interested only in
the constitutional rights of citizens, and he denied that
he was counsel for Coxey, although he had gone into
the police court to argue the constitutionality of the

---

[1] New York *Times*, May 10, 1894.
[2] Chicago *Tribune*, May 9, 1894.
[3] 53rd Cong., 2d Sess., *Senate Miscellaneous Document, No. 171*, Part 1.

Act of 1882 under which these men had been prosecuted.[1]

Senators Allen and Stewart, both eyewitnesses of the
disturbance of May 1, described what they had seen,
asserting that the men arrested were not disorderly,
and that the "banners" they carried — or wore, for
Coxey, at least, had his pinned to his coat or vest —
were three inches long and two inches wide.[2] They
inquired why, since thousands of people had trampled
the grass and shrubs, there had been only three arrests.
Allen asserted that the metropolitan police were themselves unlawfully upon the grounds when the arrests
were made. Stewart, who did not think that Coxey
walked upon the grass at all, insisted that every one
knew that Coxey was convicted when he committed no
real offense, concluding: "I say convicting this man for
an offense which he did not commit, under a technical
construction of the law which nobody else would be
prosecuted for, has created a feeling in this country
which can only be allayed by a fair investigation and a
report of the fact." [3]

In discussing the right of petition, Senator Henry
M. Teller of Colorado expressed the opinion that although probably no constitutional right was violated
by the law under which the arrests had been made,
every one concerned could get along better without
such a law. He thought that the technical violation of
the statute should have been overlooked by those in
authority. At any rate, he said, the methods of the

---

[1] *Congressional Record*, 53rd Cong., 2d Sess., pp. 4511, 4512.
[2] Browne, at least, seems to have carried his "staff of peace." See Washington
Evening Star, May 1, 1894, quoted in Hall, "An Observer in Coxey's Camp", *Independent*, Vol. XLVI, p. 616.
[3] *Congressional Record*, 53rd Cong., 2d Sess., pp. 4513, 4568, 4569.

police had been most objectionable, and it was "a matter of public notoriety that inoffensive citizens had been beaten over the head by these policemen in the most brutal and outrageous manner"; the police did things unjustifiable even in a riot, when there was no riot; and he wanted the investigation to prevent the recurrence of such affairs in the future.[1]

These speakers, however, were in the minority. Senator Sherman replied that if injustice had been done there was a remedy in the courts,[2] and Senator Hoar called attention to the fact that Coxey had announced his intention to disregard the law because he thought it was unconstitutional.[3] The majority was not disposed to spend much time sympathizing with Coxeyites, and this resolution, like the others, died a natural death. The prospect for the enactment of Coxey's bills by the Senate was by no means encouraging.

---

[1] *Congressional Record*, pp. 4566, 4567. These remarks were made in discussing a substitute motion offered by Teller, which provided for the appointment of a committee to investigate the arrests and the general conduct of the police on May 1, "and to report whether any further legislation is necessary for the protection of the Capitol and grounds about the Capitol; also whether further legislation is necessary or desirable for the protection of the citizens who may visit the National Capitol." 53rd Congress, 2d Sess., *Senate Miscellaneous Document, No. 171*, Part 2.

[2] *Ibid.*, 53rd Cong., 2d Sess., p. 4516.

[3] *Ibid.*, p. 4569.

CHAPTER VII

THE INDUSTRIAL ARMIES OF THE WEST: FRY'S ARMY

While the Commonweal was marching, while Populists in Congress were defending the proposition that poor men had a right to petition their government by unusual methods, and while, after the catastrophe of May 1, Coxey's army awaited reinforcements, there seemed to be prospects that reinforcements might arrive at Washington in large numbers, for "industrial armies", with the national capital as their objective, were advancing from the most distant parts of the United States. It has been noticed that before Coxey's plans had been announced, the unemployed in some of the far western cities had organized for mutual benefit, to demand relief or free transportation, and in many other cities the situation was ripe for such organization. Coxey's scheme, broadcasted through his advertising campaign, and aided unconsciously by the way in which the press seized upon the story and played it up, set the wheels in motion, or accelerated them if they had already started, in every part of the country except the Old South, where the unemployment problem was less acute than elsewhere.[1]

It was the western armies that represented the most extensive, spontaneous, and genuine movement of real workingmen. They were larger than the others, and

[1] Vincent states that the neighborhood of Birmingham, Alabama, one of the few industrial centers of the South, was "a recruiting ground of considerable importance", from which a few small contingents went to join northern armies. This, however, was exceptional. — Vincent, "Commonweal", p. 203.

they traveled distances which made Coxey's journey from Massillon fade into insignificance, several of them traversing the whole width of the continent. The western workmen who had learned the value of organization as a means of securing transportation on the railroads before the spring of 1894 naturally took to this means of travel when the idea of the advance upon Washington gained popularity on the Pacific coast. Aside from the distances involved, the vast expanses of mountain and desert where there was only a sparse and widely scattered population, made other methods of traversing this region seem impracticable. The largest, best organized, and most permanent of these armies were Fry's, from Los Angeles, and Kelly's, from San Francisco.

The industrial army at Los Angeles was organized during the month of February, 1894. On March 5, six weeks after Coxey had announced his plan of campaign to the public, it adopted a constitution. Its preamble began with a statement of grievances which asserted that " the evils of murderous competition; the supplanting of manual labor by machinery; the excessive Mongolian and pauper immigration; the curse of alien landlordism; the exploitation by rent, profit, and interest, of the products of toil — have centralized the wealth of the nation into the hands of a few and placed the masses in a state of hopeless destitution."

The questions were then asked:

Why is it those who produce food are hungry?
Why is it those who make clothes are ragged?
Why is it those who build palaces are houseless?
Why is it those who do the nation's work are forced to choose between beggary, crime, or suicide in a nation that

has fertile soil enough to produce plenty to feed and clothe the world; materials enough to build palaces to house them all; and productive capacity through labor saving machinery of 40,000 million man power, and only sixty-five million souls to feed, clothe, and shelter?

The conclusion was that something must be done quickly.

Therefore we, as patriotic American Citizens, have organized ourselves into an Industrial Army for the purpose of centralizing all the unemployed American Citizens at the seat of government . . . and tender our services to feed, clothe, and shelter the nation's needy, and to accomplish this end we make the following demands on the government.

1st. Government employment for all her unemployed citizens.

2nd. The prohibition of foreign immigration for ten years.

3rd. That no alien be allowed to own real estate in the United States.[1]

The leader of this army was General Lewis C. Fry, a Hoosier who had wandered to the Pacific coast. He had been in the regular army,[2] which perhaps accounts for the assertion that his organization and discipline had a more distinctively military cast than any of the others.[3] Each recruit, when he signed the muster roll, subscribed to the following obligations:

I have sworn to support the constitution of the United States and the Industrial Army.

To obey all lawful orders that may be said, sent, or handed to me by those authorized to do so.

---

[1] Vincent, "Commonweal", pp. 163–165; Major General O. O. Howard, "The Menace of Coxeyism: Significance and Aims of the Movement", *North American Review*, Vol. CLVIII, pp. 689, 690; Henry Frank, "The Crusade of the Unemployed", *Arena*, Vol. X, p. 243. For the complete text of this constitution, see Appendix B.

[2] Indianapolis *Journal*, May 3, 1894.

[3] Frank, *Arena*, Vol. X, p. 243; *Cyclopedic Review of Current History*, Vol. IV, p. 142.

To render cheerful support and assistance to all officers and comrades of the army.

To never violate any law of the United States or such state or territory in which I may be, or aid or abet any riotous conduct.

To respect the right of property and law and order.

To never act in any manner to bring discredit upon the Industrial Army or the United States.[1]

A clergyman of liberal views who delivered a Sunday morning lecture on social and religious problems at Los Angeles was surprised to find several companies of the industrial army in attendance.

They marched through the streets of the city — he wrote — in front of many of the churches, with emblematic ensigns flying, five hundred strong, and as they filed into the hall and quietly took their seats they were greeted with thunderous applause. I noticed that my most attentive and appreciative listeners were these same sallow-faced and sad-hearted unemployed.

He returned the compliment by praising the character of the men, a number of whom he interviewed. They were earnest and sincere, he said, and seemed to believe that they would succeed in reaching Washington, and that when they arrived their representatives would not dare refuse legislation for their relief. He decided that Fry, whom he questioned, was both earnest and intelligent, and entirely peaceful in his intentions. When he asked Fry what he would do if the Government should interfere with his progress, the General replied: "Lay down as prisoners of war and demand that the government provide for us." [2]

---

[1] Frank, *Arena*, Vol. X, pp. 243, 244. The same oath, according to Vincent, was administered to the recruits of Kelly's army. Vincent, "Commonweal", p. 133.
[2] Frank, "Crusade of the Unemployed", *Arena*, Vol. X, pp. 242, 243.

By the middle of March the Los Angeles army was reported to have an enlisted strength of eight hundred fifty men, and it was increasing. Its officers demanded free transportation eastward over the Santa Fé and one of them threatened to capture a train if it were refused. On March 16, six hundred men set out on foot, about two hundred remaining in the barracks as an "industrial reserve."[1] The army proceeded eastward toward San Bernardino. It was suspected that the intention was to take a freight train to cross the desert. The towns along the line of march donated food as the best method of preventing depredations, and for the most part, discipline was maintained, the only exceptions being incursions into two or three orange groves.[2] At Ontario the army boarded a freight train. Although the trainmen protested, they did not resist, and the men rode to Colton. Citizens of that place had donated three thousand pounds of hardtack, two hundred fifty pounds of bacon, two hundred pounds of beans, salt and matches. The army was now prepared to cross the desert, and it embarked on an eastbound freight on the Southern Pacific.[3] Two days later it was reported at Deming, New Mexico. "The discipline maintained is first class," said a newspaper dispatch. "Twenty miles west on the Southern Pacific officers of the army put twenty-five professional thieves off the cars on the open prairie."[4]

As the industrial army approached Texas, a panic developed at El Paso. Railway messages were received

---

[1] San Francisco *Chronicle*, March 16, 17, 1894.
[2] *Ibid.*, March 17, 18, 19, 1894. *Cf. Public Opinion*, Vol. XV, p. 595 (March 22, 1894).
[3] San Francisco *Chronicle*, March 20, 1894.
[4] *Ibid.*, March 23, 1894.

there to the effect that the army was gathering strength
and was despoiling towns along the way. The mayor
proclaimed on March 21 that these men had "plundered
and robbed people along their line of march", and he
called a meeting of citizens to organize for protection.
There was great excitement, and many bought arms.
Early in the afternoon another report came from the
Southern Pacific office that Tucson, Arizona, "was
being looted and burned by the army of tramps because
they had been refused food", and Governor Hogg was
requested to call for United States troops. The governor's telegram to the mayor and the county judge
indicated that he viewed the situation with more
equanimity than they did. He assured them that Texas
was fully able to arrest General Fry and his whole army
if they committed robbery or other violations of the
penal code; he thought that the railroads that brought
the army into the State would probably take them out;
and he asked for a report upon all criminal acts of the
industrials, promising to enforce the laws. At six P. M.
a telegram was received from the mayor of Tucson
stating that nine hundred men of the industrial army
had arrived that morning, that they had "maintained
thorough discipline", and that after they had been fed
and provided with food for the journey, they had proceeded on to El Paso. This dispatch was "hailed with
cheers", and a subscription of three hundred dollars
was raised to entertain the industrials when they arrived.[1]

When General Fry arrived in El Paso in advance of

[1] San Francisco *Chronicle*, March 22, 1894; *Review of Reviews*, Vol. X, p. 59.
A dispatch from Tucson stated that the 700 men of the army were given all they
wanted to eat by the city, that their conduct was orderly, and that reports of their
pilfering were believed to be without foundation. Pittsburgh *Post*, March 23, 1894.

his army, he was arrested on a charge of vagrancy, but the case was dismissed for lack of evidence, and he addressed a crowd on the Plaza. He gave to the press a copy of a letter which he had sent to each member of Congress, inclosing the constitution of the industrial army. Nature, he said, was not at fault for the conditions that prevailed, but they had been "brought about by vicious and ignorant legislation in the interest of the plutocrats." The army, he thought, might number four hundred thousand men, who would be a living petition for laws that would give immediate relief. They wanted the government to issue a billion dollars of legal-tender money, to employ all idle citizens "on internal improvements, such as irrigating canals to reclaim the desert waste; also to improve harbors and navigable rivers." [1]

The army arrived the next evening, and after spending the night in El Paso, it marched out of the city limits, presumably to catch a train to San Antonio. It seems, however, that the railroad had decided that it had furnished enough free transportation, and there was some difficulty about obtaining it. After three days it was reported that Fry and his men had broken a switch lock to sidetrack a train, and had been carried to Finlay, seventy miles farther on. Then their real troubles began. Near Sierra Blanca the railroad sidetracked them in the heart of the desert, and left them there. A telegram from El Paso to Governor Hogg described their location and continued:

John R. Hughes with the State Rangers is at Sierra Blanca to prevent these men from entering upon trains.

[1] San Francisco *Chronicle*, March 23, 1894.

He had telegraphed Judge R. E. Beckham here that the men are tired but orderly, having nothing to éat. The railroad refuses to haul them.

These men would move on foot but for the rangers. This country can not support them. Where they are now they can obtain nothing to eat." [1]

Some asserted that the policy of the railroad was to keep the men in the desert without food until in desperation they interfered with mail trains, and the United States troops could be called upon. The trains running through carried armed guards. A judge in El Paso County, and another at Marfa in Presidio County, issued injunctions forbidding tramps to interfere with trains. [2] General Fry, who had mysteriously disappeared, was reported to have been discovered by the conductor of an east-bound train in an empty ice box of a refrigerator car, and to have been put off "in the wilds of Texas", one hundred fifty miles west of Dallas. [3]

While the men starved, Governor Hogg was engaged in straining the relations between himself and the officials of the Southern Pacific. He not only refused to call out troops, but he withdrew the rangers who were guarding the trains at Finlay. Bitterly denouncing the heartless proceedings of the railroad, he wired his views to the Dallas *Times Herald* in no uncertain terms:

You can truthfully say that neither the cormorant nor the commune can disgrace Texas while I am Governor. When a railroad company hauls tramps or unemployed penniless men into this State it cannot dump them into a barren desert and murder them by torture and starvation without atoning

[1] San Francisco *Chronicle*, March 27, 1894. *Cf. Review of Reviews*, Vol. X, p. 59, which states erroneously that it was the Santa Fe that sidetracked the train.
[2] Pittsburgh *Post*, March 28, 1894; San Francisco *Chronicle*, March 27, 1894.
[3] San Francisco *Chronicle*, March 27, 1894.

for it, if there is any virtue in the machinery of justice. Nor will I permit them to be shot down on Texas soil by any armed force whatever, no matter how much the Southern Pacific and the other enemies of the State may howl about the commune.

J. S. Hogg

The governor told the general manager that since the railroad had brought the men into the State it must take them out, transport them to some place of refuge within a reasonable time, "or submit to the consequences from the State of Texas." The general manager rested upon his legal rights. These men, he said, had reached the place where they were by force, and the company simply refused to surrender its property to them. He offered to carry them to El Paso if the governor desired it, but this was "purely gratuitous", not a legal obligation. The governor replied, standing by his guns. Popular feeling seemed to be on the governor's side, and his stand was indorsed in resolutions adopted by a meeting at Dallas of the Central Industrial Council of Texas.[1]

The parties to the dispute were extricated from this deadlock by the discreet generosity of the people of El Paso, who, fearing that the industrials might return to them, first sent two hundred dollars worth of provisions by express, and then paid for a special train of five coaches and two baggage cars which carried the army to San Antonio.[2]

[1] Pittsburgh *Post*, March 28, 1894; San Francisco *Chronicle*, March 28, 30, 1894. A dispatch from St. Louis to the effect that the Frisco line refused to haul tramps for nothing quoted Supt. Wentworth of that line as saying: "There is no power on earth to compel us to operate our road if we do not want to." *Ibid.*, March 31, 1894.

[2] San Francisco *Chronicle*, March 30, 1894; *Review of Reviews*, Vol. X, p. 59; Pittsburgh *Post*, March 28, 1894; *Weekly Iowa State Register*, March 30, 1894.

At Austin, General Fry, who had managed somehow to escape from the wilds, wanted to march his men to the gubernatorial mansion to thank Governor Hogg for his pains, but he was prevented by the police. A freight train was provided to continue the journey. The army arrived at Longview in fourteen box cars — six hundred men packed in like sardines, so densely that none could lie down. Armed citizens escorted the industrials when they transferred to the Texas Pacific train that was to take them to Texarkana, whence the Iron Mountain road hauled them into Arkansas.

On the last day of March, Fry, having succeeded in leading his men safely out of the wilderness of Texas, saw them safely encamped at Little Rock.[1] A dispatch to the New York *Times* from that place, dated April 1, described the army as consisting of sixteen companies of fifty men each, adding that the men were "machinists, carpenters, bricklayers, printers, farm hands, and few, if any, professional tramps."[2]

Their discipline — said another dispatch — is remarkable. There was no drinking. While the army was in camp General Fry addressed five hundred people on the financial situation. His language was temperate and mild. He avows that the movement is just starting; that in less than thirty days 400,000 men will be in Washington for a common purpose. They mean to be peaceable in their actions. . . .

[1] San Francisco *Chronicle*, March 31, April 1, 1894; Pittsburgh *Post*, April 1, 1894; *Weekly Iowa State Register*, April 6, 1894. A dispatch from Little Rock in the San Francisco *Chronicle* of May 1 stated that the army arrived with 600 men. A dispatch on the next day stated that Fry's army was assuming serious proportions in the southwest, that 200 more had arrived on a stock train, and that there were 900 awaiting transportation at San Antonio; and that the main army left on the night of April 1 for Memphis with nearly 1100 men. *Cf.* New York *Times*, April 2, 1894.

[2] New York *Times*, April 2, 1894.

It is their serious and orderly demeanor that appeals to the people.[1]

Fry arrived at St. Louis with six hundred men on April 3. At the request of the police he posted sentinels about his camp in the railroad yards to keep his men from wandering into the city. The Merchant's Exchange supplied the army with food.[2] The announcement in the newspapers, however, that the crusaders refused to be deflected from their purpose by an offer of work at $1.50 per day led many to suspect their sincerity. Donations of food ceased and it began to appear as if Fry might have to carry out his threat to surrender his men to the police as vagrants in order to have them fed at the public expense.[3] The money to ferry them across the Mississippi was finally raised by subscription, but at East St. Louis the railroads refused to furnish transportation. After two days of unsuccessful attempts to get it, the industrials were ordered out by the police, and they marched away on foot. Starting across Illinois with eight hundred men, Fry's force was soon reduced to three hundred by the hardships of the march.

At Vandalia about half the men refused to walk farther, demanding an opportunity to ride. They pressed on separately under the leadership of Colonel Galvin, who thereby became commander of an army of his own. Galvin moved southward to the line of the Balti-

---

[1] San Francisco *Chronicle*, April 2, 1894; Pittsburgh *Post*, April 2, 1894.

[2] *Weekly Iowa State Register*, April 6, 1894; *Review of Reviews*, Vol. X, p. 59.

[3] Pittsburgh *Chronicle Telegraph*, April 12, 1894. The *Nation*, which was uniformly unfriendly to the movement, remarked: "These 'sojers' had the bad luck to receive an offer of $1.50 per day to work at digging trenches for the laying of pipe by the East St. Louis Water Board. They refused it, of course; but when the facts became known, the soft-headed people who had been supplying them rations free, stopped doing so." *Nation*, Vol. LVIII, p. 264. The story of the offer of work was denounced as a "fake" in the Pittsburgh *Press*, April 13, 1894.

more and Ohio Railroad, which he followed across Indiana to Cincinnati.[1]   When he was interviewed near
Cincinnati, the aims he expressed and the moderation
of his language were similar to Fry's.   He wanted government ownership of the railroads as well as government employment on western irrigation projects.   He
did not blame the Cleveland administration or any
particular act of Congress for the hard times, which he
thought were the result of twenty years of legislation
in favor of monopolies.   When he was asked whether
the Wilson tariff was the cause of the hard times, he
replied:

I can't think so.   They are not due to any one act of legislation nor to the present administration.   They are the
natural result of laws passed to favor monopolies for twenty
years past.   Both parties are managed by capital.   The
Democrats have succeeded in gaining control of the Government, and the Republican capitalists are afraid to invest.
The Democratic capitalists are uncertain as to how their
measures will result, and they are also holding their money.
In consequence of this condition the money of the country
is tied up and the workingman is starving.   We shall demand
a remedy from Congress and the Senate.

If they do not know how to give us one, we will tell them
there are millions of acres of desert land in the West that
would be fertile if irrigated.   For the unemployed workingmen in that portion of the country we will ask an appropriation large enough to give employment to the hundreds of
thousands there.   While our State [California] raises an
abundance of fruit and grapes every year, they rot because
there are not people enough there to consume them; while
the poor in the East go hungry because private monopolies
want so large a profit on operating railroads that we cannot
ship them.   The Australian Government owns and operates

---

[1] Pittsburgh *Chronicle Telegraph*, April 16, 1894; Pittsburgh *Post*, April 28, 1894;
Review of Reviews, Vol. X, p. 59.

its own railroads, and so should the American Government. If the United States Government did as well by its unemployed as the city of Cincinnati has done, this movement would never have started. That is all we shall ask them to do — to give us work.[1]

From Cincinnati, Galvin proceeded toward Columbus, but before reaching that city he engaged in an exploit which brought his army added notoriety. Near Washington Courthouse, Ohio, on the night of April 27, his two hundred men boarded a Baltimore and Ohio freight to ride into Columbus. At Mount Sterling the train was sidetracked by order of company officials, but the passengers refused to descend from the tops of the box cars. The sheriff of Madison County refused to act unless he had warrants directed against the men as individual vagrants. It seems that Galvin had resigned his position as commanding officer in order to escape possible arrest as the individual responsible for the trespass on the railroad company's property, but it was understood that he would resume command when this danger was past.

Both the sheriff and the railroad officials called upon Governor William McKinley for troops. The general agent and the superintendent of the road complained that the presence of Galvin's army had made it impossible to bring a freight train through Mount Sterling for two days, and that the sheriff, with the local company of militia under his orders, refused to act. The

---

[1] *Public Opinion*, Vol. XVII, p. 94; Washington *Post*, April 21, 1894. The next in command to Galvin, Lieut. Col. Wood, described as an old silver prospector thrown out of work by the repeal of the silver-purchase act, was asked what the army proposed to do in Washington. He said: "We will make every lawful effort to secure favorable action on our demands. If we fail we will proceed to organize the army on a permanent basis for political purposes. Organizers will proceed to visit every city in the country and start recruiting stations." Chicago *Tribune*, May 1, 1894.

governor promptly ordered Colonel Coit with one battery of artillery and four companies of infantry to the scene of the disturbance.

Early in the morning of April 28 Attorney-General Richards and Adjutant General Howe arrived at Mount Sterling to observe the situation and to prevent unnecessary violence. Galvin's men on the box cars were quiet, but they refused to budge. Galvin insisted that he had no control over the men and advised them to act according to their own best judgment. When a local police officer asked them to move and tried to read his orders from the governor, he was hooted and jeered.

Then, about noon, to the great surprise of the army, a trainload of soldiers pulled in and unloaded. A Gatling gun was trained upon the mass of men on the car tops, and an officer gave Galvin's men three minutes to get off the train in the name of the State of Ohio. None moved, and there was a tense silence. Then a company of the militia climbed to the top of a car at one end of the train. The Galvinites' color bearer jumped off, followed by others. As the militiamen moved from one end of the train to the other, they found the cars vacated before their arrival.[1]

Having vindicated the authority of the State, the soldiers permitted Galvin's men to move on, and within two days they were encamped in Columbus, gazed upon by crowds of sight-seers. Of thirty recruits who joined at Columbus, more than half were trade unionists. Populists and labor leaders assisted in their entertainment and prepared to speed them on their way. Others

---

[1] Pittsburgh *Post*, April 29, 30, 1894; Hooper, "Coxey Movement in Ohio", *Ohio Archeological and Historical Society Proceedings*, Vol. IX, p. 157; Charles S. Olcott, "William McKinley" (Boston, 1916), Vol. I, pp. 278, 279.

were willing to contribute money to free the city of
their presence, and enough was raised by subscription
to pay their way out of Ohio.[1]

On May 1, when Coxey was arrested in Washington
for walking on the grass, Galvin's men reached Wheeling, West Virginia. The city authorities fed them and
gave them lodgings in the city hall.[2] Again they were
assisted out of the State by labor organizations, whose
representatives succeeded in making a contract with
the Baltimore and Ohio to carry the army to Pittsburgh
at a rate of one cent per mile per soldier, — the railroad explaining that it was treating this as a business
matter, as in the case of any other excursion — and in
this unwonted style the army rode to Pittsburgh, accompanied by an "escort committee" of Wheeling laboring men.[3]

The Pittsburgh police authorities prepared to receive
Galvin as they had received Coxey. When the army
arrived at the Baltimore and Ohio station it was confronted by a large body of policemen and detectives
who marched it promptly through the city to Homestead. There the men encamped in Schuchman's ice
house, which not long before had housed Coxey's "petition in boots", and again the wayfarers received a
warm welcome and plenty of food. Galvin consulted
in Pittsburgh with the same group of Populists and
labor leaders who had coöperated with Coxey, but his
attempts to get railway transportation for his men to
Washington were unsuccessful.[4]

Now that a far western industrial army had ap-

---

[1] Chicago *Tribune*, May 1, 1894; Pittsburgh *Chronicle Telegraph*, April 30, 1894.
[2] *Ibid.*, May 1, 1894; Pittsburgh *Press*, May 1, 1894.
[3] Pittsburgh *Chronicle Telegraph*, May 3, 4, 1894.
[4] *Ibid.*, May 4, 5, 1894; New York *Times*, May 4, 1894.

peared in a region through which Coxey's Commonweal had recently passed, it was natural that observers should compare the two groups, and the Westerners did not suffer in this comparison. An editorial in the Pittsburgh *Chronicle Telegraph* asserted that Galvin, who had brought his army intact all the way from Los Angeles, was the most successful of the commonweal commanders; his men were not "casual recruits picked up by the way", for most of them had been members from the start.[1] Galvin impressed a reporter as a man of genial and unassuming manners — just "the kind of a man to succeed in such an undertaking." Galvin said that his division consisted of a force of picked men, most of whom had union cards, and other evidence seemed to support his assertion.

That many of the Commonwealers are brawny workmen was revealed to a *Chronicle Telegraph* reporter who visited the camp. The men were mainly employed in washing their linen in the river, and as they stood with their bare arms and chests they revealed muscles that would have done credit to a Sandow.[2]

It was noted that the men were not fed from a common kettle, as Coxey's army had been, but that each company received rations which were cooked over its own fire, and that they had better food than Coxey's men.[3] Galvin said that his men had walked only a short distance since he took his stand in favor of riding at Vandalia, Illinois.[4]

After the army had rested over the week-end and had attended church in Homestead, it was ejected from

[1] Pittsburgh *Chronicle Telegraph*, May 4, 1894.
[2] *Ibid.*, May 5, 1894.
[3] *Ibid.*, May 4, 1894.
[4] *Ibid.*, May 5, 1894.

its home in the ice house, and for want of better means of conveyance, it began to walk again.[1] This proved so irksome that soon a score of deserters were arrested for an attempt to ride on a Baltimore and Ohio train.[2] Following Coxey's route only a short distance up the Monongahela River, Galvin turned eastward towards Johnstown, but he found the towns along the way less hospitable than Homestead. Being frustrated in an attempt to board a freight at Blairsville, it seems that the army broke up into small squads which rode the freights as best they could. The men assembled at New Florence in Galvin's absence and held a council of war to determine the next step in the campaign. The alternative propositions were to walk to Johnstown and there try to secure transportation to Harrisburg, or to move on to Harrisburg in small groups, assemble there, and march by easy stages to Washington. They decided upon the latter course. It was reported that the army had disbanded; also that every eastbound freight carried its quota of Galvinites. At the time of this meeting Galvin was in Johnstown, where the chairman of the Populist State Committee [3] had been making unsuccessful efforts to secure aid for the army.[4]

After various vicissitudes Galvin reached Washington before Fry. On the night of May 30 his two hundred hungry and footsore men trudged into the District of Columbia and made their way to the Coxey camp. They found an enthusiastic reception — and an empty larder.[5]

---

[1] Pittsburgh *Chronicle Telegraph*, May 7, 1894.
[2] *Ibid.*, May 9, 1894; *Public Opinion*, Vol. XVII, p. 161.
[3] R. A. Thompson of Indiana, Pa.
[4] Pittsburgh *Chronicle Telegraph*, May 7, 18, 19, 1894; Chicago *Tribune*, May 14, 1894; *Public Opinion*, Vol. XVII, p. 183.
[5] Pittsburgh *Chronicle Telegraph*, May 30, 1894.

In the meantime Fry's army, which Galvin had left in Illinois, had been making somewhat slower progress. At Terre Haute, Indiana, the men were vaccinated by the county board of health. Although they protested, they did not resist for they were bound by their agreement to comply with the laws and to submit to the constituted authorities. They made a good impression "by the excellent camp discipline observed and by the cleanliness and intelligent appearance of the men" — an impression to which a wash day in camp doubtless contributed.[1] There were some irregularities about the process by which the army got out of Terre Haute. It seems that they chartered a car, into which they loaded their wagons, horses, and other baggage, and the officers asserted that they had paid fare for the men, who were to ride on the train. When the car was loaded, however, the train started, leaving the men behind. They camped that night about fires made from railroad fencing, and the next day they seized a Vandalia train bound for Brazil, claiming that they were entitled to the ride.[2] At Brazil a car was chartered to Indianapolis; when the train started the men climbed on, and the conductor let them ride.[3]

---

[1] Indianapolis *Journal*, April 24, 1894. "The army is composed of men of all trades, who claim they will accept employment offered to them." *Ibid.*, April 25.

[2] *Review of Reviews*, Vol. X, p. 59; *Weekly Iowa State Register*, April 27, 1894.

[3] Indianapolis *Journal*, April 27, 1894. An editorial in this issue insisted that the governor ought to have kept Fry out of the State, and that Fry should be treated as a suspect, and leader of a gang of idlers and tramps, not as a hero. It spoke of the illegal "seizure and appropriation of a train at Brazil", and censured the local authorities because they made no attempt to prevent this "outrage." A letter from the mayor of Brazil attacked this editorial, saying that neither he nor the Vandalia agent there knew anything about the "outrage"; moreover, that while in Brazil "the army under 'General' Fry was as orderly as any body of organized men that ever entered our city", and that their "individual conduct was such that not a single complaint was filed against any one of them." He said that if the railroad had regarded its property as stolen it would have notified the authorities. The facts

At Indianapolis a "Hoosier Brigade" was already formed and awaiting Fry's arrival. It soon appeared, however, that the leaders of the two contingents were not on the best of terms and the result was one of the quarrels which so frequently threatened to disrupt the very democratic organization of the industrials. One Aubrey, who had formerly quarreled with Fry, and who, according to Fry's statement, had deserted him, had been acting as a sort of self-constituted advance agent, organizing the Hoosier detachment. Although both armies were quartered in a building known as the "Porkhouse", they did not combine under a single commander until Aubrey was deposed and O. H. Ballard, "the Hoosier Kid", was elected to command both contingents. Aubrey complained that this was only a ruse to get rid of him so that Fry might regain complete control after leaving the city, and on May 1 Aubrey moved on with some fifty followers.[1]

Fry made a protracted visit at Indianapolis, but he soon wore out his welcome. The enlistments far outnumbered the desertions, and the army increased to five hundred men. The industrials paraded the streets and turned book agents as a means of raising money to continue their journey, selling copies of Vincent's "Story of the Commonweal" which had just been published in Chicago.[2] Plenty of provisions were obtained, but the presence of so many more unemployed where

he had obtained from the agent were that Fry chartered a box car to Indianapolis, and that at the time of leaving the men boarded the train. The agent wired Terre Haute for orders, and was told to let the men ride to Indianapolis. *Ibid.*, May 1, 1894. This discussion sheds some light upon the nature of the frequently conflicting reports about "train stealings." See also Vincent, "Commonweal," p. 213.

[1] New York *Times*, April 25, May 1, 1894; Indianapolis *Journal*, April 27, May 1, 1894; Chicago *Tribune*, May 3, 1894.

[2] Chicago *Tribune*, May 3, 1894; Indianapolis *Journal*, May 3, 1894.

there were already too many was soon felt to be a burden, and it appears that local labor organizations resented the presence of this new type of competition. Labor leaders petitioned the mayor to get rid of the "Commonwealers",[1] and the feeling was by no means confined to the labor unions. The mayor requested Fry to move on,[2] but the transportation question again presented itself; the army was tired of walking, and many of the men were without shoes.[3] It was intended that the money raised by the army with the aid of local Populists should be used to buy box-car transportation to Washington or to some intermediate point, but the railroads refused to accept less than regular fares.[4]

The Indianapolis *Journal*, which shared in the desire to help the army get out of town, contained an enlightening comment upon one aspect of the process of "train stealing."

An opinion was expressed by several citizens — it said — if the railroads could get a reasonable freight rate for the army without the public being aware of the fact, that a freight train might be placed in the company's yards which might be captured by the army without any resistance on the part of the company. Then the company might say that it did not take these people into another city or State of its own free will, but was compelled to because it did not have force sufficient to put them off the train. Fry says a scheme somewhat like this was followed by his army in the West.[5]

---

[1] Although the western organizations of the unemployed usually called themselves "industrial armies", at least in the earlier stages of the movement, all such organizations were popularly called "Commonwealers" or "Coxeyites." The reporter of the Indianapolis *Journal*, whose tone was by no means friendly, was unable to resist the temptation to refer to Fry's "Commonwoe."

[2] *Review of Reviews*, Vol. X, p. 59.

[3] Chicago *Tribune*, May 5, 1894.

[4] *Ibid.*, May 3, 4, 1894.

[5] Indianapolis *Journal*, May 3, 1894.

The roads in Indiana, however, were less obliging. Fry then talked of ordering a thousand mules from Texas, to be sent to Cincinnati; he had friends in Texas, he said, who would sell their farms rather than see his army fail to reach Washington.[1] It is not recorded, however, that his men ever rode in this manner. The army was finally divided because it was easier to provide for a smaller force, and it left on foot, one detachment being led by an Indiana Populist named Jennings and the "Hoosier Kid", and the other by Fry. Jennings took a more southerly route that led him into Kentucky, and Fry with two hundred men started along the old National Road.[2] Fry soon swung southward toward Cincinnati. His two hundred odd men were now housed in an old tent that formerly sheltered Forepaugh's circus, now converted into a combination of lecture hall and sleeping quarters.[3] He reached Cincinnati before the end of May. There he embarked his men in two barges, to be towed up the river. His announced destination was Pittsburgh, and the Pittsburgh Populists made ready to receive him.[4] It seems, however, that the period of six days for which the tow-

---

[1] *Ibid.*, May 5, 1894; Chicago *Tribune*, May 5, 1894.

[2] Indianapolis *Journal*, May 7, 1894. According to the Chicago *Times* of May 8, Fry said "that the roasting that the local press had given him had put $500 in his pocket; that he had 'worked' the town to its limit, and had had a good time. He will reach Washington, he thinks, with $2,000 in his treasury, a greater portion of which will come from the sale of his book."

On May 20, 65 men led by Jennings and the "Hoosier Kid" arrived on a steamboat in Frankfort, Ky. They said that they were going to Washington by way of Virginia. They were said to be the first Commonwealers seen in Kentucky. Chicago *Tribune*, May 21, 1894.

[3] Indianapolis *Journal*, May 8, 9, 10, 1894.

[4] Pittsburgh *Chronicle Telegraph*, May 29, 31, 1894; *Review of Reviews*, Vol. X, p. 59. A dispatch from Cincinnati, May 21, stated that the owner of a towboat had offered to take the army to Pittsburgh for $325, and that the Central Labor Union of Cincinnati was trying to raise the money. — Chicago *Tribune*, May 22, 1894.

boat was hired expired when the expedition was near
Parkersburg, West Virginia, and there the passengers
were landed.[1] Again the army divided, probably because small bodies of men found it simpler to subsist
and easier to steal rides. One division took the National
Road to Washington, another followed the Baltimore
and Ohio tracks, and a third remained in Parkersburg.[2]
Fry and part of his men finally reached Washington on
June 26,[3] three months and ten days after the original
six hundred left Los Angeles.

[1] Pittsburgh *Chronicle Telegraph*, June 4, 1894.
[2] *Ibid.*, June 6, 1894; *Review of Reviews*, Vol. X, p. 59.
[3] Pittsburgh *Chronicle Telegraph*, June 26, 1894; Chicago *Tribune*, June 27, 1894.

CHAPTER VIII

The largest of the unemployed armies, and in many respects the most interesting of them all, was the one conducted on its transcontinental tour by General Charles T. Kelly. This army was organized at San Francisco by Colonel William Baker. By the end of March it had an enlisted strength of fifteen hundred men. On March 27 a large delegation of the industrials called upon Mayor Ellert to ask his assistance. They planned to go to Washington to join Coxey, and they wanted transportation in barges to Sacramento, from which point they expected to go east by rail. They needed, they said, only a few hundred dollars and a wagon load or two of provisions. It seems that their spokesmen were agitators of whom the mayor was suspicious. He told his callers that this was a "scheme concocted by worthless men for private gain", and he cautioned them against several of these individuals, asking them to send their own leaders to him. The men of the army, said the San Francisco *Chronicle*, "are genuine laboring men, who are now struggling by every honest means to better their condition." [1]

On the first day of April the army paraded the streets, and had speechmaking at its headquarters, the Furniture Workers' Hall. A friend of the movement from

[1] San Francisco *Chronicle*, March 28, April 2, 1894. Vincent states that the San Francisco army was organized by Col. William Baker on April 2. This may have been the date of the formal organization. "Story of the Commonweal", p. 126.

Los Angeles told the industrials about the operations of General Fry. The following day had been set for their departure, but their plans remained uncertain, for as yet no means of conveyance had been found, and a commanding general had not been chosen. Two days after the appointed one the mayor paid for the ferry passage of six hundred men across the bay to Oakland, and the long journey had begun. Colonel Baker, who was in charge for the time being, hoped, according to the *Chronicle*, "to find bread to the right of them, meat to the left of them, and pie in front of them, on the rest of the Eastward charge."

The men were marched to the Mills Tabernacle, a large building which the Oakland authorities had placed at their disposal. After the chief of police offered them some sane advice, Colonel Baker addressed them. He was sorry, he said, that he could not go with them, but he must stay to organize other regiments. He urged them to stand together, to obey their officers, and to do nothing that would bring discredit upon the organization, for a good report left behind them would bring better treatment to those who followed. He announced that he expected to arrange for transportation by rail to Sacramento, but if that failed, the army would march in the morning.[1] The attempt to inveigle the railroad failed, however, and the matter of walking was reconsidered. Colonel Baker, when interviewed, said that he had spent the day fighting the Southern Pacific Railroad.

[1] San Francisco *Chronicle*, April 4, 1894. The officers of the army at the time when it arrived at Oakland were Col. William Baker, Majors W. W. Webster and F. O. Houbert, Aid-de-Camp A. G. Stone, Adjutant Samuel Adams, quartermaster's department: R. W. West, John Russell and Ed. Rahey. The captains of companies were: Co. A, Souci; Co. B, McKenzie; Co. C, Stock; Co. D, Wallace; Co. E, Evans; Co. F, George Robey; Co. H, Holben; Co. I, Walker; Co. J, Meehan; Co. K, Rodgers; and Co. L, McKetchner. *Ibid.*, April 4, 1894.

The company — he explained — has refused to give my men transportation to Sacramento, where our leaders have gone. Now we do not propose to walk to Sacramento, but we are going to get there all the same. . . . The Southern Pacific should give us transportation, . . . and we are going to demand it again tomorrow. I have the bone and sinew here, and I guess we can hold our own. I cannot tell you what our plans are, for we have not made any. We want our rights as poor men, and we must have them.[1]

Now Oakland was by no means pleased to have San Francisco's unemployed thrust upon her in this unceremonious manner. The mayor of Oakland protested, but in vain. The citizens, however, rose to the occasion, fed the army, and raised two hundred dollars to pay freight on it to Sacramento.[2] It soon appeared that the arrangements were not to the army's liking; stirring events followed; and in the midst of them Charles T. Kelly rose from obscurity and gained a hold upon the men which indicated that he was a born leader.

Kelly, a young man thirty-two years of age, in the spring of 1894 was a compositor in a San Francisco printing establishment. Born in New England, he had migrated westward, and had been a newsboy in Chicago, and a printer in St. Louis, in Texas, and later in California. Through his own efforts he had acquired a good education. According to a newspaper story, after a dissipated youth he fell in love with a Salvation Army girl and joined that organization to win her, thereby gaining experience very useful to him at the height of his career. He later left the Salvation Army, but he stuck to his trade. His ability placed him at the head of

---

[1] San Francisco *Chronicle*, April 5, 1894.
[2] *Ibid.*, April 5, 1894; *Weekly Iowa State Register*, April 13, 1894; *Nation*, Vol. LVIII, p. 264.

labor organizations to which he belonged. He was known among his acquaintances as a first-class workman, but a crank on the labor question. The Industrial Army affair carried him away completely. He was reported to have said: "In a matter like this a man must be a man or a serf. He must do his duty, and his family must be a second consideration. My wife and child must look out for themselves." [1] He was described as "a small, slight young man, with mild blue eyes, a soft, winning voice, and a breadth of forehead that indicates more than average intelligence", who looked "more like a divinity student or the secretary of a Y. M. C. A. organization than the commander of nearly 1500 men." [2] He seems to have had about him that intangible quality of personal magnetism, which enabled him to maintain discipline in his command with little effort. [3] The extraordinary way in which he impressed himself immediately upon the army and held it together through a series of difficult situations, marked him as something more than an ordinary printer.

Kelly seems to have joined the industrials while they were stranded at Oakland. The events of April 5 gave him a chance to assert himself. The mayor ordered the army to leave town before daybreak the next morning. The railroad offered box-car transportation to Sacramento for the two hundred dollars that had been subscribed, but the army declined to ride in that manner, and when the chief of police asked for coaches, the division superintendent said that he could not furnish them for that sum. The industrials had been marching

[1] San Francisco *Chronicle*, April 8, 1894; Vincent, "Commonweal", pp. 125, 126.
[2] *Weekly Iowa State Register*, April 20, 1894.
[3] Vincent, "Commonweal", p. 125.

GENERAL CHARLES T. KELLY

about town all day. They were at the station at eight
o'clock that evening when a train of six empty box cars
pulled in. When Kelly saw it "he shouted that they
did not propose to be pushed into such cars like hogs";
he called for a vote of the men, and they decided that
they would not go. In spite of the efforts of the police,
they marched back to the tabernacle, amidst great excitement.

Late at night diplomatic relations with the army
were broken off, and the city authorities decided upon
decisive action. The whole police force was called out,
and twenty-five policemen reported for duty. The
mayor wired the governor for the use of militia, and
two companies, with a Gatling gun, were mobilized to
act as soon as they got orders, which, however, did not
come. The sheriff agreed to swear in as many deputies
as were needed. The plan was to ring a general alarm
at two A. M., get out a large crowd, and deputize the
men. The Southern Pacific agreed to have a train of
seven box cars ready at four o'clock.

The general fire alarm brought out the fire department and a large crowd of citizens, hundreds of whom
were sworn in as deputies.[1] The chief of police and the
sheriff, backed by two hundred fifty men armed with
clubs, surrounded the tabernacle and demanded that
the army march. When the army refused to move,
police broke in and arrested Kelly and a number of
others. The men now refused to do anything until
Kelly was returned to them; he was brought back and

---

[1] The number of deputies sworn in is stated as 1,000 in a dispatch to the New
York *Times*, April 7, and the *Review of Reviews*, Vol. X, p. 57, places the number
at 1200. These numbers were larger than was indicated by the detailed accounts
in the San Francisco *Chronicle* of April 6 and April 7, which, however, did not
state the total number.

was greeted with cheers. The industrials were much astonished by these events, but although there was great excitement, there was no violence. Kelly "was taken on the men's shoulders, and from this position he addressed them, saying that they should go away peacefully." Thereupon the army marched to the railroad station, escorted by the two hundred fifty police and deputies. When it was discovered that there were only six cars instead of seven that had been promised, the men refused to go aboard until the railroad got another. Kelly made a speech from the top of a car, in which he denounced the officials of Oakland and the policemen "who choked him and dragged him to prison without cause." The completed train was surrounded so that none might escape, and it pulled out for Sacramento with the entire army.[1]

At Sacramento a branch of the industrial army was organized on April 3 by men who came from San Francisco for the purpose. The chief of police gave them permission to solicit food and clothing at business houses in the city. They expected to start as soon as the San Francisco army arrived.[2] General Houbert, a Russian who claimed to be a graduate of the St. Petersburg medical college, labored under the impression that he was the commanding officer, and that he had left Colonel Baker in charge at Oakland while he himself was making the arrangements at Sacramento. On April 6 he received the telegram: "We, the Industrial Army, emphatically refuse to ride in box cars. We are United States citizens and not hogs. When we are furnished

---

[1] San Francisco *Chronicle*, April 6, 7, 1894; *Nation*, Vol. LVIII, p. 264; *Review of Reviews*, Vol. X, p. 57; Vincent, "Commonweal", p. 126.

[2] San Francisco *Chronicle*, April 4, 1894.

proper transportation will then proceed to Sacramento, not otherwise." It was signed by General Kelly and Colonel Baker. Houbert replied: "What reasonable excuse have you to give for not taking that train? Who is this man Kelly? By what authority does he act?" He was soon to find out.

When Kelly and Baker arrived with seven hundred or more men, arrangements had been made to care for them in the Agricultural Park, where they encamped under the grand stand. After they had eaten, Houbert harangued them. He denounced Kelly as a socialist and an imposter, criticized his actions at Oakland, and threatened to reduce him to the ranks. But before he had continued long he discovered that the new leader's popularity was too great to be withstood. One of the men said: "Kelly eats and sleeps with us, and is one of us, and we won't go back on Kelly." Thereupon General Houbert perceived how the land lay, consented to serve thenceforth as an advance agent, and departed for Ogden. Kelly's ascendency was unquestionably established.[1]

At Sacramento about three hundred fifty recruits were obtained, some of the laborers at work on the streets leaving their jobs to join, and the strength of the combined contingents rose to something more than a thousand men. They received provisions for several days, and arrangements were made by the State and local authorities to send them over the mountains to Ogden, Utah.[2] Kelly disappeared for a time, and Baker

---

[1] San Francisco *Chronicle*, April 7, 1894. This account states that the men were "orderly and well behaved."

[2] *Ibid.*, April 7, 8, 1894; Vincent, "Commonweal", p. 127. Their fare seems to have been paid by the mayor of Sacramento and the governor of California. See below, p. 157, Note 1.

seemed quite at a loss during his absence, "claiming that he depended upon him entirely, and that he did not know how they were going to get along without him." [1]

While the army sped toward Utah, the authorities of that territory prepared a cold reception. Governor West notified the Southern Pacific that it was forbidden to bring the army into his jurisdiction. He called out the three companies of militia at Ogden, and he started from Salt Lake City on a special train with his staff, two companies of militia with a Gatling gun, a company of Salt Lake City police, and two thousand loaves of bread consigned to the Ogden Relief Society. [2]

On Sunday, April 8, Ogden was at high tension. The governor arrived at eight o'clock in the morning. The city presented the appearance of an armed camp. During the day ten thousand people gathered to see the trainload of industrials come in. Most of the sightseers carried guns.

While this great concourse of people waited, the first round in a legal battle between the Utah authorities and the Southern Pacific Railroad was being fought. The governor said afterwards that when he had served notice on the road that it must not bring the army into Utah, he had been given to understand that the train was to be sidetracked in Nevada pending a settlement of the difficulty, and that it was not until four o'clock in the afternoon that he learned what the company was doing. He immediately took steps to get out an in-

---

[1] San Francisco *Chronicle*, April 7, 1894. It is not clear what happened to Kelly. The Sacramento dispatch quoted here said that there was a report that he was in jail at Oakland. A later dispatch from Ogden said that he "was lost in the shuffle at Sacramento." *Ibid.*, April 9.

[2] *Ibid.*, April 8, 1894.

junction to prohibit the road from bringing the men into Ogden, or from allowing them to leave the cars. It was not served until twenty minutes before the train arrived. On the next day, after a hearing, another injunction ordered the Southern Pacific to take the men back to the places from which they came.[1] Thus the Southern Pacific was enjoined from bringing the industrials in after they were already in, and when they were in, it was ordered to take them out. The railroad refused to take them back, and the men refused to return.[2]

The main question, according to Governor West, was whether the State and local authorities of California could load vagrants upon trains and dump them upon Utah without liability on the part of these authorities or of the carrier.[3] From another point of view the legal battle was between the Southern Pacific, which wanted to get the army off its hands, and the Union Pacific and the Rio Grande Western, which had western termini at Ogden, and which doubtless feared the consequences if it hauled these men to some point farther east and unloaded them there.[4] Governor Waite of Colorado invited Kelly into his State, but Rio Grande

[1] San Francisco *Chronicle*, April 8, 9, 10, 1894; *Weekly Iowa State Register*, April 13, 1894; *Appleton's Annual Cyclopedia*, 1894, p. 761.

At the hearing for the injunction, "It appeared from the evidence of the officers of the army that it was composed of vagrants and tramps who had no money or means of support, and who started from San Francisco without either food or bedding, and with but scanty clothing; that their transportation was paid from San Francisco to Oakland by the Mayor of San Francisco; that their fare from Oakland to Sacramento in cattle cars was paid by contributions from the citizens of Oakland, and that their fare from Sacramento to Ogden was paid by the Governor of California and the Mayor of Sacramento, but that nothing whatever was paid by any member of the army." — San Francisco *Chronicle*, April 10.

[2] San Francisco *Chronicle*, April 9, 1894.

[3] See *Appleton's Annual Cyclopedia*, 1894, p. 761, for a quotation from the governor's message to this effect.

[4] San Francisco *Chronicle*, April 10, 1894.

Western officials pointed to a Colorado law which imposed a fine of two hundred dollars for each indigent person brought into the State by a common carrier.[1] The Union Pacific refused to carry the men except at full passenger rates,[2] and the attorneys of that road obtained from the court an order that United States deputy marshals should protect its property.[3] On the afternoon of the 11th, the court handed down a decision against the Southern Pacific. The earlier injunction was modified to authorize the use of force by the territorial officials in ejecting the industrials unless the latter moved out before ten o'clock the next morning. In announcing the decision, the judge said that this was one of the most difficult questions that he had ever been called upon to decide. "There is," he said, "but little authority directly in point, if any. . . . There are no precedents. The court is obliged to travel over a road that has never been traveled before to my knowledge." [4]

The people of Ogden, after they had had a chance to see the industrials and observe their behavior, were more favorably disposed toward the army, — and the city government represented the citizens. Soon after their arrival the mayor took Colonel Baker and other officers to call upon Governor West, who told them that they must return. Baker seemed helpless and "mentally unequal to the task of railroading his men through to Washington"; Kelly seemed to be the only man in whom they had confidence. He was reported to be on his way to join them. The men were allowed to occupy

[1] San Francisco *Chronicle*, April 8, 1894; *Review of Reviews*, Vol. X, p. 57.
[2] San Francisco *Chronicle*, April 9, 1894.
[3] *Ibid.*, April 10, 1894.
[4] *Ibid.*, April 12, 1894.

a railroad roundhouse, where they were furnished with
plenty of food. "The industrial army today has been
quiet and orderly," said a dispatch of the day after its
arrival, " — cleanly, too, as evidenced by the varie-
gated garments which were seen hanging out to dry in
the warm sun." [1] It soon began to appear that popular
sympathy in Ogden was with the army. The governor
was denounced for "attempting to bulldoze a thousand
unarmed, unemployed men who ask nothing but help
to forward them on their way to Washington", and for
foisting Salt Lake City militia and police upon Ogden.
When the decision of the court that the army could be
forced to return was announced, there was much excitement. The labor element sympathized with the
industrials, and men paraded the streets with banners
which indorsed the movement.[2] Threats of a riot were
heard, and wild rumors that armed men from Salt Lake
were on their way to liberate the Kellyites.[3]

In the meantime, Kelly was coming. When he arrived on the fourth day of the army's sojourn in Utah,
he was greeted by his men "as though he were a veri-

[1] San Francisco *Chronicle*, April 10, 1894. According to this account the men
were well pleased by their treatment at the hands of the mayor and citizens of
Ogden. But in one of Kelly's speeches after he reached Iowa, in which he described
the various kinds of treatment received by the army and the terrible sufferings in
some places, he said that at Ogden the camping place was low, swampy ground
covered with garbage, and that in three days three men died and 30 were taken to
the hospital. *Weekly Iowa State Register*, May 4, 1894. The poorly clad men suffered severely from the cold, and this was probably the cause of most of the illness.

[2] San Francisco *Chronicle*, April 10, 11, 1894.

[3] *Ibid.*, April 12, 1894. At Salt Lake City "Several hundred men claiming to
represent 1900 workingmen of the city met and adopted resolutions denouncing
Governor West and the Mayor for their efforts to prevent the industrial army from
entering the Territory. They were particularly harsh in their criticisms of the
Governor and called upon President Cleveland to remove him from his position."
Ibid., April 13, 1894. The inclusion of the mayor in this indictment was perhaps
due to the fact that the City of Ogden, as well as the two adjoining counties, had
been parties to the injunction suit, but the city soon withdrew its name from the
suit. *Ibid.*, April 11, 1894.

table Napoleon." He conferred with the governor. Newspaper men were kept out, but when Kelly emerged he said that the governor had told him that he would have to return to California, and he had asked for two hours to confer with his men. At their leader's suggestion, the men voted to go to Washington, by rail if possible, but on foot if necessary. The mayor of Ogden, after a stormy interview with the governor, now decided to take matters into his own hands. In the middle of the afternoon he hurried to the camp, accompanied by the city attorney, and called upon Kelly to prepare to move immediately. Within three quarters of an hour all was ready, and the army marched out toward Uintah, led and followed by detachments of cavalry, and accompanied by a great crowd and much enthusiasm. The poorly clad men, who had been suffering severely from the cold, continued to receive wagon loads of blankets and provisions from the relief committee when they paused four miles from the city. Ogden, "after nearly four of the busiest days of its history", was now free to resume its customary pursuits, although it still presented a martial appearance. It was estimated that the cost of the entertainment had been ten thousand dollars, and there were speculations as to whether it could be collected from the Southern Pacific.[1]

Colonel Baker, who rode to Uintah on the last load of supplies, hinted at the possibility that it would not be necessary to walk far. At midnight the army captured a Union Pacific train of twenty-six box cars, the train crew offering no resistance to the twelve hundred men. The "theft" appears to have been with the connivance

---

[1] San Francisco *Chronicle*, April 12, 1894; *Our Day*, Vol. XIII, p. 378.

of the Union Pacific officials.[1] Kelly took charge, and the train moved rapidly eastward. The industrials carried three days' rations, and they received food at the larger cities. Cheyenne refused to allow the train to stop within its limits, but furnished supplies that included thirteen thousand loaves of bread and five beeves.[2] At Topeka, Kansas, the People's Party League appointed a committee on arrangements to welcome and feed the army when it came through.[3] Kelly talked along the way. He expressed regrets that he had not been able to call upon Governor Waite to thank him for his sympathy. The army, he said, was composed of respectable men and all undesirable characters were excluded; — six tramps found among them at Green River, Wyoming, had been left with the local authorities. He stated among other things that the industrial movement had nothing to do with the Coxey movement in Ohio.[4]

While Kelly's freight cars were rolling toward the Missouri River, preparations were being made at the eastern terminus of the Union Pacific, similar to those that had been made in Utah. The people of Omaha, where the Union Pacific ended, and of Council Bluffs, on the Iowa side of the river, when they faced the approach of what they believed to be an army of tramps and desperate characters, were duly perturbed.[5] The

---

[1] *Outlook*, Vol. XLIX, p. 733; *Midland Monthly*, June, 1894, quoted in Haynes, "Third Party Movements", p. 341; *Our Day*, Vol. XIII, p. 278; Vincent, "Commonweal", p. 129.

[2] San Francisco *Chronicle*, April 13, 1894; *Weekly Iowa State Register*, April 20, 1894.

[3] San Francisco *Chronicle*, April 16, 1894.

[4] *Ibid.*, April 14, 1894.

[5] "As usual in labor matters, the reports telegraphed over the country differed widely from those given in the local papers, even of the most conservative character. According to the Omaha 'Bee' [the leading Republican paper of Nebraska],

industrials arrived in Omaha on Sunday morning, April 15. Their appearance and their perfect discipline, reinforced by moderate language on the part of the commander, soon changed the fear into sympathy, tempered, however, by discretion on the part of conservatives.[1] The people of Omaha were soon relieved of whatever apprehensions remained, when the train was run across the bridge to Council Bluffs — probably because the Union Pacific wanted to be sure of getting the army off its hands.[2]

If the Union Pacific was anxious to pass the army on, the roads that extended eastward from Council Bluffs were equally anxious to avoid receiving it, and they had been making strenuous efforts to prevent the crossing of the river. On Saturday, Judge M. N. Hubbard, attorney for the Chicago and Northwestern, called upon Governor Jackson at Des Moines and showed him a telegram from the general manager of the Union Pacific to the general superintendent of the Northwestern, announcing the theft of the train and the approach of the army. Hubbard asked protection for the railroads at Council Bluffs, and offered to furnish trains for troops

when 'General' Kelly's army arrived from San Francisco and Ogden . . . the people of Omaha expected to find a body of tramps, if not of desperadoes. They soon learned, however, that the reputed 'capture' of a Union Pacific train was with the knowledge and consent of the managers of the road, and that the army was made up of law-abiding workingmen out of work." *Outlook*, Vol. XLIX, p. 733.

[1] See extract from the Omaha *Bee*, quoted in *Public Opinion*, Vol. XVII, p. 94, which concludes: "The inoffensive conduct of the men, the courtesy and forbearance of commander Kelly under the most trying circumstances, have won for them sympathy and aid. General Kelly is a modest, active business man of excellent judgment and good taste. He blames no party for the deplorable condition his men were in. He says it is a question of humanity, not of politics. Whatever may be said of the folly and futility of Kelly's expedition, it will be admitted by all that he is a capable leader and a gentleman."

[2] "At the request of the railway the train was run across the river into Council Bluffs." — Rev. Joseph T. Duryea, "The 'Industrial Army' at Omaha", *Outlook*, Vol. XLIX, p. 780.

if they were called out. The governor also received a wire from the sheriff of Pottawattomie County, which announced that Kelly's army was expected and that the railroads were demanding protection.[1]

The governor at once set out for Council Bluffs on a special train, accompanied by Judge Hubbard. Shortly after his arrival that evening he called into consultation the attorney-general, the agents of the railroads, the mayor, and the sheriff. General Manager Hughitt of the Northwestern wired a request that the governor use all possible means to prevent the army from entering the State; he also instructed local officials of the road to run all engines and empty cars out of the city. It was suggested that the Union Pacific bridge might be barricaded, but since that road was in the hands of receivers appointed by the Federal courts, the idea was not taken seriously. The governor called out seven companies of militia that had already been instructed to hold themselves in readiness, but at midnight he decided that no effort should be made "to prevent the landing of the pilgrims on Iowa soil", and that the troops would be used only to preserve order.[2]

When Kelly's army arrived in Council Bluffs before noon on Sunday, April 15, the men stayed near their train, building fires of old ties which had been distributed along the track for that purpose by the Union Pacific. Many, worn with fatigue from the journey, slept on the damp ground. The three hundred militiamen were encamped a few hundred yards away, but the industrials, except for the moral effect of the pres-

---

[1] "Report of the Adjutant General of Iowa," 1895, pp. 8, 9; *Weekly Iowa State Register*, April 20, 1894.

[2] "Report of the Adjutant General of Iowa", 1895, p. 10; *Weekly Iowa State Register*, April 20, 1894.

ence of these troops, were under no restraint except
that imposed by their own discipline. This discipline
was described as perfect in a dispatch to the *Iowa State
Register*, which added: "While here they roamed at
will over the city, and not an act was committed that
was not praiseworthy." It was estimated that thirty
thousand people came to see the army during its first
day in the city.

The impression that the army had a serious purpose
was strengthened by its manifestations of religious zeal
on that Sunday afternoon.

After dinner — said the same reporter — the army gathered into little knots and religious services were conducted
in half a dozen places at once. Prayers were offered up by
the men so earnest and full of touching pathos that tears
were brought to the eyes of hundreds of people. The religious element seems strongly to predominate, and when
some good old Methodist hymn was started it was carried
through by hundreds of voices that appeared to be well
trained for congregational singing.

Kelly boasted that there was not a tramp nor a
drunkard in the army, and that three fourths of his
men were mechanics. The report that on the first day
in Council Bluffs only one hundred fifty-five recruits
were accepted out of several hundred who applied indicates that discrimination was used in the admission
to membership in the organization.[1] A newspaper
description of the enlistment of a new company after
the army reached Des Moines explained the selective
process:

The recruits are taken before Gen. Kelly's adjutant, Sam

---

[1] *Weekly Iowa State Register*, April 20, 1894; *cf.* Duryea, "Industrial Army",
Outlook, Vol. XLIX, pp. 781, 782.

Adams. He questions them closely as to their past life and occupation; their habits and objects in joining the army; whether they are unemployed, and if so for what reason. If they have any concealed weapons they are taken away, and if there is anything wrong with the applicant a way is found to get rid of him. If he is under the influence of liquor that settles it; he doesn't get in.[1]

Kelly's men subscribed to the same obligations which were administered to the members of Fry's army, requiring them to observe the laws of the land, to respect property rights, and to obey the orders of their officers.[2]

On Monday afternoon the army marched to the Chautauqua grounds three or four miles east of the city, the column, nearly half a mile long, headed by several wagon loads of donated provisions, and followed by two of the militia companies. The rest of the militia was moved to the Chautauqua grounds during the night.[3] The next day there was a cold rain, with flurries of snow; the industrials stood wet and shivering in the mud where they had spent the night. On top of Chautauqua Hill was the ampitheater, a large unused building which might have afforded ample shelter, but part of the militia had encamped in it, and the officer in charge, nervously apprehending a disturbance if the industrials got too close to his men, kept them out.

After a night in the mud and a day in the rain, Kelly's men were suffering acutely. The owner of the building, taking pity upon them, went to a lawyer's

[1] *Weekly Iowa State Register*, May 4, 1894. "General Kelly has instructed his adjutant, Sam Adams, to be careful in examining candidates for admission. Bums are rigidly excluded. A dozen or more applicants were rejected today." Chicago *Times*, May 2, 1894.

[2] Vincent, "Commonweal," p. 133.

[3] "Report of the Adjutant General of Iowa", 1895, pp. 11, 17; *Weekly Iowa State Register*, April 20, 1894. The *Register* account said that the militia companies "were gotten control of by the railroads in some manner."

office and had a permit drawn up which allowed them to use the building for forty-eight hours if they built no fires there, but when the sheriff received the permit at the Chautauqua grounds, he discovered that this document had been dated the fifteenth instead of the seventeenth by mistake, and the time had expired before it began! The sheriff was unable to persuade the officer in charge of the building to admit the suffering men, and the militiamen "boasted that they would shoot if the Kellyites attempted to come in out of the storm." [1]

There was great indignation at this inhuman treatment of a body of men for whom much sympathy had already been aroused. A committee of citizens demanded that the governor withdraw the troops. The governor blamed the sheriff (the governor was a Republican and the sheriff was a Democrat), saying that the militia was under the sheriff's orders when it was sent to the Chautauqua grounds. He took the companies out of the sheriff's hands, and relieved them from duty shortly afterwards. [2] The indignation of the people, however, was directed not so much against the governor as against the railroads, which were held responsible for the calling out of the militia. Judge Hubbard, in particular, was the object of general execration as the personification of corporate heartlessness. It was said that he was not only callous to the sufferings of the unfortunate industrials, but that he advocated the

[1] Duryea, "Industrial Army", *Outlook*, Vol. XLIX, p. 781; the *Weekly Iowa State Register*, April 20, 1894, says that "Only the heroism and good sense of Kelly's men prevented bloodshed."

[2] *Weekly Iowa State Register*, April 20, 1894; *Outlook*, Vol. XLIX, p. 733, which states that the militia was withdrawn "in accordance with the demands of public sentiment."

most bloodthirsty methods to thwart their designs; if a train were captured, he wanted to send a wild engine down the track to meet it, and let the wreck solve the problem whether the railroads must haul these men without remuneration. He was described as the most unpopular man in town, and a meeting of "judges, lawyers, and prominent citizens" sent resolutions condemning him to President Hughitt of the Northwestern, with the request that the unpopular judge be removed from the locality.[1] A meeting of laboring men in Omaha on Wednesday denounced the inhumane treatment of Kelly's men, and it was said that one speaker offered to furnish two thousand rounds of ammunition to clean out the militia before the public broke up the meeting. A similar gathering was held at Council Bluffs.[2]

That night, at Omaha, occurred what was to have been the first of a series of meetings under the auspices of the Knights of Labor, for the object of diffusing "knowledge of the principles of civil government and political economy", at which Doctor Joseph T. Duryea was to deliver an address. Kelly was invited to speak and to take up a collection. Laboring men crowded in until it was necessary to adjourn to the public square. Kelly told the story of his army and explained that the aim of his men "was to impress the government at Washington as mere petitions would not, and that the Government might understand and appreciate the condition of the multitude of laborers and devise some measures of relief."[3] He did not suggest any definite

[1] *Weekly Iowa State Register*, April 20, 27, 1894; Vincent, "Commonweal", pp. 137, 140.
[2] *Weekly Iowa State Register*, April 20, 1894.
[3] Duryea, "Industrial Army", *Outlook*, Vol. XLIX, p. 782.

program of legislation — perhaps he had none worked
out as yet — but he expressed a sort of mystical faith
in the willingness and ability of Congress to do what was
necessary when his army called attention to the need
for it.

When we reach Washington — he said — and present our
living petition to Congress — a petition that cannot be
pigeonholed, referred, or put in the waste-basket — something must happen. You ask me, What will we do? My
answer is: What will the other fellows do? Do you not
think that in California tonight there are thousands of
women and children kneeling by their bedsides, praying to
God for the success of the Industrial Army? So long as these
prayers are ascending we will not turn back, nor will we
abandon our purpose.[1]

Less temperate speeches were made by others, with
pointed thrusts at Governor Jackson, the railroads, and
Wall Street, and the meeting adopted resolutions which
pledged all present to boycott all merchants who patron-
ized any railroad refusing to haul the army. Several
hundred dollars were raised to supply the army's needs.
Other meetings of a similar character were held in
Council Bluffs.[2]

Meanwhile Governor Jackson and the mayors of the
two cities were making efforts to induce the railroads
to carry the army to the Mississippi, or to Chicago,
offering to pay the cost of running the trains. But the
railroads did not want to set a precedent that would
encourage other bodies of unemployed to move east-

[1] *Outlook*, Vol. XLIX, p. 733; Vincent, "Commonweal", p. 136. *Cf.* Kelly's
speech at Des Moines, reported in *Weekly Iowa State Register*, May 4, 1894. A
writer who had heard Kelly and his officers speak at Ogden said: "Their prevailing
idea seemed to be that whenever a man cannot for himself find work at two dollars
a day, it is the duty of the Federal government to find it for him. Paternalism in
government was the watchword, not self help." *Our Day*, Vol. XIII, p. 278.
[2] Vincent, "Commonweal", p. 136.

ward. They also feared the displeasure of the people of Illinois, and they asserted that they had no right to carry men without means of support into that State.[1] The possibility of steamboat transportation down the Missouri was also considered, but there were suspicions that this was merely a ruse of the railroads.[2]

Matters began to come to a head on Thursday, the nineteenth. Early on that morning Kelly called his officers into council. He had been notified by the county authorities, he told them, that he must move on, and that since the railroad managers were inexorable, the army must start its journey to Chicago on foot. After breakfast the camp was in a bustle of preparation. An hour before noon the long column started with flags and banners flying, General Kelly at its head mounted on a fine black horse presented him by an admirer in Council Bluffs. There were a dozen or more wagons to carry the provisions, the camp equipment, and the invalids. That night the army camped at the village of Weston, on the Rock Island and Milwaukee railroads, about nine miles from Council Bluffs, the men finding shelter in a grain elevator, in barns and in any other buildings available.[3]

Meanwhile a crisis had been reached in Omaha and Council Bluffs. The laboring men of the two cities

[1] Duryea, "Industrial Army", *Outlook*, Vol. XLIX, p. 782; *Weekly Iowa State Register*, April 27, 1894; Haynes, "Third Party Movements", p. 340. "The process of reducing the army to the pass of tramping cost the railroad companies 'slathers' of money; but they established what they knew was an important precedent." — London. "Book of Jack London", Vol. I, p. 58.

[2] *Weekly Iowa State Register*, April 27, 1894. The feeling against the railroads appears in the statement: "At a meeting in Council Bluffs it was proposed to raise money to pay full fare, but the sentiment was against such a concession to the railroads, at whose demands the militia was called out." *Outlook*, Vol. XLIX, p. 733.

[3] Vincent, "Commonweal", pp. 136, 137; Jack London, "A Jack London Diary: Tramping with Kelly through Iowa", *The Palimpsest*, Vol. VII, pp. 140–142.

were inflamed by the treatment which the industrials had received at the Chautauqua grounds, by the refusal of the railroads to transport them eastward, and especially by the remarks attributed to Judge Hubbard. At a workingmen's meeting in Omaha that night it was decided to march to Council Bluffs and apply to the railway managers for a freight train. On Friday morning a large body of men, with drums, fifes, and flags, marched across the bridge,[1] and joined the crowd already gathered before the Grand Hotel. The streets were filled by thousands of shouting, determined men, bent on obtaining transportation for Kelly's army. The situation began to look ominous. The railroads pulled their engines and cars out of town, and train service was cut off.

There were conferences between the governor, the mayor, leaders of the army, and a committee of citizens in which Editor Tychenor of the Omaha *Evening News*, and Doctor Duryea, who came over with another Omaha minister to try to allay the excitement, were prominent. The railroads unanimously declined to accept anything less than regular fares. Unless the army walked, the alternatives were to pay full fares, amounting to about fifteen thousand dollars, which was too expensive, or to send the industrials down the river. The army declined the governor's offer to provide a steamboat as soon as possible.

Meanwhile the men in the streets demanded action. Part of the mob captured an engine and some cars, but the engine was cut loose by its crew and was run into a roundhouse. The Rock Island agent dispatched a

---

[1] *Weekly Iowa State Register*, April 27, 1894; *Outlook*, Vol. XLIX, p. 733; Duryea, "Industrial Army", *Ibid.*, p. 782.

section boss to tear up the track in order to prevent the passage of a train, but Kellyites persuaded the section hands to quit work, and replaced the rail that had been removed. The Milwaukee tracks were reported torn up at Neola. Late in the day a train was captured. A mob, egged on by some excited women, induced an engineer's son to steal his father's engine, several box cars were picked up which were soon filled with enthusiastic citizens, and the train started for Weston.

At Kelly's camp his men had observed trains of empty cars, cabooses, and extra engines flying past without stopping, as the Chicago, Milwaukee, and St. Paul Railroad moved its rolling stock eastward to a safer place. Soon the Reverend J. G. Lemon, of the Christian House, arrived in haste, "covered with mud & with steaming horses", to tell the army that the people of Omaha and Council Bluffs had risen to demand transportation for it on the railroads.[1] Messenger after messenger arrived with reports of the progress of the mob until the announcement came at last that a train was being made up to carry the army eastward that night. Rations were issued for a hurried meal and preparations were made for a prompt departure. About eight o'clock, when a headlight was seen approaching on the Milwaukee tracks, the industrials heaped their remaining fuel on the campfires and they flared up amidst shouts of rejoicing. The foreman of the section and one of his men were found trying to tear up the rails, and the train crept slowly along the remaining mile with scouts in advance to make sure that the track was safe.[2]

When the train pulled into Weston it immediately

[1] London, "Diary", *Palimpsest*, Vol. VII, p. 142.
[2] *Ibid.*, pp. 142, 143.

became apparent that it was entirely inadequate to carry the whole army, and Kelly was too wary or too conscientious to accept it. He was not willing, he said, to break the law and put his army in the wrong by accepting a stolen train. While the visiting delegation and the army shouted and sang songs, sometimes accompanied by the whistle of the engine, Kelly, in consultation with the leaders of the former group, declined an invitation to ride back and accept the hospitality of Council Bluffs. He used the train, however, to send back his sick, of whom there were many after the exposures at Chautauqua Park.[1]

As a result of the disorder on Friday the militia was called out again. On Saturday, Omaha Trade Unionists again invaded Council Bluffs, looking for a train, but nothing of the kind was to be found but a few Union Pacific switch engines and flat cars.[2] Then the excitement subsided, and by Sunday morning when the army proceeded eastward from Weston the militia was again relieved from duty. Another of the dramatic episodes of Kelly's march was closed.

[1] Vincent, "Commonweal", pp. 140 ff.; *Weekly Iowa State Register*, April 27, 1894; Indianapolis *Journal*, April 21, 1894; Duryea, "Industrial Army", *Outlook*, Vol. XLIX, p. 782; London, "Diary", *Palimpsest*, Vol. VII, p. 143. London states that "after the citizens & Kelly held a consultation it was decided to march back the next day to Council Bluffs where the people would get us another train." This may have been the impression of the men rather than the decision of the leaders: in either case it was not acted upon.

[2] "Report of the Adjutant General of Iowa", 1895, p. 12; *Weekly Iowa State Register*, April 27, 1894. The latter states that the intention was to capture a train, take it to Weston, and force Kelly and his army to ride through the State, which suggests that these trade unionists were not only sympathetic toward the army, but anxious to get rid of it as well, probably for fear of the competition of so many unemployed workers.

CHAPTER IX

THROUGH IOWA AND ON TO WASHINGTON

Just before Kelly's army started from Chautauqua
Park to Weston a nineteen-year-old youth from the
Pacific coast by the name of Jack London made his
way into camp and found his place in the rear rank of
the newly arrived "first Regiment of the Reno Industrial Army." Jack London had not yet attained
fame as a writer, but he kept a diary of his journey from
San Francisco until he left the army at Hannibal,
Missouri.[1] He had already had more than his share of
adventures: as a mere boy he had left the monotonous
work of a canning factory to become an "oyster pirate"
at San Francisco, and then a member of the fish patrol,
and he had had a long sea voyage on the Pacific. He
had just quit shoveling coal at thirty dollars a month,
revolting against the injustice of it when he discovered
that he was doing two men's work for one man's pay,
and he had decided to see more of the world with the
industrial army.[2]

[1] Jack London, "A Jack London Diary, Tramping with Kelly through Iowa",
Palimpsest, Vol. VII, pp. 129–158 (May, 1926), edited by John Ely Briggs. This
diary was published by the State Historical Society of Iowa from a copy of the
pencilled original furnished by Charmian London, with her special permission. An
interesting account based largely upon this diary and including some of Jack
London's later comments upon his experiences with Kelly's army is to be found in
Charmian London's "Book of Jack London", Vol. I, Chapter XI. The picturesque
side of his experiences in catching Kelly's army is related in Jack London's article:
"Hoboes that Pass in the Night", *Cosmopolitan*, Vol. XLIV, pp. 196, 197, and his
experiences with the army in "The March of Kelly's Army", *ibid.*, Vol. XLIII,
pp. 643–648. His book, "The Road" contains the same material.
[2] London, "Book of Jack London", Vol. I, Chaps. V–X.

After he had missed the army at Sacramento, as many others did because of its early departure from that place, London pursued it in box cars, in the ice box of a refrigerator car, on blind baggages or on the roofs of coaches, dodging or tipping brakemen and suffering from heat, cold, and other discomforts of this method of travel, until he caught up with Kelly at Chautauqua Park. He was out on a lark, as others in the army doubtless were, seeing new sights and gaining new experiences of a kind well calculated to give him an insight into the characteristics of some of the lower strata of society. He discovered that in the desert "the days are burning hot & the nights freezing cold"; he played cards with a Chinaman and found that there "was not a game he did not understand"; and he observed two cowpunchers in a saloon "raising cain generally." The journey was not one for the physically unfit: the diary contains such entries as "woke up at 3:30 A. M. half froze to death"; "My feet were so cold that it took half an hour's brisk walk to restore circulation"; and again, "It was so cold on the train that night that the brakeman did not care to bother me." [1]

Some of the tribulations of the non-paying passenger on an Overland Limited are indicated by the following extract, couched in the rather technical language of the road:

We made a 45 mile run to Elko & a 23 mile run to Peko where they tried to ditch us. We went out ahead but the brakeman rode the blind out. We waited till the train had almost run by when two of us jumped the palace cars & decked them while the third went underneath on the rods. I climbed forward two cars to the other fellow & [invited

[1] London, "Diary", *Palimpsest*, Vol. VII, pp. 130–139, *passim*.

AN ENCAMPMENT OF KELLY'S INDUSTRIAL ARMY, 1894, JACK LONDON IN LOWER RIGHT-HAND FOREGROUND

From "The Book of Jack London," by permission of The Century Company, and Mrs. Charmian K. London

him] to come on along the decks to the blind but he said that it was too risky. I went forward about five cars & as the brakeman was on the platform I could proceed no further and escape observation. I waited & when the train stopped I climbed down & ran ahead to the blind. The brakeman rode her out but I took the next one behind him, & when he jumped off to catch me I ran ahead & took the platform he had vacated. The fellow on the roof with me got ditched, but I made her into Wells, the end of the division where they put on a double header. The brakeman was after us like a blood hound, so I climbed on the engine & passed coal through to Terrace, the end of that division.[1]

An entry in the diary on the third day of the journey noted that ever since leaving Oakland London had seen "hundreds chasing the first detachment of the industrial army", and another on the following day that he had met "swarms of people going east & but one going west."[2] Shortly after leaving Laramie, Wyoming, riding the blind baggage through a blizzard with snow so thick that "one could not see over a rod ahead", he overtook the "Reno Detachment of the Industrial Army", consisting of "eighty-four husky hoboes" lying in a dense mass on the straw-strewn floor of an empty refrigerator car attached to a through freight, and he climbed in to join them. After thirty-six hours without food a collection was taken up to wire ahead a request for a free meal. At Grand Island, Nebraska, London relates, "we were taken to the Restaurants and given a fine dinner, though we were well guarded by the local police so that none would escape." Arriving at Omaha on Thursday, April 19, they were met by a platoon of policemen who saw to it that the Reno con-

[1] London, "Diary", *Palimpsest*, Vol. VII, p. 134.
[2] *Ibid.*, p. 130.

tingent crossed the river intact. At Council Bluffs, however, London slipped out of the ranks to avoid a five-mile night march through rain and mud to Kelly's camp at Chautauqua Park. After sleeping in an empty barroom he stole a ride to Omaha and saw the town until a "sympathizer" provided him with a quarter and a ride to the camp.[1] His experiences on the road were probably similar to those of many others who joined Kelly from time to time.

While the disturbances in Council Bluffs had been at their height, the army had grown by the addition of western contingents such as that from Reno, and from enlistments from among the local unemployed. At Weston the enrollment reach nineteen hundred,[2] and the column started eastward across Iowa with fully fifteen hundred men in line. It was greeted by a continuous ovation. Farmers came as far as twenty-five miles, with brass bands, to see the army, to bring provisions, and to give the men rides.[3] At Neola a troop of boys and girls and young women, carrying flags and wearing sashes inscribed "Neola's Militia", came out to meet them. "It was an apt comparison," wrote London, "with the Ogden & Council Bluff's militia."[4] He continued:

All afternoon the ladies & gentlemen of the town thronged the camp, mingling with the boys, & in the evening there was a general rejoicing. In all the camps singing & speaking was going on, the ladies mingling their sweet voices with those of the boys all hoarse from the cold weather & sleeping out

[1] London, "Diary", *Palimpsest*, Vol. VII, pp. 139, 140; London, "Hoboes that Pass in the Night", *Cosmopolitan*, Vol. XLIV, pp. 196, 197.

[2] *Review of Reviews*, Vol. X, p. 57; Vincent, "Commonweal", p. 136.

[3] *Weekly Iowa State Register*, April 27, 1894; Indianapolis *Journal*, April 23, 1894.

[4] Vincent, "Commonweal", p. 147; London, "Diary", *Palimpsest*, Vol. VII, p. 146.

nights. . . . In one portion of the camp church was held
& a local minister officiated. In another, about a score of
germans sent their old country songs echoing throughout
the camp. We had our own little time, the principal feature
of which was songs & dances by the cooks.[1]

A Catholic priest secured for the army the loan of
one hundred fifty teams to assist it to the next town.[2]
There were similar experiences in some of the other
towns. Long afterwards Jack London remarked in
retrospect of this part of the journey:

> It was circus day when we came to town and every day
> was circus day, for there were many towns. Sure; they en-
> joyed it as much as we. We played their local nines with
> our picked baseball team; and we gave them better vaude-
> ville than they'd often had, for there was good talent left in
> some of the decayed artists of the army.[3]

All this spontaneous enthusiasm was utilized by careful organization. The secretary of the Central Labor
Union of Council Bluffs and the president of the Nebraska Federation of Labor had agreed to act as advance
agents for the army, keeping one town ahead of it and
arranging for its entertainment. The mayor of Council
Bluffs appointed an officer of the local Knights of Labor
to act as his representative in coöperation with these
two. The Sovereign Grand Consul of the Woodmen of
the World, who had lodges in most of the towns along
the line of march, offered to provide teams and wagons
to carry the provisions and the sick.[4] With such assistance as this, Kelly was usually able to keep his commissary well stocked.

[1] London, "Diary", *Palimpsest*, Vol. VII, p. 147.
[2] New York *Times*, April 23, 1894.
[3] London, "Book of Jack London", Vol. I, p. 158.
[4] *Weekly Iowa State Register*, April 27, 1894.

In an army in which authority and discipline depended largely upon the consent of the members rather than upon force imposed from above, it would have been strange if there had been no questioning of the authority of the leaders.[1] The officers were elected by the men, and depended largely upon their favor for continuance in office. Jack London's company twice deposed a captain and elected a lieutenant in his place. The principal grievance in both cases, apparently, was the failure of the officer to get supplies, food, and accommodations for the privates.[2] It was difficult to avoid suspicions of favoritism when there was not enough for all. There seems to have been no open break in the harmonious relations of the leaders until the army reached Neola, where Colonel Baker was the offender. London related that at the end of the evening's celebration with the townspeople, his company began its march to the stable where it was quartered for the night, but it was stopped by the sentries; then "Col. Baker came along with quite a jag on and a woman on his arm and passed us through." Baker had previously been suspected of misconduct. The next morning that redoubtable officer, doubtless because he was still suffering from the effects of his spree, started a row and, according to London's statement, tried to break up the army. Baker was then charged with flagrant violation of the rules which prohibited im-

---

[1] According to Vincent's statement the army at Atlantic consisted of something more than 1300 men, divided into 23 companies. The company officers seem to have been a captain, and one or two lieutenants. There were three colonels, who together constituted General Kelly's staff. There were also majors, a commissary department, a quartermaster's department, and a chaplain with the appropriate name of Mr. Parsonage. Vincent, "Commonweal", pp. 133, 153; Chicago *Tribune*, May 6, 1894; *Weekly Iowa State Register*, April 27, 1894.

[2] London, "Diary", *Palimpsest*, Vol. VII, pp. 144, 149, 155.

morality and the use of liquor. He was ignominiously dismissed and was started back towards Council Bluffs with the assistance of the village marshal,[1] but he re-appeared with acceptable explanations of his conduct, in time to participate in another quarrel.

The Sacramento division of the army was commanded by Colonel George Speed. He was described by Vincent as "a sort of socialist agitator" who had made speeches on street corners to drum up recruits when the Sacramento contingent was being organized, and who had been elected its colonel when it started eastward. Speed's influence over his regiment was greater than Kelly's, and there had developed a fierce rivalry between the Sacramento men and the men from San Francisco. This rivalry developed into a violent quarrel between Kelly and Speed, in which Speed's men took his side, and about two thirds of the army supported Kelly. Kelly called it a mutiny and tried to disband the Sacramento company and distribute its members among the others, but it refused to disband. Kelly accused Speed of violating the rules by permitting his men to leave camp without a pass, and Speed invited Kelly to account for several thousand dollars that had been contributed to the army. Kelly reduced Speed to the ranks, whereupon Speed was elected General of a separate command of some three hundred men. A fight between the supporters of the two leaders was narrowly averted by the intervention of the mayor of Atlantic, and the followers of Baker and Speed threatened to leave the main body. The key to the situation, however, lay in the control of the food supply, which

[1] London, "Diary", *Palimpsest*, Vol. VII, p. 147; Vincent, "Commonweal", pp. 147, 148.

was in Kelly's hands, and the mutineers received nothing from the commissary. A reconciliation was effected before the army left Atlantic, and both Speed and Baker resumed their previous positions, with the understanding that thereafter all important matters should be considered by the whole staff, and that the accounts should be open to inspection.[1]

In view of Kelly's lack of any military training, the discipline of his army, as it was described by those who saw it, was remarkable. His men could form a column of fours with precision, and they could march in a very creditable manner, although on the long marches no attempt was made to keep them in formation. But it was in the camp arrangements that his organizing ability showed best results.[2] A correspondent of the Chicago *Tribune* described them as follows:

Once the camp is reached . . . things move along at a lively rate. The first to arrive seize their axes and make for timber. There are good woodchoppers among them, and little time is required to cut enough for the night. Each company carries its share to its camp circle, and almost before it can be realized the commissary has served the rations, and big juicy steaks are frying in pans on fire beds of live coals. There is no confusion over this work and the men are not permitted to quarrel over camp locations or supplies. After supper guards are placed, with a relief every two hours, and no man is allowed to leave the grounds without a pass. The town authorities are requested to arrest all men not supplied with these passes. . . . In breaking camp everything is done in a methodical way. Only a few minutes are required to clean, roll, and tie up everything. A wagon

---

[1] Vincent, "Commonweal", pp. 148–150; London, "Diary", *Palimpsest*, Vol. VII, pp. 148, 149; New York *Times*, April 25, 26, 1894; *Weekly Iowa State Register*, April 27, 1894.

[2] Chicago *Tribune*, May 6, 1894; *Weekly Iowa State Register*, April 27, 1894.

comes up, when there are wagons, and each company loads its blankets and pans, falls in behind, and takes up the march. If there is a sick man in the company, he rides. When the grounds are deserted there isn't even a pin to be found. Only the smoldering fires tell the tale.[1]

The reporter just quoted described Kelly's persuasive art in taking up collections, but he noted that that shrewd leader kept his Salvation Army tricks bottled up at Neola, where the population was ninety per cent. Catholic. He added that the bugbear of the army was Pinkerton's secret service. Although many were suspected of being railroad detectives, he asserted that there were none, for the railway employees were as suspicious of "Pinkertons" as the army was, and their presence would have caused strikes. The army, however, sent out men to spy upon the railroads, army telegraph operators listening in on the messages at the stations when they got the chance.[2]

Two sleuths of a very different variety camped with the army one night and tramped twenty-two miles with it the next day. They were Labor Commissioner O'Blenes of Iowa and his clerk, who had joined the army in disguise, at the suggestion of Governor Jackson, to find out what it was like. They reported that they had started with little respect for the men, "but thinking the leaders were well meaning but misguided zealots." They returned with their opinions reversed, —

satisfied that the majority of the men composing the 'army' were men who would work if they had an opportunity; and

[1] Chicago *Tribune*, May 6, 1894.
[2] London relates that at Weston a private in one of the San Francisco companies "was tried by a drum head court martial & on being found guilty was drummed out of camp. He was supposed to be a railroad detective, reporter, or Pinkerton," and a few days later he wrote: "If any Pinkertons or detectives are caught it will go hard with them." — "Diary", *Palimpsest*, Vol. VII, pp. 144, 150.

that, chimerical as the movement was, they believed in it. . . . The men could not be properly classed as tramps or vagrants, as these terms are commonly understood, although they had no means of support either visible or prospective other than the charity of the public, and their banding together made their continued presence in any community both a burden and a menace.

They brought back a poor opinion of the leaders, saying that Kelly, Baker, and Speed were "thorough frauds, fakirs, and schemers for their own selfish ends."[1]

A "war correspondent" for the Des Moines *Capital*, who viewed the whole affair as "a piece of monumental folly" expressed more cynical views. "The army," he said, "is now getting down to a purely business basis. We do not intend to starve, nor do we intend to work, and we do not intend to walk unless we cannot help it. . . . We are getting along so well that we have been led to wonder why this plan of civilization had not been thought of before." No one was robbed or killed: "We could not afford to do these things, as General Kelly says, and General Kelly knows what we can afford to do." The singing, the carrying of flags, and other similar performances, made a good impression on the honest farmers who furnished food. The army had the sympathy of laboring men, and trades unions were passing resolutions in its favor. The result, he concluded, was that no one could criticize the industrials without criticizing those who indorsed them, and this shut the mouths of politicians who wanted the labor vote.[2]

At Avoca, Kelly gave to a representative of the Associated Press a more definite statement of his

[1] *Weekly Iowa State Register*, May 18, 1894.
[2] Des Moines *Capital*, quoted in *Public Opinion*, Vol. XVII, p. 38.

army's demands than had been hitherto expressed. He does not seem to have started from San Francisco with any clear-cut program like that worked out by Coxey, and probably the arduous work of conducting his army had left him little leisure to think, a process of which he was by no means incapable. He had now had time to consider what it was all about and to formulate his ideas. The principal item was a scheme for putting the unemployed to work on projects for the reclamation of arid lands. His idea was that by the time the work was done, the workers could have saved enough to carry them through a year of farming on the lands that they had reclaimed, thus developing "from homeless wanderers into steady farmers and property owners." "If we can only get to Washington," he said, "if we can let the lawmakers see that we are bread-winners, honest and sincere, we will be successful in our mission, for our demands are not unreasonable." He added that Congress was not to be asked to issue any "special funds or bonds"; the financing of the project was to be left entirely to the discretion of the law-makers.[1]

As the column neared Des Moines the farmers were no longer so enthusiastic as in the western part of the State, and wagons were becoming scarce. Desertions reduced the force for a time to little more than a thousand, many dropping out to catch rides on trains. They caused the Rock Island road so much annoyance that it issued a printed circular to the industrials in their camp at Adair to the effect that stolen trains would be obstructed, and would be run at the peril of the occupants. This caused intense excitement, for

[1] *Weekly Iowa State Register*, April 27, 1894; Vincent, "Commonweal", p. 154.

the men felt that the railroads were trying to worry them into unlawful acts which would make it possible to call out United States troops. They were soothed, however, by the officers, who reminded them that the army was pledged to keep the peace and obey the laws. Many of the trains carried as many as twenty extra men to throw off Kellyites who swung themselves onto the brake beams when the freights were forced to pull slowly up a steep grade. Except for the throwing of a few rocks, however, there was no resistance by the ejected stragglers.[1] Kelly firmly refused to allow any of his men to capture a train, insisting that such action would ruin the cause. The army managed to keep up its pace of twenty miles a day for five days, and finished by attempting a forced march of forty miles into Des Moines, lasting through the night of April 28 and 29.[2]

Des Moines had been making preparations, but of a less alarming nature than those at some of the previous stops.[3] The People's Party Political Club met on April 23 at the Trades Assembly Hall, to hear a paper on "The Governmental Social Experiments in New Zealand." At this meeting a committee was appointed

[1] Vincent, "Commonweal", pp. 156–158. Jack London's shoes wore out and he walked six miles barefooted before he got another pair. Before he reached Des Moines he was walking on "eight blisters and more a coming." Often he could not get a ride in a wagon and his attempts to ride trains were unsuccessful except once when he went to the station and obtained a ticket by "playing on the sympathies of the people." London, "Diary", *Palimpsest*, Vol. VII, pp. 144–152, *passim*.

[2] *Weekly Iowa State Register*, April 27, 1894; *Review of Reviews*, Vol. X, p. 59.

[3] At Atlantic "General Kelly received a statement from Des Moines laboring men to the effect that a bureau for the army would be opened there tomorrow and recruits invited from the entire state, similar to the headquarters at Lincoln, Neb., which was already forwarding small bodies of soldiers to the army. Kelly was assured by Des Moines labor leaders that if he would remain there a week he would be well cared for and receive probably five hundred men from the surrounding towns." — Vincent, "Commonweal", p. 152.

to arrange for the entertainment of Kelly's men, headed by the ex-presidential candidate of the party, General James B. Weaver. General Weaver sent word to Kelly at Atlantic that sentiment in Des Moines was very favorable to the army, and that he was endeavoring to secure for it railroad transportation from Des Moines to Washington, with every prospect of success.[1] The city authorities, on the other hand, who felt less of this favorable sentiment than the Populists did, prepared to prevent any demonstrations when the army arrived. Apparently Kelly planned to arrive in the city in time for a great ovation on Sunday morning, but he reckoned without his host. It was a long, hard march, and the farmers gave little aid; it rained; and the General got lost. Morning found the men in camp at Walnut Creek, where they were visited by General Weaver. When they made for the city they were held in the outskirts by the police, shivering in the rain, while the stragglers came up. It was late in the afternoon before they were marched to the stove works, an unoccupied three-story brick building rented by the city authorities for the purpose, where the Kellyites were quartered during the twelve days of their sojourn in Des Moines. Brass bands and parades were forbidden, which excited sympathy for the army and led labor organizations to denounce the city authorities. The thousands who watched the wet and hungry men march by gave little evidence of either enthusiasm or disapproval.[2]

[1] Vincent, "Commonweal," p. 152; *Weekly Iowa State Register*, April 27, 1894.

[2] H. L. Stetson, "The Industrial Army", *Independent*, Vol. XLVI, p. 681 (May 31, 1894); *Weekly Iowa State Register*, May 4, 1894; Indianapolis *Journal*, April 30, 1894; Chicago *Tribune*, May 1, 1894. An editorial in the *Register* entitled "Kelly and Newspaper Lies" branded as falsehoods the statements in Associated Press

A meeting held in the interest of the army in the Trades Assembly Hall on Monday night was crowded to suffocation. When General Weaver was called upon to speak, he compared the situation with the French Revolution; and he told how in Congress he had seen petitions on the clerk's desk carted off by the janitor without having been looked at: American citizens were denied the right of petition. "Here", says the reporter, "the crowd yelled for air", and the meeting was adjourned to the Courthouse yard, where General Weaver explained what the army wanted: free silver to right the crime of '73, and appropriations to irrigate arid lands in the west; the east got appropriations for harbors, and it was time that the laboring man got his share. Kelly announced that he intended to be in Washington on May 1, but that although he had not been able to do so, he would persist if it took until Christmas, and he added an anti-Chinese note to his previous expressions. He was followed by Mr. Nedrea of Omaha, who said that he would rather be a dead Kelly than a live Cleveland, that he was for Weaver for president, that such uprisings as this made plutocracy tremble, and that he wanted workingmen to assert their rights and vote together. The Industrial Quartette sang the army's favorite song, "Where is My Wandering Boy Tonight." [1] A later meeting was

reports that the army was not well treated when it arrived, and that the indignation was comparable to that at Council Bluffs. The *Register* had a tender regard for the reputation of its city and its State. Nebraskan reflections upon Iowan hospitality on the former occasion had led it to remark: "Those Omahogs . . . who refused to let the army stop on the Nebraska side and commenced instructing Iowa what to do with the men the minute they were safe across the river, beat the world for gall. Their resolutions of sympathy are worth as much as so much pulp." *Weekly Iowa State Register*, April 27, 1894.

[1] *Weekly Iowa State Register*, May 4, 1894.

addressed by Generals Kelly and Weaver, and by J. R. Sovereign, General Master Workman of the Knights of Labor.[1] Kelly also spoke to the students of Drake University, which made it seem advisable to the trustees of the institution somewhat later to issue a denial that they had any special sympathy for him.[2] The industrial baseball team played the Des Moines Stars and "put up a surprisingly good game", winning two out of three games, one by the interesting score of twenty-seven to nineteen.[3]

The Drake students did more than listen to Kelly, for they investigated his army. They recorded the information that they were able to obtain from the men, and President Aylesworth compiled statistics from this material. His results showed that of 763 men questioned as to their nationality, 549 professed to be American born. Of the foreign born, two fifths came from the British Isles or British colonies,[4] and more than a fourth from Germany. Most of the remainder were from western Europe, the list being completed by three Poles, one Russian, one Greek, one Turk, and one from the Argentine Republic. Eighty-three trades and occupations were represented among the 425 men examined who claimed to have any, the miners being more numerous than those of any other occupation.[5]

---

[1] *Weekly Iowa State Register*, May 4, 1894.

[2] *Ibid.*, May 18, 1894; Chicago *Tribune*, May 1, 1894.

[3] Chicago *Tribune*, May 3, 1894; London, "Diary", *Palimpsest*, Vol. VII, p. 153.

[4] England 30, Ireland 28, Scotland 12, Canada 12, Wales 2, Australia 2.

[5] Assuming that the remainder of the 763 men of Kelly's army had no trades, the percentage with trades or professions that required more or less skill was no greater than that found by McCook in his census of 1349 tramps. See J. J. McCook, "Tramp Census", *Forum*, Vol. XV, p. 754. But other evidence has been cited to indicate that most of Kelly's men were not of the professional vagrant type. The *Weekly Register* of May 4 tells that when one of the men persistently refused to wash, his company stripped him, boiled his clothes, and scrubbed him with hot water.

As to politics, 240 were Populists, 218 were Republicans, 196 were Democrats, 81 were undecided, and 11 were independents. There were 358 Protestants and 280 Catholics, with 114 who said that they had no religion. The average time since the men had been last employed was six months.[1] The *Iowa State Register* printed summaries of its reporter's interviews with about fifty of the men. About half of them stated the wages at which they were willing to work; half a dozen wanted "union" or "standard" wages, and the rest stated amounts varying from a dollar to two dollars a day. Seven others said they were willing to do any work offered.[2]

At Des Moines, as elsewhere, the behavior of the men caused no little astonishment.

The Army — wrote the president of Des Moines College — exhibited some marked peculiarities. The men kept sober. There was no report of any drinking. They were quiet and orderly, and gave the police no trouble. Tho a few of them advocated the doctrines of the anarchists, there was no attempt to destroy property, nor was there any stealing. They carry the flag of the United States at the head of the column, and on the lapel of the coat, if the wearer was fortunate enough to have a coat, a small flag would usually be pinned. They profess great love and loyalty to the country.

---

[1] *Weekly Iowa State Register*, May 4, 1894; Stetson, "Industrial Army", *Independent*, Vol. XLVI, p. 681; *Our Day*, Vol. XIII, pp. 280–282.

[2] For example, Col. George H. Speed, who had led the Sacramento mutineers, was single, a hatter, had no religion and no politics, and would accept nothing less than regular wages; he would not accept a position at this time because of the effect that it might have on his men. William Smith, of Los Angeles, was single, an engineer, had no religion on an empty stomach, was a Populist, had been unemployed for ten months, and would not accept less than standard wages in any line of work; he said that "the government would demand service in time of war, and must be brought to the realization that something was radically wrong when men could not find employment in time of peace." *Weekly Iowa State Register*, May 4, 1894.

They have a chaplain and a chorus which sings very effectively the familiar religious hymns.[1]

The Coxey fiasco at Washington occurred while Kelly was in Des Moines. Kelly had at first asserted that the industrial army movement had no connection with the Coxey movement in Ohio. Then he had said that he would coöperate with Coxey if he arrived in Washington on time. Now he attacked Coxey's lack of generalship. Coxey should have waited, he said, until the western armies came up, to get their support for his demonstration. "His whole fate," said Kelly, "depends upon my army. . . . The whole west, especially the laboring element, is with me and my men in our mission. . . . The laboring men form the bulk of the voting population, and these demonstrations have already had their effect upon the Western congressmen. . . ." It was therefore Coxey's own fault if he failed.[2]

The army did not fare as well in Des Moines as on the earlier part of the march through Iowa. The food supply, obtained by a daily house-to-house canvass made under the direction of a citizens' committee, soon ran short, and donations came in slowly. The excellence of Kelly's camp arrangements for the march was not perpetuated in the more permanent quarters in the stove works, and after a few days the camp was reported to be so filthy and insanitary that there was danger of a pestilence.[3] Nevertheless the army grew;

[1] Stetson, "Industrial Army", *Independent*, Vol. XLVI, p. 681.

[2] He added that Browne and some others in Coxey's army were "in bad odor in the East and in Coxey's own army. I know Carl Browne well. He used to run a little would-be comic paper in Los Angeles, and it was the general subject of ridicule. Carl Browne is a conceited ass and he has no one to support him." *Weekly Iowa State Register*, May 4, 1894; see also Chicago *Tribune*, May 3, 1894.

[3] Chicago *Tribune*, May 1, 2, 3, 4, 5, 1894; Stetson, "Industrial Army", *Independent*, Vol. XLVI, p. 681.

a new company was formed, and a count of the men on May 3 showed 1350 in camp.[1] The city council asked Kelly to move on, and labor organizations feared that the disbanding of the army would swamp the labor market,[2] but the men were tired of walking and the transportation question was again the crucial one, both for the industrials who wanted to go east, and for the citizens who wanted to get rid of them.

It has been noted that General Master Workman Sovereign of the Knights of Labor spoke at Kelly's second meeting. He had appeared unexpectedly in Des Moines, saying that he was going to take a hand in the fight, and that the army would not walk out of Des Moines even if it were necessary "to tie up all the railways in Iowa" in order to get concessions from them. He asserted that President Eugene V. Debs of the American Railway Union supported him in this stand. He opposed the seizure of trains, but he thought that if the railroads were paid a fair price they ought to accept it, and he said that the Knights of Labor would help raise the money. A telegram from Debs, however, denied the assertions about the American Railway Union, saying that it would not strike without a grievance, and this disposed of the matter.[3] On May 3 a delegation of three hundred laboring men, headed by General Weaver and local labor leaders, called upon the governor and urged him to find some way to move the army. Governor Jackson agreed to make another attempt to get it to the Mississippi if it would agree to get on a steamboat and go down to Cairo and up the

[1] Chicago *Tribune*, May 4, 1894; *Weekly Iowa State Register*, May 4, 1894.
[2] Chicago *Tribune*, May 2, 1894; Pittsburgh *Chronicle Telegraph*, May 3, 1894.
[3] Chicago *Tribune*, May 1, 2, 3, 1894; Chicago *Times*, May 3, 1894; *Weekly Iowa State Register*, May 4, 1894; Pittsburgh *Chronicle Telegraph*, April 30, 1894.

Ohio, from which it appears that he was less concerned about what the people of the East thought about having the army with them than he was about the reaction of the neighboring State of Illinois. The railroads declined unanimously to furnish a train for anything less than passenger rates.[1]

The scheme finally hit upon for moving the army was to build flat boats, transform it into an industrial navy, and send it down the Des Moines River. Des Moines carpenters helped in the construction and furnished tools, and the industrials worked busily in "Kelly's navy yard", visited by thousands of people who rejoiced in "the prospect of the departure of the enormous white elephant that has squatted down upon the city." [2] Kelly had stayed too long. His army and its friends in Des Moines had begun to get on each other's nerves. On the eve of his departure he quarreled with General Weaver and the citizens' committee, complaining that they had promised to take proper care of his army, but that they had failed to make good their promises — all this to the great enjoyment of those who had no love for Populists. Sovereign and Debs issued an appeal to organized labor to help the industrials, and the State Master Workman of the Knights of Labor accompanied Kelly to Keokuk. The embarkation was on May 9, with one hundred thirty-four boats and about a thousand men. Des Moines breathed a sigh of relief: the *Register* headline was "Rid of at Last." [3]

[1] Chicago *Tribune*, May 4, 1894; *Weekly Iowa State Register*, May 4, 1894.

[2] *Weekly Iowa State Register*, May 11, 1894, which said: "It was an argument in favor of Kelly's men that they took such an active part in such a busy scene." The boats were 18 feet long, 6 feet wide, and 1 foot deep, Kelly paid more than $500 for the materials. See also Chicago *Tribune*, May 7, 1894.

[3] *Weekly Iowa State Register*, May 11, 1894; Chicago *Tribune*, May 9, 10, 1894.

Kelly's discipline began to relax before he left Des Moines, and there were indications that his hold upon his men was slipping. He was accused of spending entirely too much time showing the ladies about,[1] and of passing too much of the responsibility for the work to Baker and Speed. Lack of discipline, or the difficulties of navigation, or both, soon scattered the fleet along many miles of the river.[2] Many of the boats were damaged in shallow rapids, and repairs meant delay. The food supply was uncertain; four days after leaving Des Moines most of the crews had had only one meal a day, and one had gone forty-eight hours without food. Several boats, manned chiefly by Sacramento men, got away before the others and picked up provisions intended for the whole army. When Kelly tried to break up one of these recalcitrant crews and distribute its members among the other boats, they threatened to leave in a body, and they escaped with a reprimand.[3] The army arrived famished at Ottumwa, where it was

Chicago *Times*, May 8, 1894. The *Review of Reviews*, Vol. X, p. 59, states the number of boats at 104, each carrying 8 or 10 men.

[1] The two young women who had been prominent in the mob that captured the train for Kelly in Council Bluffs had left to escape arrest, and had accompanied the army on its march. Kelly explained that they had lost their positions because they had tried to help him, and he felt responsible for them, and that he would let them accompany the army so long as they did no wrong. He said that since one of them was a Daughter of Rebecca and he was an Odd Fellow, he could have them cared for at the home of some Odd Fellow at each town where the army stopped. When the mother of one of them came after her, Kelly said that he told both of them that they could not accompany the army farther, but they were in his boat when the army started down the river. Commissioner O'Blenes heard grumbling about the presence of these women among the criticisms of Kelly by the men on the march. *Weekly Iowa State Register*, May 4, 18, 1894; Chicago *Tribune*, May 1, 1894; New York *Times*, May 1, 1894.

[2] Chicago *Tribune*, May 10, 1894; *Weekly Iowa State Register*, May 11, 25, 1894; *Review of Reviews*, Vol. X, p. 59.

[3] London, "Diary", *Palimpsest*, Vol. VII, pp. 155, 156; Chicago *Tribune*, May 12, 1894. Jack London seems to have been the ringleader in the crew that received the reprimand. See Jack London, "The March of Kelly's Army", *Cosmopolitan*, Vol. XLIII, pp. 645 *ff*.; Charmian London, "Book of Jack London", pp. 159, 160.

well fed and visited by some ten thousand people. Its popularity as a spectacle had not yet declined; London wrote on the third day of the voyage that all along the river since they had left Des Moines the banks had been lined so continuously with spectators that the industrials sometimes had to go miles to find a secluded spot to bathe or make their toilets. [1]

Some distance below Ottumwa, "Kelly's Marines" had an engagement with some of the Rock Island Railroad's special deputies. Clubs and stones were used, and some of Kelly's men were injured. Two of the deputies were arrested, but were at once bailed out by officials of the road. When the news of their encounter came to the camp that night, the excitement was intense. "If any Pinkertons are captured," wrote London, "Woe unto them for the men are getting desperate." The next morning when one of the boats tried to cross the river, a force of twenty-five "Pinkertons" prevented their landing, doubtless fearing an attempt upon a train. Immediately a host of warlike Kellyites started across in boats or plunged into the stream and waded through. Most of the deputies beat a hasty retreat, but two were caught, their pistols were taken away, and they received severe punishment. Kelly soon restored order, and the two captives seem to have escaped with what damage they had already received and "a good talking to" from the General. [2]

On the lower stretches of the river, where it serves as the boundary between Iowa and Missouri, the weather changed for the worse, and after "a miserable

[1] London, "Diary", *Palimpsest*, Vol. VII, p. 155.
[2] *Ibid.*, pp. 156, 157; Chicago *Tribune*, May 17, 1894.

day on the water with a chilling wind & driving rain"
the men spent a miserable night on the inhospitable
Missouri shore.[1] Eleven days out from Des Moines the
army reached the Mississippi.[2] The navigation in
flat-bottomed scows of more than two hundred miles of
shallow stream over dams and shoals and through
rapids, in the space of eleven days, had been a very
creditable performance.

On the Mississippi the boats were lashed together
into a sort of raft and were taken in tow by a steamboat. Large crowds from the three adjoining States
flocked to see them. At Quincy, where Kelly had once
lived before he went west, Alderman Thad Rogers had
invited the army to stop at his hotel, promising a
thousand pounds of meat and a thousand loaves of
bread for their entertainment. Kelly addressed two
thousand people in the city park for half of the gate
receipts. The hospitality of Quincy seems to have
been too much for some of the men, for a captain was
indicted for the theft of a watch and ten men were
arrested for being drunk and disorderly.[3] A number
deserted at Hannibal, Missouri, among them Jack
London who, having had his fun out of the army, decided that starvation was not to his taste, and that he
was ready for other adventures.[4]

The reception at St. Louis was flattering. Several
hundred dollars was subscribed to help Kelly, and

[1] London, "Diary", *Palimpsest*, Vol. VII, p. 158.
[2] On May 20. — Chicago *Tribune*, May 21, 1894.
[3] Chicago *Tribune*, May 21, 22, 1894; *Weekly Iowa State Register*, May 25, 1894.
The *Tribune* said that for three days before the arrival of the army the city had
been full of tramps who said they were waiting for it.
[4] Chicago *Tribune*, May 26, 1894; London wrote in his diary: "We went supper-
less to bed. Am going to pull out in the morning. I can't stand starvation."
London, "Book of Jack London", Vol. I, p. 161.

arrangements were made to meet the flotilla some miles up the river with an excursion steamer bearing a brass band and a number of labor leaders.[1] When the fleet arrived on May 28, the men camped on the levee, and were given the freedom of the city while their general was being received by labor unions. An encounter between some of the industrials showed that there was still discipline left in the army. A fight occurred in which a man had his skull fractured; there were cries of "Lynch him", but the captains kept their men under control and held the crowd back until the police arrived to take charge of the assailant.[2]

From St. Louis, Kelly continued down the Mississippi to the mouth of the Ohio, where the boats were destroyed, but his army was barred out of Cairo and some of the neighboring towns.[3] He then started up the Ohio in barges. It seems that for a time the recruits still balanced the desertions, for at Evansville, Indiana, it was reported that he still had eleven hundred men.[4] The army was forbidden to enter Louisville. Jeffersonville and New Albany on the Indiana side, alarmed at the report that Kelly was ascending the river with twelve hundred men in barges, swore in deputies and special police to keep him out. At Louisville Kelly and Baker were arrested as vagrants, and, although released, they were prevented from speaking.[5]

The whole ascent of the Ohio was a struggle with ad-

---

[1] Chicago *Tribune*, May 27, 1894.

[2] *Ibid.*, May 30, 31, 1894; *Review of Reviews*, Vol. X, p. 59.

[3] Chicago *Tribune*, June 8, 1894.

[4] *Ibid.*, June 12, 18, 1894. The Indianapolis *Journal* of April 23, 1894, reported that J. H. Swift, of Terre Haute, was raising recruits for Kelly's army, and that he expected to have two hundred men in two days. Kelly was probably joined by a number of such detachments along the way.

[5] Chicago *Tribune*, June 18, 19, 20, 21, 22, 1894.

versity. By the second week of July the men seem to
have been scattered in various parts of Kentucky, Ohio,
and West Virginia, many in a destitute condition, to
the great annoyance of farmers upon whom they foraged. There were reports that the army was disbanding, that it was reassembling, and that Kelly with two
hundred men in barges was being towed by a small
steamer, trying to make Parkersburg before low water.[1]

On July 12, three months and seven days after the
affair in the Oakland Tabernacle, Kelly appeared in
Washington and announced that he still had six hundred men on the way between the Capital and Ports-
mouth, Ohio. Two days later a detachment described
as "the remnants of Kelly's industrial army" was arrested at Wheeling, West Virginia, and sentenced to
fifteen days in the workhouse, and it was intimated that
others who were expected would receive the same treatment.[2] Other remnants straggled into Washington, but
only a fraction of the number that Kelly had succeeded
in holding together from California to the lower Ohio.
His army had attained its greatest strength and the
height of its popularity in western Iowa, during the
latter part of April. After May 1, Kelly's cause, like
Coxey's, had declined.

[1] Chicago *Tribune*, July 8, 1894; *Review of Reviews*, Vol. X, p. 59; Washington
Post, July 11, 1894.
[2] *Ibid.*, July 13, 15, 1894.

CHAPTER X

The attempt to trace in detail the movements of all the bands of industrials that formed, traveled, dissolved, and sometimes reappeared, would be tedious and perhaps unprofitable. But several of the armies other than Coxey's, Kelly's and Fry's held together long enough or had careers sufficiently dramatic or significant to deserve special mention.

The departure of Fry and Kelly was by no means the end of the industrial army movement in California, a State which was perhaps more active in producing these organizations than any other. On April 2, before Kelly's army had left San Francisco, a second regiment of the Los Angeles army set out to join Fry — one hundred sixty-seven men under the command of General Arthur Vinette. They wanted to ride on the Sante Fe Railroad to Kansas City, and offered to pay their way in work for the road. When this plan fell through they set out on foot to San Bernardino, the army increasing on the way to something more than two hundred. The conduct of the men was similar to that of their predecessors; they were reported to be orderly and well behaved; at Whittier they went to church, seventy professed religion, and all took a pledge not to drink intoxicating liquor.[1]

It appears that in most cases the passage through a

[1] San Francisco *Chronicle*, April 1, 2, 3, 1894; Vincent, "Commonweal", p. 199.

locality of a single industrial army was enough to exhaust the hospitality of the community, and Vinette had the misfortune to follow Fry. Delayed by the difficulty of obtaining transportation and food and by the hostility of local authorities, the second Los Angeles regiment progressed in three weeks only as far as the first had traveled in two days. Vinette's men encountered their first formidable opposition at San Bernardino. There the citizens agreed to boycott the army, refusing to give or to sell it any food. When the men tried to board an overland freight at three o'clock one morning, they were driven off with the aid of a drenching from the city fire hose. Then fifty deputy sheriffs marched several of the leaders to jail. Released on the promise to leave the locality, they were again incarcerated at Colton, where they were held for trial on the charge of attempting to defraud the railroad of fares, and of inciting a riot. They ingeniously pleaded not guilty, demanded trial by jury, and tried to subpoena all the members of the army as witnesses, hoping thereby to get them employment at the usual *per diem* throughout the trial of eight cases.[1] The further adventures of this army are difficult to trace, for the attention of the leading newspapers does not seem to have been focussed upon it as upon some of the others, but Vinette himself ultimately reached Fry's camp near Washington.[2]

Other contingents from San Francisco, Oakland, and Sacramento followed in Kelly's wake. On April 28

[1] Vincent, "Commonweal", pp. 199, 200; San Francisco *Chronicle*, April 14, 16, 1894; *Weekly Iowa State Register*, April 20, 1894; *Public Opinion*, Vol. XVII, p. 69 (April 19, 1894); Pittsburgh *Chronicle Telegraph*, April 14, 16, 18, May 9, 1894.
[2] The Washington *Post* of July 25, 1894, reported that Col. Vinette had just arrived with 10 men and that about 30 others were already in the camp.

eleven hundred industrials were reported on their way from Oakland to Sacramento, one band of five hundred commanded by Mrs. Anna F. Smith, who was described as an elderly woman of decisive manners and commanding presence.[1] The activity of the California industrials continued until June, and a train was stolen in that State as late as June 8.[2]

The most intractable and troublesome of all the industrial armies were those formed in the mountains and the Pacific Northwest. In the regions where the frontier condition had not yet passed away, the hardy miners and mountaineers were less accustomed to the restraints of civilization than the workingmen of the industrial regions, and they were more dangerous when thwarted. For two or three months they kept United States marshals, militia, and even the regular army, busy protecting railroad property.

The first blood of the industrial army conflict was shed in the clash between deputy marshals and Hogan's Montana army. By the middle of April about five hundred men, most of them unemployed miners, had organized at Butte to obtain transportation eastward. They negotiated with the Northern Pacific for a ride to

---

[1] New York *Times*, April 29, 1894; Pittsburgh *Chronicle Telegraph*, April 28, 1894; Vincent, "Commonweal", pp. 199, 200. Vincent mentions the presence of four women in a contingent of 850 waiting for transportation at Oakland on April 22, and adds: "The interest taken by the women of Oakland in the Commonweal was, perhaps, greater than that recorded of any other city. Here two hundred women signed a recruiting list which provided for their immediate passage, by rail, to Washington City." See also *Weekly Iowa State Register*, April 13, 1894. The San Francisco *Chronicle*, April 3, 1894, states that Vinette's regiment started with an express wagon "filled with all sorts of munitions contributed by the women's branch of this organization." A train was captured at Washington, Iowa, on May 15 by 150 Commonwealers, fifty of whom were women. — Chicago *Tribune*, May 15, 1894.

[2] 53rd Cong., 2d Sess., *Senate Executive Document*, No. 120, p. 17. For notices of some of the later California armies see Pittsburgh *Chronicle Telegraph*, April 30, May 9, 1894.

St. Paul, but without success. That road was then in
the hands of a receiver appointed by the Federal Court,
and the receiver pointed to a Minnesota statute, which
forbade the importation of indigent persons into that
State, as the reason for his refusal. The people of Butte,
feeling that the hard times were caused by the Federal
legislation against silver, were in hearty sympathy with
Hogan's purpose. As his men grew desperate the situation alarmed the railroad, and the United States marshal was called upon to protect its property. On April
21, United States Marshal William McDermott telegraphed the Attorney-General of the United States
that the Commonweal army had taken possession of the
railroad, preventing trains from leaving; and that excitement ran high, with public sentiment strongly in
favor of the industrials. He asked for instructions,
inquiring whether he had authority to call in the aid of
militia or regular troops, and whether he should employ
a large number of deputies at high pay. Attorney-
General Olney instructed him to employ as many
deputies as were necessary to execute the orders of the
Federal Court, and he proceeded to swear in a large
number of them — but not enough.[1]

When Hogan's final request for transportation was
refused, his army began to act upon its own initiative.
It contained a number of experienced railroad men.
Early in the morning of April 23 some of them broke
into a roundhouse, manned an engine, got up steam,
and coupled it to a freight train. In the meantime
the railroad officials applied to the Federal judge for an
injunction to restrain the Hoganites from stealing the
train, on the ground that the court was responsible for

[1] 53rd Cong., 2d Sess., *Senate Executive Document*, No. 120, p. 3.

the management of the road by the receiver it had appointed. The injunction was granted; Hogan's men disregarded it, and warrants were issued for their arrest. According to one version of the story, when the marshal tried to serve the writs, he and his deputies were locked up by the Hoganites, who thereupon started east at the rate of forty or fifty miles an hour.[1]

An account of this affair in a letter from a Butte Populist denied that the train was stolen, as was stated in Associated Press dispatches printed in the East. A committee of business men, he said, had tried to arrange transportation for Hogan's men to St. Paul, but the railroad would not carry them for money; the business men then told Hogan to take a train, guaranteeing that no one would interfere with him, and although it took two hours to get up steam in a dead engine, he was not disturbed, for the committee had "fixed" the railroad agent; and although the United States marshal knew what was going on, he did not try to follow until he thought the army would be out of the State before he and his deputies could reach it. The writer added that under the circumstances no one would serve as a deputy marshal but "the vilest and most disreputable men in the community", and moreover that it was an open secret that the militia, if they had been called out, would have stacked their arms.[2] Whether this writer's state-

---

[1] Indianapolis *Journal*, April 26, 1894. The New York *Times*, April 25, 1894, stated that after two days' struggle between the local authorities and the mob, the officers were overawed, and no opposition was offered to the army's departure.

[2] Letter of T. B. Sullivan, Butte, Mont., April 30, 1894, to H. E. Taubeneck, Washington, D. C. [chairman of the People's Party National Committee], printed in *National Watchman*, Vol. IV, p. 799 (May 11, 1894). A case similar to this was reported from Bismarck, N. D., on June 20, when the marshal brought in from Dawson five business men of that city who had been arrested and charged with conspiracy in aiding Coxeyites to steal a Northern Pacific train. — Chicago *Tribune*, June 21, 1894.

ment of facts was more accurate than the Associated Press reports or not, the marshal's observations on the condition of public sentiment in Butte suggest that this letter represented the state of mind of the greater part of the community.[1]

At any rate Hogan's army made away with the train, and, having an exceptionally fast locomotive, they took the mountain curves at unprecedented speed. Hogan had warned the division superintendent of his intention to hold the right of way, and the track was cleared of other traffic.[2] The train sped on past Bozeman, where recruits and food appeared, until it was blocked by a bank of earth at the end of a tunnel. Finding tools left by laborers on the track, the industrials worked energetically for six hours until the obstruction was removed, and proceeded on to Billings.[3]

Division Superintendent Finn, of the Northern Pacific, wired the sheriff of Yellowstone County, instructing him to arrest the army at Billings. It seems that Finn had once failed to be elected sheriff of that county, and the under-sheriff who received the telegram, refusing to take him seriously, wired in reply:

County attorney and sheriff are out in Bull Mountains laying out additions to Billings. All of our ablebodied men are busy selling real estate. Stop Coxey's Army at Livingston.[4]

Marshal McDermott, with about seventy-five deputies, had followed the industrials in a passenger train. Overtaking them at Columbus, he demanded an un-

---

[1] See also Vincent, "Commonweal", pp. 201, 202, 216, 217.

[2] "It is all we can do," said the general manager, "for we have too much regard for human life to do anything else." — Vincent, "Commonweal", p. 217; *Weekly Iowa State Register*, April 27, 1894.

[3] Vincent, "Commonweal", pp. 201, 202; New York *Times*, April 26, 1894.

[4] Vincent, "Commonweal", p. 219.

conditional surrender, but when Hogan returned a decisive refusal, the marshal, whose deputies were greatly outnumbered, contented himself with following Hogan to Billings. Both trains arrived at that place about noon of April 25. At the station a hundred recruits were waiting with a large crowd of excited citizens whose sympathies were clearly with Hogan's army. The deputies jumped from their train and charged toward Hogan's men into a shower of rocks, brickbats, and other convenient missiles propelled by the sympathetic citizens as well as by the industrials. Several of the deputies opened fire with their revolvers, and before the brief battle ended a citizen was fatally wounded, and several of Hogan's men and at least one of the deputies were injured. The deputies, finding the infuriated mob too much for them, soon beat a hasty retreat to their cars. The victorious Hoganites, now furnished with running orders from the railroad, fled to Forsyth, where they stopped to spend the night.[1]

Meanwhile the wires had been busy between Montana and Washington. Besides the complaints of the United States Marshal to the Attorney-General, President Cleveland received a telegram from the Governor of Montana to the effect that deputy marshals, trying to serve an injunction of a Federal Court, had been mobbed.[2] After a consultation between the President, the Attorney-General and General Schofield, it was decided that since the Governor of Montana had no authority to act under these circumstances, United States troops should be used to restore order.[3] Lieutenant

---

[1] Vincent "Commonweal", pp. 201, 202, 217, 218.
[2] *Outlook*, Vol. XLIX, p. 714; New York *Times*, April 26, 1894.
[3] Indianapolis *Journal*, April 26, 1894; *Weekly Iowa State Register*, May 4, 1894.

Colonel J. H. Page was ordered from Fort Keogh with six companies of infantry, to proceed to Forsyth and arrest Hogan's army.[1]

About midnight, while Hogan's men slept in their cars, his sentries perceived a train approaching from the east at high speed. It stopped before they could arouse the sleeping army and soldiers swarmed out of it, surrounding Hogan's train so completely that only about two hundred and fifty men escaped. Hogan promptly surrendered the rest to Colonel Page.[2] The three hundred thirty-one prisoners were taken to Helena, where they were brought to trial two weeks later.[3] Since there was no Federal law on the subject of train-stealing, the only clear case against the Hogan-

---

[1] Four troops of the Tenth Cavalry were also sent from Fort Custer to coöperate with him. The infantry did its work without assistance, capturing 331 prisoners. Troops were also ordered to other points along the line of the Northern Pacific to assist the United States marshals in executing the orders of the courts. — "Report of the Secretary of War", 1894, p. 119.

[2] Vincent, "Commonweal", pp. 218, 219; Pittsburgh *Post*, April 28, 1894; *Weekly Iowa State Register*, April 27, 1894; *Public Opinion*, Vol. XVII, p. 115 (May 3, 1894). Vincent's circumstantial account has been followed in most of its details. In regard to the newspaper dispatches about the Hogan affair, the *Outlook* commented: "The telegraphic reports are . . . confused, if not contradictory. The dispatches upon which the troops were called out depicted an armed force of desperadoes which proved too much for an armed force of a hundred deputies, while the dispatch announcing the unresisting surrender of the 'army' to the troops stated that only three men in the body had revolvers." — *Outlook*, Vol. XLIX, p. 714 (May 5, 1894).

[3] Chicago *Tribune*, May 1, 15, 1894; Vincent, "Commonweal", p. 208. On the difficulties of the marshal in guarding his prisoners and in providing quarters and subsistence for them and his deputies, see 53rd Cong., 2d Sess., *Senate Executive Document*, No. 120, p. 6. This document consists of a request by the Attorney-General of the United States for an increase in the deficiency appropriation for the fees of deputy marshals from $50,000 to at least $125,000, made necessary by the unusually large number of them employed during April, May, and June, 1894, because of disturbances in fourteen States and two territories. This request was accompanied by a number of extracts from his correspondence with United States marshals showing the necessity for the increase. About four fifths of the disturbances which made the use of deputies necessary were caused by attempts of industrial armies to seize trains on roads in the hands of receivers; the others were mostly caused by strikers.

ites was that they were guilty of contempt of court.[1] The judge who had issued the injunction against interference with trains at Butte refused to accept Hogan's defence that he and his men had taken the train with the tacit consent of the managers of the Northern Pacific. On May 14 Hogan was sentenced to six months in jail, and the engineer and fireman of his train and forty of his officers received lighter sentences of thirty days each. The remaining three hundred men were brought into court and were released upon their promise to discontinue the practice of train-stealing.[2]

The conviction of the leaders, however, did not result in the dissolution of the army. A month later it appeared at Bismarck, North Dakota, going down the river in flat boats. Here it was rumored that these men were in the employ of silver mine owners of Butte and other Montana towns, sent out on a crusade for free silver.[3] Occasional newspaper items indicate their progress as far as Missouri. At Pierre, South Dakota, one hundred and fifty special police were armed with rifles and a committee was appointed to inform Hogan — they were apparently ignorant that he was supposed to be in jail — that he could have two days' rations if he would consent to accept them several miles downstream. The leaders expressed the intention of continuing down the Mississippi and up the Ohio, ex-

---

[1] *American Law Review*, Vol. XXVIII, p. 426 (May–June, 1894); 53rd Cong., 2d Sess., *Senate Executive Document*, No. 120, p. 6. According to a dispatch from New York, an eastern attorney for the Northern Pacific wired instructions to attorneys at St. Paul, Minn., and Helena, Mont., asking them to proceed against the prisoners before Judge Knowles of the United States Court for contempt of court; also to prefer charges of grand larceny for the theft of the train, conspiracy under the laws of Montana, and felonious assault for firing on United States deputy marshals. — Pittsburgh *Chronicle Telegraph*, April 26, 1894.

[2] Chicago *Tribune*, May 15, 1894.

[3] *Ibid.*, June 11, 17, 18, 19, 1894.

pecting to reach their destination about September 1.[1]
When they arrived in St. Joseph, Missouri, on July 9,
they were described as four hundred miners from Butte
on their way to Washington to demand free silver of
Congress.[2] The sources that have been examined do
not indicate how much farther they went or what became of them.

Sanders' Cripple Creek brigade of Colorado miners
spent two days of the wildest railroading recorded during this period.[3] Arriving at Pueblo early in May,
Sanders made the usual demand for free transportation
on the railroad, and received the usual reply from the
Missouri Pacific that his men would be carried only if
they paid full fare.[4] This seems to have been one of
the better type of unemployed armies; it was found to
contain three locomotive engineers, five firemen, three
telegraph operators, and one civil engineer.[5] Thomas
Bates, one of Sanders' men who joined him at Pueblo,
told long afterwards that Sanders, in his speeches, was
insistent that he wanted only genuine unemployed workingmen in his army, and that none of his men should
carry weapons.[6]

---

[1] Chicago *Tribune*, June 21, 24, 1894.

[2] Washington *Post*, July 11, 1894.

[3] This brigade was founded in the Cripple Creek mining region before the end
of April. S. S. Sanders, the leader, was an electrician, a native of Missouri, who
had recently been a personal friend of Charles T. Kelly at San Francisco. Vincent,
"Commonweal", p. 211; Chicago *Tribune*, May 3, 12, 1894.

[4] Chicago *Tribune*, May 8, 1894.

[5] *Ibid.*, May 12, 1894.

[6] Statement by Mr. Thomas Bates, of Madison, Wis. Mr. Bates was a young
Welshman who had been working in the Cripple Creek mining region until he found
himself among the unemployed in the spring of 1894, and joined Sanders' army at
Pueblo. In the summer of 1923 he gave the writer a detailed account of his adventures. His memory seems to have been unusually accurate, for the facts he stated
check with the newspaper accounts so far as the latter give them. Notes taken
from Bates' relation have been used in the preparation of this account, cited as
"Bates."

When Sanders decided to take a train, the Missouri Pacific had already taken the precaution to run all its good engines and its passenger cars out of town, and nothing remained but an old Rio Grande Western switch engine that leaked badly, and a few flat cars. Sanders told his men that the railroad had given him permission to borrow the engine, and it was promptly manned by members of the army. The engineer, old Lewellyn, had made this run for thirty years. The flat cars were coupled on. Sanders gave orders to pack up tents and board the train, where the four hundred and fifty men found little more than standing room. They pulled out, the men waving their flags and the crowd cheering, for the whole country seemed to be sympathetic. As the water leaked out of the old engine, frequent refilling was necessary, but the railroad had emptied the water tanks. The energetic industrials, however, filled the boiler with water obtained from the nearest stream or farmer's pump, carried in buckets, dinner pails, or tin cups. After a twenty-mile run a derailed engine was found in a cut, ditched by the railroad to block the passage of the army. Nothing daunted by this obstruction, the men found tools in a section foreman's shanty, tore up the track behind them, built it around the wreck, and continued their journey, taking enough rails along with them to discourage pursuit. A second wrecked engine in another cut was found lying across the track. Again they went to work, even Sanders himself taking a hand, until the track was built around. By this time the men were famished, for in their haste they had forgotten to bring any food. Three miles from Chivington they encountered a third wreck which was the worst of all — an engine and some cattle cars piled up on the track, so that it would take hours to build around them.

The army marched to Chivington to obtain food. There they found a number of deputies, — all good fellows, said Bates, who did not molest them. A steer was killed and cooked for Sanders' men and after a hearty meal they returned to build the track around the wreck. The telegraph operator at Chivington told them that they would find the water tanks full, and that there would be no militia or deputies to interfere with them until they reached Scott, Kansas, where the marshal and his deputies were waiting to arrest them. Having passed the third wreck, they went on to the end of the division. They found the passenger trains waiting and the track clear. Here the army's train crew went to the roundhouse and selected the best engine they could find. "Treat her right, Lewellyn," said the deposed engineer, "she's good for seventy miles an hour", and old Lewellyn soon had her going so fast that the men on the flat cars could not hold their flags up against the wind.[1]

While Sanders and his men were on their way out of Colorado, the United States marshal in Denver was informed that the presence of the industrial army on the track interfered with the movement of the mails. Counsel for the Missouri Pacific was told to apply for an injunction to prevent further interference with the railroad's property. The Colorado marshal did not catch the army, but the officials of the Missouri Pacific had planned, as the report of the telegraph operator at Chivington had indicated, to have it intercepted soon

[1] Bates; Chicago *Tribune*, May 10, 1894; New York *Times*, May 10, 1894; *Weekly Iowa State Register*, May 11, 1894.

after it crossed the Kansas line.[1] United States Marshal S. F. Neely and his deputies had come from Topeka to Scott, where Sanders found them waiting for him. When Sanders had interviewed the marshal and held a conference with his captains, he advised his men to submit, and thereby get a ride in Pullmans to Topeka, more than three hundred miles nearer their destination. Some of the men, in spite of their commander's orders, had guns and wanted to resist, but the majority prevailed upon them to submit peaceably. Those who were armed must have disposed of their guns promptly, for a newspaper report stated that not a weapon of any kind was found among them.[2] A cow was killed and the men were so ravenous that they devoured it half-cooked within a few minutes.

Sanders told his men to behave, promising them that at Topeka they would meet the Populist governor, L. D. Lewelling, who was known to sympathize with the Coxeyites, and who had refused to call out the militia to recapture the stolen train.[3] The deputies, scattered throughout the cars to maintain order, seem to have been somewhat officious, and they were in the minority; most of them, said Bates, had bloody noses before the end of the journey.

[1] Chicago *Tribune*, May 10, 1894; Pittsburgh *Chronicle Telegraph*, May 9, 1894.
[2] Pittsburgh *Chronicle Telegraph*, May 12, 1894; Bates.
[3] *American Law Review*, Vol. XXVIII, p. 426. The writer of this note on the industrial armies made caustic comments upon the following telegram from "the caricature who disgraces the office of governor of Kansas" to a sheriff "who evidently had some conception of his official duty":

"*James Hunt, Sheriff, Horace, Kansas:*
Telegram asking for troops to arrest 500 men who have stolen Missouri Pacific train received. Was train stolen in Kansas? Have any depredations been committed in your county? Have warrants been issued and processes been resisted? Are the men still in your county?

L. D. Lewelling, Governor."

At Topeka the train was surrounded by an enthusiastic crowd; tobacco, money, and bread were tossed in through the car windows. Governor Lewelling was there, inquiring of the marshal when the men had been fed last, and telling him to get tents and food for them immediately.[1] The governor, Secretary of State Osborn, and other Populist leaders had already held a conference and had summoned a mass meeting in the public square to discuss the problem of the unemployed, and the governor extended permission to use the courthouse grounds as a camping place for the army.[2]

Perhaps Marshal Neely was as badly scared by these demonstrations as Bates thought he was; at any rate he disregarded the governor's invitation and kept the men locked up in cars. On his way to Topeka he had wired Attorney-General Olney that the jail capacity of that city was inadequate to house the army, and he obtained permission to quarter his prisoners on the Fort Leavenworth military reservation, whither they were promptly removed.[3] They were placed in a camp in a triangle inclosed by railroad tracks, guarded by deputies in the surrounding hills. The soldiers at the fort, said Bates, were sympathetic and good fellows, and the deputies were for the most part mere boys, not to be taken seriously. Sanders and his captains were permitted to go to Leavenworth when they chose, but the men were kept within the inclosure.[4]

Sanders appears to have been an optimist; he assured his men that they had done nothing for which they could be convicted, and that it was not their fault that

---

[1] Bates.
[2] Chicago *Tribune*, May 12, 1894.
[3] 53rd Cong., 2d Sess., *Senate Executive Document*, No. 120, p. 8.
[4] Bates.

the Missouri Pacific had destroyed several thousand dollars of its own property and had obstructed the mails in the attempt to prevent the army from getting out of Colorado. "We are much obliged to Uncle Sam," he had boasted at Topeka, "for helping us this far on our journey, providing us with comfortable cars, and keeping us from hunger.[1]" He obtained free legal service, collected money for his army, and informed his men that he had bought a steamboat, the *Mayflower*, on which they would ride to Kansas City when they were acquitted; there they would take on Bennett's army and proceed on down the river. Bates' captain returned from town one night, however, with the report that President Cleveland did not want the army in Washington, and that he had sent word to the courts to find the men guilty; this would probably mean jail sentences, and the captain proposed to leave before it was too late, taking with him all who wanted to go. When he took a vote of the company one man preferred to stay and get three square meals a day.

That night the captain and the other twenty-nine men slipped past the guards in small groups, assembled on the railroad tracks, and caught a train to Kansas City. There some of them joined Bennett's army, and marched through the streets with it, singing a song to the tune of "John Brown's Body", which, Bates said, aroused the spectators to a high pitch of enthusiasm. The last stanza ran:

So now my story's ended, but to you I have not said
That when they closed our silver mines they made our
country dead.

[1] Chicago *Tribune*, May 12, 1894.

We voted for free silver so that we could earn our bread,
As we go marching on.[1]

Meanwhile the authorities who had arrested Sanders'
men seemed to be puzzled as to what to do with them.
A newspaper dispatch surmised that there would be
more difficulty in convicting them than in making the
arrests.[2] There had been some difficulty in the beginning because of the absence of Federal law covering
cases of this kind; it seems that when the State authorities of Kansas refused to make the arrest the railroad
sued out a writ of replevin in a Federal Court for the
recovery of its property.[3] One of Sanders' attorneys
asserted that the warrants on which the men were arrested were worthless, and he threatened not only to
have the industrials released by writs of *habeas corpus*,
but also to sue the railroad for heavy damages. By
this time the intention seems to have been to try the
men for interfering with the mails.[4] At the time of the
arrests Attorney-General Olney had told Marshal Neely
to take the prisoners before a court at once if possible,[5]
but there was delay of more than a month. The judges
seemed too busy to try these cases:[6] perhaps they felt
that Populist Kansas was no place to convict industrial

---

[1] Bates. Bennett's army from Denver had traveled through Nebraska and south
ward into Kansas, expressing the intention to float down the Missouri River to
join Kelly. At Seneca, Kansas, where Bennett was refused transportation in
wagons, he refused to walk, boasting that his men had not walked more than sixty
miles since they left Denver. — Chicago *Tribune*, May 16, 23, 1894. According
to Bates, Bennett's army disbanded in Kansas City. It was still there, although
declining in numbers, in the middle of June. — Pittsburgh *Chronicle Telegraph*,
June 14, 1894.

[2] Chicago *Tribune*, May 13, 1894. It estimated that Sanders' army had already
cost the government $18,000.

[3] *American Law Review*, Vol. XXVIII, p. 426.

[4] Chicago *Tribune*, May 18, 1894.

[5] 53rd Cong., 2d Sess., *Senate Executive Document*, No. 120, p. 8.

[6] Chicago *Tribune*, May 20, 1894.

armies of train-stealing. For a time it appeared that Sanders' optimistic statements that his army could not be convicted were justified. The president of the Platte County Anti-Horse-Thief Association, anticipating the release of the industrials, ordered the five hundred members of the association to hold themselves in readiness to protect property if Sanders' men invaded Missouri.[1] On June 18, however, the two hundred men who had not yet escaped were convicted. They were distributed among county jails with sentences of various lengths to prevent them from reassembling when released.[2]

Colorado produced several other armies besides Sanders'. General Bert (or Bart) Hamilton, alias Joe St. Clair, described as a civil engineer and actor, organized a "Silver Legion" at Denver before the end of March. He held meetings of the unemployed, proposing to go to Washington to demand free silver, a new railroad from Ohio to the Pacific coast, and other measures of interest to the western States. He also proposed to demand free transportation on the railroads. The railroads failed to coöperate and it was soon reported that Hamilton was threatened with arrest if he assembled his army within the city limits, and that he would have to walk out of town if he moved his men. Presently General Hamilton was arraigned before a court on the charge of stealing a suit of clothes and other articles from a boarding-house keeper. He explained the charges on the ground of his landlady's unreciprocated affection for him, and thereafter he seems to have failed to interest the leading newspapers.[3]

---

[1] Chicago *Tribune*, May 23, 26, 1894.

[2] *Ibid.*, June 19, 20, 1894.

[3] Pittsburgh *Post*, March 25, 26, 28, April 1, 1894; San Francisco *Chronicle*, March 26, 31, April 3, 1894; *Weekly Iowa State Register*, March 30, 1894.

Grayson's Colorado division, starting from Denver, moved northward through Greeley during the latter part of April,[1] and Bennett's army, already mentioned in connection with Sanders' exploits, was progressing through eastern Kansas in the latter part of May,[2] and was in Kansas City when Sanders' men were convicted at Leavenworth. Early in June a body of Coxeyites was reported to have tried to navigate boats from Denver to the Platte, when the rivers were swollen by rains. Some of the boats capsized and a number of men were drowned.[3]

Another aggregation of several hundred industrials from the mountain region, that proved to be especially troublesome, left Salt Lake City on April 30, led by General Carter. The General and a score of his followers were soon arrested for the theft of a Rio Grande Western train, but the rest continued their journey, and bands of "Carter Commonwealers", near Julesburg in the northeastern corner of Colorado, continued to worry the railroads until the middle of June.[4]

A number of train stealers captured in the neighborhood of Julesburg and Ogalalla were confined in abandoned military barracks at Fort Sidney, Nebraska. They were a truculent lot of prisoners and hard to handle. As a result of a break for liberty on June 19, several of them were severely clubbed by the deputy marshals. It seems probable that their unruliness was caused by the treatment they received.[5]   A month

[1] Vincent, "Commonweal", p. 202.

[2] Chicago *Tribune*, May 16, 23, 1894.

[3] Pittsburgh *Chronicle Telegraph*, June 8, 1894.

[4] Chicago *Tribune*, May 1, 13, June 14, 16, 1894; 53rd Cong., 2d Sess., *Senate Executive Document*, No. 20, p. 91.

[5] Chicago *Tribune*, June 18, 20, 1894; 53rd Cong., 2d Sess., *Senate Executive Document*, No. 120, p. 19.

later a dispatch from Sidney to the Indianapolis *Journal* stated that these men were confined in a small building inadequate to house half their number, where they were compelled to sleep without blankets on bare floors overrun by vermin; their food was poor, many were sick, and in addition to the danger of a typhoid epidemic there were at least three cases of scurvy among them; they had been confined in this "pen of filth" for two weeks before a farcical trial, which was described as an example of "kangaroo justice", and they had not yet been informed what their sentences were.[1] It is not surprising that under the circumstances these prisoners, when they began to be released in small squads to prevent their reassembling, were reported to be in an ugly frame of mind.[2] A similar case occurred at Boise, Idaho, where the jails were full and captured Coxeyites were quartered in a roundhouse. When the governor investigated it, he wired the Attorney-General at Washington, advising tent camps.[3] The marshals had their troubles in caring for unexpectedly large numbers of prisoners without proper facilities for housing them, and often without funds on hand, and they were continually cautioned to be economical.[4] When they or the other authorities in charge of prisoners were callous, inefficient, or corrupt, the result must have been deplorable.

The armies from the cities of the Pacific Northwest swarmed along the railroads extending eastward from Seattle, Tacoma, and Portland, meeting the same difficulties and causing the same vexations to the con-

[1] Indianapolis *Journal*, July 21, 1894.
[2] Chicago *Tribune*, July 17, 1894.
[3] *Ibid.*, May 21, 1894.
[4] See 53rd Cong., 2d Sess., *Senate Executive Document*, No. 120, *passim.*

stituted authorities as their brothers from the mountains. Many of them seem to have been rough and ready lumberjacks from the forests of the Pacific slope, or railroad laborers, who had been attracted to the Northwest by high wages; now, finding themselves unemployed after the panic, they were eager to return to the regions whence they had come.[1] In noting their many conflicts with deputies and troops, it must be remembered that they found more obstacles placed in their way than did Kelly and Fry. All the transcontinental railroads along which they tried to pass, except the Great Northern, were in the hands of receivers appointed by Federal Courts,[2] and consequently the courts interfered with the borrowing of trains throughout the Northwest much as they did in Hogan's case.

At Tacoma and Seattle there were reported to be fifteen hundred men enrolled in the industrial army as early as the end of March.[3] The Seattle regiment organized by General Shepard announced its intention to go to Washington by rail, hoping to raise enough money to charter a freight.[4] By the latter part of April it consisted of about a thousand men, most of them railroad laborers.[5] Anticipating that they might be offered work on the Great Northern Railroad as strike breakers, they showed their sympathy for organized labor by resolutions stating that the army would uphold the American Railway Union, and that any member of the Commonweal who accepted work on a road against

[1] E. Benjamin Andrews, "Last Quarter Century of United States", p. 329.
[2] "Report of the Secretary of War", 1894, p. 152.
[3] San Francisco *Chronicle*, March 30, 1894.
[4] *Ibid.*, April 11, 1894.
[5] *Weekly Iowa State Register*, April 27, 1894.

which the Union had declared a strike would at once be given a dishonorable discharge.[1]

The Seattle regiment prepared to march eastward on April 25, with the obvious intention of boarding a train.[2] At Tacoma, an army of about four hundred was preparing to move at about the same time, and another contingent of the same size was at Spokane.[3] The United States Courts took measures to protect the railroads in the hands of receivers, and to prevent depredations against other property. On April 24 the Circuit Court at Spokane ordered the marshal to protect the Northern Pacific depots at Seattle, Tacoma, and Spokane, where it was feared that the industrials would seize trains. Two days later Marshal Drake reported that he had two hundred deputies guarding the Northern Pacific and the Union Pacific. The industrials of Seattle had already set out on foot, and he feared that it would be more difficult to protect moving trains than the property at the terminals.[4] The militia companies at Tacoma and Seattle were ordered to be ready for immediate action to protect property.[5]

Meanwhile a similar situation developed in Oregon. The five hundred men of "a branch of Coxey's army" took possession of a Union Pacific freight at Troutdale. On April 27 United States Marshal H. C. Grady informed the Attorney-General that he had no arms to equip enough deputies to recover it; the people were in

[1] Vincent, "Commonweal", pp. 200, 201.

[2] The *Weekly Iowa State Register*, April 27, 1894; 53rd Cong., 2d Sess., *Senate Executive Document*, No. 120, p. 4.

[3] Vincent, "Commonweal", p. 210; 53rd Cong., 2d Sess., *Senate Executive Document*, No. 120, p. 4.

[4] 53rd Cong., 2d Sess., *Senate Executive Document*, No. 120, p. 4.

[5] Vincent, "Commonweal", p. 209; Pittsburgh *Chronicle Telegraph*, April 27, 1894.

sympathy with the Coxeyites; the Populist governor, when called upon by the sheriff, had refused to call out troops to protect property and it was useless to make further appeals to him. "The situation is critical," he wired, "and the men are desperate." He had served an injunction of the United States Court on the Coxeyites, but he was powerless to enforce it, and he asked for troops to aid him.[1]

It soon became apparent that the civil authorities would not be able to prevent train-stealing and disorder. The Portland army of nine hundred men marched a few miles along the Union Pacific tracks, threatening to seize a train unless the railroad would furnish transportation gratuitously.[2] The marshal, with the sheriff and his deputies, succeeded in preventing the capture of a train for three days while the army camped at Troutdale. Then, on April 28, when a special train carrying the general manager and other officials of the railroad appeared, the army suddenly surrounded it, manned the engine, ran the cars upon a siding, coupled the engine to the box cars which they had occupied the night before, and started east, disregarding the protestations of the marshal and the deputies about an injunction against train-stealing.[3]

These disturbances, coming at the same time as the affair of Hogan's army in Montana, precipitated reluc-

---

[1] 53rd Cong., 2d Sess., *Senate Executive Document*, No. 120, pp. 4, 5. Governor McGraw of Washington seems also to have felt some hesitation about interfering with Commonwealers. When he was notified that Cantwell's army had seized a Northern Pacific train he was reported to have replied that the road was in the hands of a United States Court, and that the Federal Government was prepared to protect it; he would deal with other cases as the emergency arose. — Pittsburgh *Chronicle Telegraph*, May 4, 1894.

[2] "Report of the Secretary of War", 1894, p. 152.

[3] *Ibid.*, 1894, pp. 152, 153; *Weekly Iowa State Register*, May 4, 1894. In the former account the date of the capture of the train is given as April 28.

tant action by the Federal Government. It was reported that on April 27 Attorney-General Olney wired the soliciter of the Northern Pacific in Boston, recommending that if Commonwealers interfered with railroad property, application should be made to local or State authorities for protection. This would give the governors of the States an opportunity to exert their powers; but if they failed to act, as when Governor Pennoyer of Oregon refused to call out the militia, the Federal Government would find it necessary to take action through the United States Courts.[1]

The regular army was soon called upon to enforce the mandates of the courts.[2] Brigadier General Elwell S. Otis, in command of the Department of the Columbia, anticipating that regular troops would be needed to assist in the enforcement of the mandates of the Federal courts, had already instructed the commanding officers of the posts at Fort Walla Walla, Fort Sherman, and Fort Spokane, to hold their commands ready for immediate duty. It was only two days before this that the Government had sent troops to capture Hogan's army, and now orders came from the headquarters of the army, directing General Otis to assist the United States marshal in the State of Washington. Within a few hours troops from Fort Walla Walla had captured

---

[1] Pittsburgh *Post*, April 28, 1894.

[2] An editorial in the Pittsburgh *Chronicle Telegraph* of May 15, 1894, stated that the Attorney-General and the Secretary of War had held another conference on the industrial army situation in the West, and had decided to continue the policy already adopted. "While general instructions had been sent to the military commanders in the troubled districts to give all lawful and necessary assistance to the officers of the United States courts in repressing train stealing outrages, it was felt necessary to send specific instructions to Gen. Otis at Vancouver Barracks, and to Gen. Brooke, commanding the department of the Platte, to take active steps to head off the marauders in their districts."

the Portland army with its stolen trains, and were as-
sisting the marshal in guarding his prisoners on the way
back to Portland.[1]

From this time on the industrials and the larger part
of the population that sympathized with them were in
a state of mind that made further military precautions
seem necessary to General Otis. The immediate objective of most of the northwestern armies on their way
eastward was Spokane, where the Great Northern and
the Northern Pacific converged before they entered
Idaho. The whole infantry force at Fort Sherman was
ordered to Spokane on April 29, where it camped along
the line of the Northern Pacific, and other troops in
Washington and at Boise, Idaho, were held in readiness
for immediate action. They soon found something to
do.[2]

The Tacoma army started its journey on May 1;[3]
Dolphin's army was then at Spokane, trying to pass the
troops stationed there;[4] and "Jumbo" Cantwell's
Seattle army was trying to charter a freight to St. Paul.
As they moved eastward many trains were stolen and
recaptured in a series of conflicts that kept much of this

[1] "Report of the Secretary of War", 1894, p. 152.
[2] "Ibid., 1894, pp. 153, 154. At Clealum, Washington, on the main line of the
Northern Pacific, sixty Coxeyites, lacking a locomotive, released the brakes on a
gondola coal car and coasted down grade to Ellensburg. The division superintendent, to avoid accidents, ordered all trains sidetracked and gave the gondola
the right of way. — Chicago Tribune, May 11, 1894. A fight occurred at Yakima
between deputies and industrials who refused to leave a train, in which several
men were shot, one of the deputies fatally. — Ibid., May 11, 1894. The return
to Seattle of about two hundred prisoners captured by deputies after a conflict
near Ellensburg led to demonstrations in Seattle so serious that the civil authorities felt unable to protect property, and the district judge called for troops.
—"Report of the Secretary of War", 1894, p. 154. When a train was stolen near
Spokane the railroad company tore up the track, causing a wreck in which several
Coxeyites were injured. — Weekly Iowa State Register, May 25, 1894.
[3] Review of Reviews, Vol. X, p. 59.
[4] Chicago Tribune, May 2, 8, 1894.

region in a state of continued excitement. Here the industrials, the railroads, and the representatives of authority appear to have shown less self-restraint if not more determination than in regions farther east or south. It was only when the Coxeyites were confronted by regular troops that their resistance ceased.

General Otis reported that of the three or four thousand men who composed the armies of Washington and Oregon, only a few were able to pass beyond the bounds of those States. By the latter part of May the scattered fragments of these organizations were no longer regarded as dangerous, and the return of the troops to their regular stations was begun.[1] Those who made their way around the troops at Spokane passed on towards Helena, Montana, causing disturbances in Idaho, Montana, and Wyoming, augmented by local contingents threatening the Northern Pacific and occasioning the inevitable injunctions, arrests by Federal marshals, and the occasional use of troops.[2] Until the middle of June, and in some cases even as late as July, the marshals of the mountain States were beset by many difficulties in protecting trains, capturing Coxeyites, and guarding prisoners.[3]

The principal army from the Pacific Northwest to emerge on the eastern side of the mountains with its

[1] "Report of the Secretary of War", 1894, p. 155.

[2] *Ibid.*, p. 154. A detachment of about 150 men was arrested by the Wyoming marshal, assisted by troops, at Green River, Wyoming, with a train stolen in Idaho. It was described as consisting of Portland Industrials discharged by the United States District Court there, who had made their way into Southern Idaho, reinforced by "tramps collected along the line of travel." 53rd Cong., 2d Sess., *Senate Executive Document*, No. 120, p. 11; Chicago *Tribune*, May 16, 1894. The account stated that the men wanted the marshal to arrest them so that they would be fed and taken on to Cheyenne.

[3] 53rd Cong., 2d Sess., *Senate Executive Document*, No. 120, pp. 11–18, *passim.* — See Appendix C.

organization intact was led by "Jumbo" Cantwell of
Seattle. Early in May Cantwell tried to charter a train
to St. Paul. He seems to have had money, for Mrs.
Cantwell appeared in a parade at Tacoma wearing
"eight large diamonds and a nobby spring suit", and he
was reported to have offered the Chicago, Milwaukee
and St. Paul Railroad as much as ten thousand dollars
to transport his men to the Mississippi.[1] The refusal of
this offer caused his men great inconvenience. On May
11 he reported that two hundred of them were starving,
and that three hundred more had been arrested or cited
to appear before the courts for contempt of injunctions
restraining them from interference with railroad property.

In order to elude the vigilance of marshals and troops
Cantwell adopted the device of sending his men in small
groups from one rendezvous to another. On June 16 he
was in Minneapolis with about three hundred men,
whom he ordered to move on in squads to the next
meeting place.[2] At La Cross, Wisconsin, however, the
whole army seized a stock train and rode into Milwaukee. The police of that city inconsiderately surrounded
the train, locked the doors, ran it a few miles south from
the city, and left the industrials there for some time
without food.[3] Meanwhile at Racine a body of special
police imported from Chicago by the Northwestern
road attacked a party of laborers going to work through
the railroad yards, having mistaken them for an industrial army. The laborers drove the police back into
their cars, and, passing by again, offered to kill any of

---

[1] Chicago *Tribune*, May 3, 1894.
[2] *Ibid.*,, June 17, 18, 1894.
[3] *Ibid.*, July 20, 1894.

the police who showed themselves. The police dis-
crectly remained under cover. A Populist meeting that
night censured the railroad for bringing in an outside
police force, and the chief of police for his inhumane
treatment of Cantwell's men.[1] Having escaped from
this predicament Cantwell soon appeared in Chicago
and started across Indiana, asserting that although his
men were scattered, he would have seven hundred when
he reached Fort Wayne.[2] Several days after Cantwell
himself had arrived in Washington a body of six hundred men, described as the Seattle contingent of Coxeyites, were making their way across Michigan.[3]

Many of the armies, when they started eastward, left
organizations behind them to continue recruiting and
to send on later contingents. In addition to these "industrial reserves" other organizations of sympathizers
with the movement were formed, calling themselves
"home guards." Late in April it was asserted that ten
thousand men were enrolled in the Coxey Home Reserves in Colorado, those in Denver alone numbering
twelve hundred.[4] At a meeting of the home guard at
Topeka, Kansas, held in the rooms of the Populist
League, one of the speakers declared: "I do not hesi-
tate to say that one of the objects I had in view when I
advocated raising home guards was to have a force
available so in case troops or the National Guard were
ordered out to stop Commonwealers anywhere east of
the Mississippi river we can stop the troops or the
National Guard." [5] This meeting denounced the action

[1] Chicago *Tribune*, June 24, 1894.
[2] *Ibid.*, July 24, 1894.
[3] Washington *Post*, July 11, 1894.
[4] Chicago *Times*, May 1, 1894; Chicago *Tribune*, May 18, 20, 1894; Vincent,
"Commonweal", p. 202.
[5] *Weekly Iowa State Register*, June 1, 1894.

of the Federal Court in sending Sanders' men to jail. Some of those present "proposed to buy rifles, and meet force with force", but nothing more violent seems to have been done than to go to the jail and give three cheers for the Commonwealers confined there.[1]

The Populist habit of regarding the courts as instruments of capitalistic interests in the oppression of the plain people led Populist organs to seize greedily upon all real or alleged examples of judicial corruption or irregularity. A case of "judicial infamy", exposed in connection with the arrest of Carter and some of his men in Utah, certainly deserved criticism if the facts were stated accurately in the Populist organ at Washington, which described the affair as "the most damning evidence yet brought out, showing the corruption of the courts."[2] This evidence consisted of some telegrams sent by Judge H. W. Smith to Judge S. A. Merritt, which were obtained and published by an Ogden newspaper. Judge Smith wired Judge Merritt that because of other court proceedings he would be unable to have a hearing of Carter and his confederates for contempt, and continued:

It is all-important that they be found guilty and held for contempt, because we have detectives among them, and they intend to carry things with a high hand if their leaders are discharged, and it seems to be the understanding among them that they will disband if their leaders are held. . . . A special effort will be made to get Carter off. It should not prevail. He is the most guilty of all, although there may be some difficulty in showing it.

"The like of this," said the editor of the Salt Lake *Tribune*, "was probably never before written by one judge to another. It is a direct call on Judge Merritt

[1] Chicago *Tribune*, June 22, 1894. For a note on home reserves at Springfield, Mo., see *ibid.*, May 7, 1894.　　　　[2] *National Watchman*, June 8, 1894.

to find the accused guilty whether they are guilty or not." [1] If this account of the affair was authentic, Judge Smith was, to say the least, guilty of unjudicial and very irregular action in the case.

There were other critics of the courts than the Populists. The use of "blanket injunctions", of the type soon to become famous in connection with the Pullman strike at Chicago, called forth the following comment from the *Nation:*

There was probably never so droll a use made of the writs of a court of equity as the injunctions which various Western judges have issued to the Coxeyites forbidding them to seize and carry off trains on the railroads now in the possession of receivers. The injunction has hitherto been supposed by the lay world to be a process intended to restrain one of the parties to a suit in equity from committing, or persisting in committing, some act prejudicial or likely to be pronounced prejudicial by a final judgment, to the other party's rights. But in these cases it has been issued to prevent parties in no way before the court from committing highway robbery. If we are not mistaken, too, it is usually not applied for or issued without notice to the other side. In other words, the Coxeyites ought to show cause why the writ should not issue — that is, to be "heard by counsel." Their "cause" probably would have been that the seizure of the trains was necessary to enable them to discharge a great public duty at Washington by urging on Congress the issue of $500,000,000 of irredeemable greenbacks to supply work to the unemployed.[2]

---

[1] Quoted in *National Watchman*, June 8, 1894. This account in the *National Watchman* stated that the facts had been obtained from the Hon. W. A. McKenzie, editor of the *Utah Populist*, who said that the telegrams had been printed in the Ogden *Standard*, and that a representative of the Salt Lake *Tribune* had called upon Judge Merritt and verified their accuracy.

[2] *Nation*, Vol. LVIII, p. 336 (May 17, 1894). There were other complaints of too free a use of the injunction in other than industrial army cases. A note in the *American Law Review* complained of the action of a judge in Florida who issued an injunction against the sheriff to prevent his interfering with a prize fight. — *American Law Review*, Vol. XXVIII, p. 429 (May–June, 1894).

This power of the courts was used freely to prevent interference with trains, and in many cases already noted members of industrial armies were arrested and imprisoned for contempt of court.[1] None of these cases seem to have been appealed to the higher courts, and consequently they are not reported, but it appears that a series of precedents was developing in these industrial army cases, for court action very similar to that in the well-known Debs case that was decided shortly afterwards. In addition to the injunctions issued to protect property in the hands of receivers, there are some indications that the government was asked to arrest Coxeyites, and perhaps did so, on the ground that they interfered with the carrying of the mails.[2] The employment of marshals and of the regular army was repeated at Chicago in July. Whether the legal decisions involved in the Chicago strike were consciously based upon these industrial army cases or not, the fact remains that the judicial and executive branches of the Federal Government, in their handling of the problem of industrial army train stealers during April, May and June, 1894, set precedents for most of their better-known actions in the Pullman strike in July.

[1] For a number of cases of this kind in addition to those already cited, see 53rd Cong., 2d Sess., *Senate Executive Document*, No. 120, *passim.;* San Francisco *Chronicle*, March 27, 1894; Chicago *Tribune*, June 14, 16, 17, 1894.

[2] See Chicago *Tribune*, May 18, 1894; 53rd Cong., 2d Sess., *Senate Executive Document*, No. 120, pp. 8, 9, 19.

CHAPTER XI

The hardy, resourceful, and intractable workers who formed the armies from the mountains and the Pacific Northwest seem out of place in a movement with any suggestion of an industrial proletariat about it. Coming from the passing frontier, they suggest Boones, Seviers, or Kit Carsons, taken from their proper habitat and thrown into a setting of modern industrialism. At the opposite extreme of the movement were the small New England armies. They were led by men described as "labor agitators",[1] and their demands were more colored by theoretical socialism than were those of the Westerners.

The small body of industrials that left Boston on April 22 was led by Morrison I. Swift, an individual of a different stamp from the Western leaders. He was reputed to be a graduate of Williams College, and he had studied in Germany. He had been one of the speakers who had styled themselves "social-anarchists" at a meeting of the Boston unemployed in February, which had become turbulent and had been broken up by the police.[2]

Swift's men were joined on their march by still

[1] *Journal of Social Science*, Nov., 1894, p. 8; *Weekly Iowa State Register*, April 13, 1894; New York *Times*, April 18, 1894.

[2] *Outlook*, Vol. XLIX, p. 734; G. E. Hooker, "The Unemployed in Boston", *Independent*, Vol. XLVI, pp. 487, 488 (April 19, 1894), and editorial on Morrison I. Swift, *ibid.*, Vol. XLVI, p. 264 (March 1, 1894); New York *Times*, April 23, 1894; Indianapolis *Journal*, April 23, 1894; Pittsburgh *Chronicle Telegraph*, May 23, 1894; Vincent, "Commonweal", pp. 204 *ff.*; *Cyclopedic Review of Current History*, Vol. IV, p. 140. For the views of the leader, see Morrison I. Swift, "Capitalists are the Cause of the Unemployed" (Boston, 1894).

smaller bands from other parts of New England. At New Haven the fifty-eight men of the Boston contingent found the Connecticut division of twenty-six, led by General Michael Fitzgerald,[1] and the Rhode Island division of fourteen, commanded by Captains Sweetland and Murray.[2] The students of the Yale Law School raised a purse of fifty dollars for Sweetland's men, and intended to cut classes and march in the parade, but they reconsidered their decision after they were interviewed by the Dean.[3]

At New York the leaders of the combined New England armies read to reporters a petition to Congress formulating their demands. After a preamble describing the hard lot of laborers, the national legislature was requested:

First, to provide farms and factories where the unemployed now and at all times hereafter may be able to employ their labor productively for the supply of their own wants; second, to take steps to amend the Constitution of the United States so that it shall affirm the right of everyone to have work; third, to abolish interest-bearing bonds; fourth, to furnish immediate employment for the unemployed by beginning the construction of good roads on a large scale throughout the country; fifth, to nationalize the railroads, the telegraph and mines; sixth, to see that all land not in actual use is thrown open to cultivation to those willing to cultivate it; seventh, to establish a commission to investigate the desirability of nationalizing trusts.[4]

This was the most radical and comprehensive program presented by any of the industrial armies, but it

[1] Fitzgerald was about 40 years old, Irish born, a former hotel man and real estate dealer, a good talker, and an outspoken socialist agitator. — Pittsburgh *Chronicle Telegraph*, May 23, 1894.

[2] Chicago *Tribune*, May 3, 1894.

[3] *Ibid.*, May 1; New York *Times*, May 1, 1894.

[4] *Public Opinion*, Vol. XVII, p. 137.

represented the views only of the leaders of a few very small groups of marchers, hardly those of the movement as a whole. It was in the regions west of the Appalachians that Coxeyism found its principal support and developed its dominant characteristics.

Although the largest and most significant bodies of industrials originated west of the Rockies, the Middle West produced several armies besides Coxey's original Commonweal of Christ. Of these Randall's Chicago army, closely related in its origins to the Coxey movement in Ohio, was the most important. The story of its beginnings, as it is told by Henry Vincent, goes back to August of 1893, when Carl Browne appeared in Chicago and began to lecture on the lake front with the aid of his financial panorama. How he started to organize the Commonweal there, how he was banished by the mayor, and how he returned in disguise, has already been related.[1] Coxey soon called him to Massillon to assist in perfecting the arrangements for the march from that place. As it turned out, therefore, Browne had merely prepared the way for an army in Chicago, without having perfected any permanent organization there.[2]

Among the Chicagoans who "caught the inspiration" of the Commonweal movement was Henry Vincent, of the Chicago *Express*. After having devoted considerable space in his paper to this movement he decided to join Coxey, and for two weeks after it left Massillon he followed the march of the Commonweal army. Then, returning to Chicago, he addressed a meeting on April 16 at the People's Party headquarters, called to take

[1] See above, pp. 34 *ff.*
[2] Vincent, "Commonweal", pp. 174, 175.

action in regard to the expected arrival of Kelly's army in Chicago. This meeting appointed a committee to arrange for the entertainment of Kelly's men. Vincent was elected chairman and Doctor J. H. Randall, secretary. It seems to have been through the work of this committee that the Chicago army was organized. The secretary, Doctor Randall, opened headquarters for the Chicago Coxey Commonweal, receiving the coöperation of a number of labor organizations.[1]

The committee opened a correspondence with Kelly, whose army was then encamped in the mud of Chautauqua Park, offering to provide for his men when they arrived in Chicago and to assist them eastward. An appeal was issued asking all citizens for donations of food, clothing, money, or quarters for the Kellyites when they reached the city. The proprietor of an empty barrel factory tendered the use of his building for their accommodation. In his letter making this offer he explained that his employees were out of work because of the competition of convict-made barrels, and that he had learned that his son in Montana, along with thousands of other workers, had been "thrown out of employment by legislation demonetizing silver"; he wanted to do something to aid the unemployed, and to protest against "the infamy of officials sworn to protect and enforce the law for the general welfare" who permitted the use of prison-made barrels, in violation of the State constitution, thereby crushing out honest industry.[2]

[1] Vincent includes in his list of "central bodies" that responded immediately to Randall's request for coöperation, District Assembly No. 24 of the Knights of Labor, the Carpenters' Council, the Building Trades' Council, the Central Labor Union, the New Century Club, and the Allied Woodworkers. — "Commonweal", p. 175.

[2] Vincent, "Commonweal", pp. 176, 177.

The City Council of Chicago instructed the police
to keep Kelly and his men out of the city. The Coxey
committee replied in resolutions denouncing the action
of the council "as entirely un-American and illegal",
as opposed to the rights of citizens to free assemblage,
free speech, and free travel, and as "a cheap trick of
the political panderer to the prejudice of the self-elected
upper classes who form corporations, trusts, syndicates,
and run political rings." Kelly's inability to get railroad transportation delayed the necessity of entertain-
ing him in Chicago, but it was not until the Chicago
army had marched on to join Coxey that Kelly's army
started down the Des Moines River. In the meantime
the Chicago committee was enlisting recruits, and on
April 23, when some eight hundred men were enrolled,
the Commonweal went into camp in the barrel factory.[1]
During the week following, the organization was perfected, the men were drilled, and the leaders collected
what meager camp equipment they could obtain, in
preparation for the beginning of the journey on May 1.

On April 24 Doctor Randall was chosen General.[2] He
had been a Union soldier in a Connecticut regiment,
a dentist, a labor organizer, and a Greenback editor.
His age of fifty-four years perhaps explains the inclusion
of a horse for the General in a list of the essential equip-
ments of the army.[3] The regulations which General
Randall drew up for his men required them to be

---

[1] Vincent, "Commonweal", pp. 178–181; *Weekly Iowa State Register*, April 27,
1894.
[2] As in Coxey's own Commonweal, the General seems to have been selected for
the men rather than elected by them as in many of the far western armies. Vincent states that "Dr. J. H. Randall was chosen general . . . and the announcement of the fact was received with cheers by the contingent." "Commonweal",
p. 181.
[3] *Ibid.*, pp. 181, 182, 192.

"orderly, peaceful, and law-abiding", as well as cleanly and obedient to their officers; to avoid "boisterous, profane, and obscene talk"; and to conduct themselves in a manner calculated to impress upon the public the idea that they were American citizens, proud of their country.[1] Randall seems to have been a reformer of rather moderate views, opposed to violence in action or speech. Like Coxey he emphasized the peaceful character of the movement in his addresses. He appeared to be much annoyed when an anarchistic agitator, Mrs. Lucy Parsons, broke in upon the program of speeches at one of his meetings, with an uninvited tirade. She told the Commonwealers "that they were belched up from the hearts of the people and indicated a condition"; that they had built America and now "they deserved the good things of the earth." As soon as she retired the General ended the speechmaking to prevent the intrusion of any more discourses of this character. Another meeting was addressed by James R. Sovereign of the Knights of Labor.[2]

An investigation of the character and composition of Randall's army before it left Chicago showed results very similar to those of the investigation of Kelly's army at Des Moines by the students of Drake University. It was made by Professor Hourwitch, of the University of Chicago, with the assistance of a trained sociological worker who claimed to be satisfied that the results obtained were reliable. Of two hundred ninety men questioned as to their nativity, half were born in America and the greater part of the others in the British

---

[1] Stead, "Coxeyism", *Review of Reviews*, Vol. X, p. 51. For the complete text of these regulations, see Appendix D.

[2] Vincent, "Commonweal", pp. 192, 194, 196, 197.

Isles. Only two thirds of them, however, were described as English-speaking, a discrepancy which, if these proportions are stated accurately, might be explained on the supposition that many born in America of foreign parents still spoke foreign languages. The average age was between thirty and thirty-two years. Of two hundred sixty-two questioned about their occupations, one hundred eighty-one were skilled mechanics, representing seventy trades; seventy-four were unskilled laborers; and seven were tradesmen. About one fourth of the total number investigated were members of unions. The average wage earned when at work had been $2.50 per day for the union men, $1.75 per day for the non-union mechanics, and $1.50 for the unskilled laborers. Of one hundred fifteen examined as to education, twenty-six had attended high schools, academies, business or professional colleges, or universities, and only two were described as totally uneducated. The statements of one hundred ninety-eight men as to their political affiliations showed that eighty-eight were Democrats, thirty-nine Republicans, and ten Populists — a larger proportion of Democrats and a smaller proportion of Populists than were found among the Westerners of Kelly's army; twenty-five abstained from voting, and twenty-eight others were not naturalized. The average time since the two hundred sixty-one questioned on the subject had had employment was five months; two thirds of these said that they had saved enough to tide them over this period, but that their savings were spent; most of the others had been helped through the winter by charity. Professor Hourwitch's conclusion was that it was "not the tramp, but the unemployed working man — the unfortunate citizen — who was turned into the ranks of the Commonweal." [1]

The feeling against detectives, so strong among Kelly's men, appears to have been absent from the Chicago Commonweal — at least so far as the leaders were concerned. According to Vincent's statement, the police department sent a number of World's Fair detectives to the barracks to join the army and find out what was going on. Several of them became officers — one, captain of a company. "It is not hard to discover them, however," wrote Vincent, "for they insist that they are out of work and at the same time smoke meerschaum pipes and wear yachting caps. They have a cunning look and are inclined to be attending to the business of every company in such an interested manner, not for the purpose of work, but for information." General Randall, however, refused to be alarmed by them, saying that he was not concerned with their presence so long as they behaved themselves.[2] The police apparently found no one to arrest. After futile negotiations with the railroads, the Commonweal officers made a study of cross-country routes.[3]

Randall marched out of Chicago on May 1 with about four hundred fifty men. The populace does not seem to have manifested an enthusiasm comparable to

[1] Stead, "Coxeyism", *Review of Reviews*, Vol. X, p. 51; Stetson, "Industrial Army", *Independent*, Vol. XLVI, p. 681. The New York *Times*, of April 24, 1894, stated that the character of the men then enlisted seemed superior; many were trade unionists, the iron-molders having taken an especially active part in forming the organization. An editorial in the Chicago *Tribune*, May 2, 1894, said of the men in the procession when the army marched out of the city: "The personnel of the army was of a higher type than had been anticipated. A small percentage might have been of the professional vagrant class, but in the main the men were fairly dressed and displayed intelligence", showing signs of "having been workingmen who are now out of employment."

[2] Vincent, "Commonweal", p. 195.

[3] *Ibid.*, p. 220.

that aroused by marchers in some of the cities farther west. The inevitable flags and banners were in evidence, many with mottoes and inscriptions to show the character of the army and its objects. Some of these inscriptions were indicative of the close connection of the Chicago organization with the Ohio type of Coxeyism. Among them were: "Chicago Contingent, Coxey Commonweal"; "No Charity but Work and Fair Wages"; and "Let No Man Call God His Father Who Calls Not Me His Brother." The last suggests a mild form of the religious characteristics of the "Commonweal of Christ", without Browne's "theosophy." [1]

The army seems to have encountered no serious difficulties in entering Indiana, the principal disturbances being internal. The General made efforts to exclude undesirable members. He authorized his medical director to eject men suffering from any objectionable ailments, which included one who had fits and another who had a wooden leg, and at Hammond Randall not only dismissed four officers and twenty-one privates for drunkenness, but he received applause when he lectured the rest of his men on the subject.[2] The first serious opposition appeared at Valparaiso, where the people feared an epidemic of smallpox. Citizens met and passed resolutions demanding that the army be kept out of the town. It was reported that in one of the neighboring villages where four hundred of its five hundred voters were sworn in as deputy marshals, the local tinsmith was kept busy making stars for them; and similar preparations were made in Valparaiso.

---

[1] *Review of Reviews*, Vol. X, p. 59; Chicago *Tribune*, May 2, 1894; Chicago *Times*, May 2, 1894.
[2] Chicago *Tribune*, May 3, 4, 1894.

The panic subsided when the peaceful character of this Commonweal became apparent, and arrangements were made to vaccinate its members. The men of the army, reported to have had only one meal a day on their five days' march from Chicago, were now well fed in their camp at the fair grounds. Another Coxey precedent was followed when the visitors at the camp were requested to pay an admission fee. The only serious disturbance was caused, not by the army, but by the students of the Indiana State Normal School. Some six hundred of them marched to the fair grounds and cheered the army. On their return, when a policeman tried to interfere with them, the students "set upon him and used him badly." [1]

A week's journey from Chicago Randall's men divided into two separate bodies. When the General expelled Judge Advocate William H. Sullivan, nearly a hundred of the men followed Sullivan, and the danger of a conflict between these two bodies led a sheriff and his deputies to follow them for a time, to prevent trouble. [2] Thenceforth Randall's army and Sullivan's army remained apart, with Sullivan, who captured at least one freight train, [3] usually in the lead. Randall suffered a slight delay at La Porte, where a hostile mayor had him arrested, charged with conspiracy to commit larceny by trying to compel citizens to give him bread. [4] A report from his next stopping place

---

[1] Chicago *Tribune*, May 4, 5, 6, 1894.

[2] *Ibid.*, May 8, 1894. "Jerry" Sullivan seems to have been the leader of a body of recruits from Racine, Wis. — See Vincent, "Commonweal", p. 197. If he was the same man as the judge advocate, this quarrel may have been caused by a rivalry similar to that between Speed's Sacramento men and Kelly's San Francisco followers.

[3] Chicago *Tribune*, May 16, 1894.

[4] *Ibid.*, May 9, 10, 1894; *Weekly Iowa State Register*, May 11, 1894.

stated that the mayor, having learned a lesson from the mayor of La Porte, had concluded that "it was cheaper to feed Randall's army and get rid of it than to have an army of deputies at $5 a day." [1]

The army moved on across northern Indiana and Ohio, sometimes discouraged and sometimes lionized by Populists.[2] At Mansfield, Ohio, said a Pittsburgh newspaper, Randall's three hundred men "had a glorious time", and it printed an enthusiastic letter from R. B. Floyd of the Chicago army to J. H. Stevenson, the Pittsburgh Populist and friend of Coxey's army, which showed the close connection between the Commonweal movement and Populism:

I presided at the People's Party meeting here last night. The papers say the attendance was 7,000; so you can imagine what kind of a crowd we had. We held the meeting in the park and spoke from the stands. The whole town was up in arms because the mayor refused to grant the permit. One clothing merchant told the mayor that Randall would speak if it cost him $5000, so at 4 o'clock the council held a meeting and decided to grant the permit. The crowd in front of the mayor's office at that hour blocked the streets, and included many of Mansfield's best citizens, so you can imagine the feeling of the crowd when I stepped down on the stand under the electric light and looked out on that great audience. I worked off your idea on the Commonweal joining the other hoboes in Washington, and it went with a yell; but General Randall held them over one hour and a half, and he is one of the best stump orators in the business. He is a veteran soldier, and a number of the soldiers of Mansfield occupied seats on the stand. He would like to know what route you think he had better take, and as he makes a straight People's Party appeal, he fancies New Castle and the oil country. . . .

[1] Chicago *Tribune*, May 11, 1894.
[2] *Ibid.*, May 13, 14, 16, 1894.

He has seven fine horses, two new Studebaker wagons, all presented to him by Indiana Populist farmers, and a buggy and saddle horse given him by a Populist doctor at Laporte, Ind., to take to Washington and use as he sees fit. He has fine big flags and a number of fine banners and two red umbrellas. The army makes a great show.[1]

Ten days later a report emanating from the Populist headquarters in Pittsburgh indicated that Randall's route through Pennsylvania was to be determined by the People's Party State Committee, for the purpose of arousing interest among the voters.[2]

Sullivan reached Toledo, Ohio, while Randall was being entertained by labor organizations at Fort Wayne, Indiana. A dispatch from the former city stated that after the explosion of a smallpox hoax intended to drive Sullivan's men out of the city, they were royally entertained. They were described as consisting almost entirely of trade unionists, and one of the officers, Macauley (or McCauley, or McAuley) posed as the originator of the Knights of Labor and the oldest Past Grand Master Workman of that order.[3]

Two weeks later they were in Cleveland, whence they rode on an Erie freight train to Youngstown, arriving on June 6. They marched on foot across the State line to New Castle, Pennsylvania, where a citizen was arrested for breach of the peace when he tried to drive the army out of the town, and where the men listened to an address by a Populist nominee for Congress.[4] By

---

[1] Floyd asked Stevenson to write to Randall at Youngstown, addressing his letter to "J. H. Randall, Chicago contingent, Coxey's Commonweal Army", and his communication concluded: "I trust you can advise and counsel Mr. Randall." Floyd's initials are printed both "A. B." and "R. B." — Pittsburgh *Chronicle Telegraph*, June 4, 1894.

[2] Pittsburgh *Chronicle Telegraph*, June 14, 1894.

[3] Chicago *Tribune*, May 20, 21, 1894.

[4] Pittsburgh *Chronicle Telegraph*, June 6, 8, 9, 1894.

the middle of June Sullivan was in Pittsburgh; at Homestead he was welcomed by Elmer Bales, head of the Coxey organization at that place; [1] and on June 23 he was reported to be in Johnstown with sixty men.[2] Some of them ultimately arrived at their destination.[3]

Randall's army approached Pittsburgh from the north, by way of Beaver Falls and Economy before Sullivan left Homestead. On June 18 a "grand rally of Commonweal leaders" was held at the Populist headquarters. J. H. Stevenson acted as genial host. Coxey, appearing unexpectedly, told the others that he had not walked on the grass or carried banners on the Capitol grounds. Mrs. Randall was there, acting as advance agent for her husband's army. Sullivan was also present, now on the best of terms with the Randall family.[4] Three days later General Randall and his army marched into Allegheny. Times had changed since the police of that city had confined Coxey's men in the ball park. The army with several hundred sympathizers and a drum corps marched without interference to a meeting where they listened quietly to some "straight Populist talk." [5] The army marched on through Homestead and ceased to interest the Pittsburgh papers. Randall with fifty of his men reached Washington about the middle of July.[6]

Later bodies of Commonwealers who marched out of Chicago were less successful. A band described as Parkes' Chicago Commonwealers, leaving Chicago early

[1] Pittsburgh *Chronicle Telegraph*, June 14, 18, 19, 1894.
[2] Chicago *Tribune*, June 24, 1894.
[3] Washington *Post*, July 18, 1894.
[4] Pittsburgh *Chronicle Telegraph*, June 18, 1894.
[5] *Ibid.*, June 22, 1894.
[6] Washington *Post*, July 13, 18, 1894.

in June, found that the people who had already provided for Randall's men had little hospitality left for
late comers. Near La Porte, Indiana, these men, desperate from hunger, entered a farmer's yard, slaugh-
tered his cow, and devoured it before his eyes.[1] Another
Chicago contingent of Poles and Bohemians who had
worked on the drainage canal, progressed at least as
far as Ohio, where it, too, suffered from hunger. At
Clyde, Ohio, these men threatened violence when their
demand for food was refused, and the militia drove them
from town "at the point of the bayonet."[2]

St. Louis contributed to the Coxey movement an
army somewhat smaller than Randall's. General J. K.
Morrison led it across the Mississippi on May 2, and on
through Illinois and Indiana, following the route taken
earlier by Fry and Galvin. They found it necessary to
walk most of the way to Indianapolis. At Vincennes,
Indiana, they attempted to raise money by selling copies of McCallum's curious pamphlet entitled "Dogs and
Fleas, by One of the Dogs" — the one that Carl Browne
was accustomed to quote in his speeches.[3] Fragmentary
dispatches in the newspapers show that a number of
other bands of industrials marched from various cities
of the Middle West. The later armies seem to have
received less sympathy and support than the earlier
ones. Kelsey's army was crossing Iowa early in June,
and two weeks later the police barred it out of Indianapolis.[4] Others were reported in Milwaukee,[5] in Minneap-

---

[1] Chicago *Tribune*, June 13, 1894.

[2] *Ibid.*, June 5, 1894; Washington *Post*, July 24, 1894. The former gave the leader's name as John Rybowkoski. The latter's account of "Rey Bakowski's army" doubtless referred to the same organization.

[3] *Review of Reviews*, Vol. X, p. 59; Chicago *Tribune*, May 3, 4, 8, 12, 1894.

[4] *Ibid.*, June 3, 11, 17, 1894; Indianapolis *Journal*, July 15, 17, 1894.

[5] Chicago *Tribune*, May 4, 1894.

olis,[1] in Iowa,[2] and at Omaha.[3]   An incident at Fairfield, Illinois, in the middle of June, recalls the disturbances in the Far West.   Fifty men, who claimed to be a part of Kelly's army, seized a fast freight and demanded a free ride on the Louisville, Evansville and St. Louis Railroad.   The mayor refused to aid the railroad and the sheriff was absent; consequently the receivers of the road petitioned the Federal Court at Springfield to restore its property.   A score of the marauders were arrested by the United States marshal and his deputies, and were imprisoned for contempt of court.[4]

Any attempt to determine with any accuracy the total number of men who marched in the industrial armies is beset with difficulties, as the wide discrepancies in various contemporary estimates show very clearly.   *Public Opinion* stated that at the beginning of May there were probably not more than three thousand men on the way to Washington;[5] a newspaper "roster" of the armies published at about the same time, including several groups that appear to have been "reserves" or strikers, placed the total at 11,450;[6] a list in the New York *Times* placed it at 6,500.[7]   W. T. Stead in his widely quoted article in the *Review of Reviews*, stated that there were probably never more than five thousand on the road at any one time.   He gave a list of maximum strength of the six principal armies as follows:[8]

---

[1] *Journal of the Knights of Labor*, May 31, 1894.
[2] Chicago *Tribune*, May 15, July 14, 1894.
[3] *Ibid.*, May 4, 1894.
[4] Chicago *Tribune*, June 14, 16, 17, 1894.
[5] *Public Opinion*, Vol. XVII, p. 115 (May 3, 1894).
[6] New York *Recorder*, quoted in *Weekly Iowa State Register*, May 4, 1894.
[7] New York *Times*, April 26, 1894.
[8] W. T. Stead, "Coxeyism", *Review of Reviews*, Vol. X, p. 49.   He called atten-

Coxey, Massillon, Ohio.... 500
Fry, Los Angeles........1000
Kelly, San Francisco......2000
Randall, Chicago.........1000
Hogan, Montana......... 500
Oregon army............ 900
——————
Total   5900

The inadequacy of Stead's estimate, however, at once becomes apparent when it is noted that his list omits such armies as Sanders', Cantwell's, or Morrison's; and when his nine hundred men of Oregon are compared with General Otis' report that the armies of Oregon and Washington were composed of some three or four thousand men.[1] It was asserted that at one time early in May there were forty bands of various sizes on their way to Washington,[2] many of them small, no doubt, but adding considerably to the total. The President of Des Moines College, in an article published at the end of May, spoke of organized bands "numbering fully 8,000" marching toward the national capital.[3] Perhaps the estimate that there were never more than about ten thousand men engaged in this pilgrimage at any one time [4] is as accurate a guess as can be made; the total must have approached this number. In view of the shifting personnel of the armies, the number of individuals who participated in the marching must have been considerably greater than this; how much greater it is impossible to say.

tion to the fact that this was only a small fraction of the number of tramps (about 60,000) who were supposed to be continually on the road in the United States.
   [1] See above, p. 221.
   [2] *Cyclopedic Review of Current History*, Vol. IV, p. 312.
   [3] Stetson, "Industrial Armies", *Independent*, Vol. XLVI, p. 681 (May 31, 1894)
   [4] *Cyclopedic Review of Current History*, Vol. IV, p. 312.

Before the industrial armies ceased to exist they had stolen or borrowed twoscore trains or more, most of them during May and the earlier part of June.[1] When it is noted that the first five armies mentioned in Mr. Stead's list took only three of these, the incompleteness of his estimate becomes at once apparent.

Without doubt the dominant element in most of the larger armies was composed of unemployed working-men. To what extent many of the smaller bands that marched or rode eastward, stealing trains when they could facilitate their progress by this means, were composed of professional vagrants, it is impossible to determine. Perhaps the newspapers, having overcome their early tendency to refer to the members of all the armies as "tramps" or "hoboes", later went to the opposite extreme and referred indiscriminately to "Coxeyites" in some cases where the term "tramp" would have been more accurate. Nevertheless, this whole unique movement, with the many characteristics that distinguish it from the activities of ordinary vagrants, was essentially a workingmen's affair.

[1] The following references to two Middle Western newspapers give at least 34 cases of "train stealing": Chicago *Tribune*, May 5, 7, 8, 10, 11, 12, 13, 14, 15, 16, 20, 23, June 3, 13, 14, 16, 17, July 14; *Weekly Iowa State Register*, April 20, May 4, 11, 18, 25. Three other cases not included in the above list occurring on April 27, May 18, and June 8, are mentioned in 53rd Cong., 2d Sess., *Senate Executive Document*, No. 120 — which seems to indicate that the list compiled from these two papers is by no means complete. Adding one train apiece for Fry, Kelly, and Galvin, whose cases have not been included in this list, the total is 40. Of the 40, five were taken in March or April, 24 in May, 10 in June, and one in July. Trains reported taken by strikers have not been included.

CHAPTER XII

THE DECLINE OF THE MOVEMENT AND THE END OF THE ARMIES

The "on to Washington" movement reached its height in May. By the middle of June it was played out.[1] Armies from the Far West that eluded arrest found the population east of the Mississippi inhospitable, even if the authorities let them alone. Other events were transpiring, moreover, that attracted public attention away from the Coxey movement, that made traveling more difficult, and that gave workingmen something else to think about. Early in May a strike was declared by the employees of the Pullman Company. Before the end of June the American Railway Union was involved, and the great Pullman strike and its various ramifications began to paralyze the railroads.[2] A cartoon in the Chicago *Tribune* of July 6 showed Coxey crying after his whipping, and Uncle Sam, switch in hand, turning to master Debs, saying, "Come on, sir: I am ready for *you* now." The American public had had its fun out of Coxeyism and had done its worrying about it: attention now turned to the great struggle between labor and capital which centered about the Chicago strike. The Government showed its teeth to the unions as it had to the train

---

[1] *Cyclopedic Review of Current History*, Vol. IV, p. 311. Train stealings by Coxeyites, which may be taken as a sort of index to the movement, had practically ceased by the middle of June. Only three of the 40 cases referred to above occurred after June 14.

[2] James Ford Rhodes, "From Hayes to McKinley" (New York, 1919), p. 424.

stealers. On July 2 a Federal Court at Chicago issued a "blanket injunction" to restrain Eugene V. Debs, other officials of the American Railway Union, and all other persons whatsoever, from interfering with railroad property — an injunction very similar to those that western judges had issued to prevent Coxeyites from interfering with the property of roads in the hands of receivers, or from interfering with the mails. As in these earlier cases, both deputy marshals and troops were used to enforce the processes of the courts.[1]

Aside from the fact that the novelty of the thing had worn off, the arrest and conviction of many Coxeyites had made it evident that train-stealing had become a dangerous occupation. The railroads, moreover, were tied up by strikes in the regions through which all western armies had to pass. Without railroad transportation industrial armies could hardly hope to travel the long distances that Fry, Kelly, and others had attempted, and in those regions where distances were short or where river transportation was available, the people were more unfriendly. But the remnants of the armies that had started in April and May continued to straggle into Washington, and to subsist in camps in the outskirts of the District of Columbia for two months after the public had lost interest in the movement which they represented.

On May 1, after the police had temporarily deprived Coxey's army of its marshal, Jesse Coxey and his sister led the submissive Commonwealers back to a camp in a most undesirable part of Washington. The men won the praise of those who watched them by the will with which they went to work, cleaning up the "noisome

[1] Rhodes, "From Hayes to McKinley", pp. 425, 426.

refuse" covering the ground, and trying to make the place inhabitable. Coxey and Browne, who stayed at a hotel, seemed to view the situation with more complacency than did the health authorities and some of the reporters.[1] The camp was finally condemned as a nuisance, and it was moved, first to Hyattsville, Maryland, where the inhabitants were alarmed and protested, and then to Bladensburg.[2] Instead of dispersing immediately, as many had expected, it seems that the army held its own, or even increased in numbers.[3]

Fitzgerald's small New England army arrived in the latter part of May; on the twenty-ninth these "Boston Commonwealers" listened to an address by Senator Peffer at their headquarters in the Mount Pisgah Negro chapel.[4] Galvin arrived before the end of the month, establishing a separate camp near Coxey's.[5] Fry appeared on June 26 with about two hundred men, and went into camp with Galvin.[6] Cantwell ar-

[1] Washington *Post*, May 2, 3, 1894; Chicago *Times*, May 3, 7, 1894.

[2] Chicago *Tribune*, May 8, 13, 15, 1894; *Public Opinion*, Vol. XVII, p. 161. The camp was moved to Hyattsville on May 12, and to Bladensburg on May 14.

[3] According to the Chicago *Tribune* of May 8, there were 529 men in camp on May 7, and the number was increasing. The *National Watchman*, May 11, stated that the number was increasing rapidly, and that there were fully 800. The *Journal of the Knights of Labor*, May 31, gave the number at Bladensburg as 500. *Public Opinion*, Vol. XVII, p. 161, reported that there were only 215 men in camp shortly after the move to Bladensburg.

For descriptions of the character of the army after May 1, see S. P. Austen, "The Downfall of Coxeyism", *Chautauquan*, Vol. XIX, pp. 448 *ff.*; *Outlook*, Vol. XLIX, p. 824; Tracy, "A Mission to Coxey's Army", *Catholic Review*, Vol. LIX, pp. 665 *ff.*

[4] Chicago *Tribune*, May 30, 1894.

[5] *Journal of the Knights of Labor*, May 31, 1894. On June 15, when it was reported that Galvin contemplated a march back to the Pacific coast, he was said to have between 150 and 200 men. — Chicago *Tribune*, June 16, 1894.

[6] Chicago *Tribune*, June 27, 1894. This account states that Fry and his army were turned away by Browne, whose provisions were low, after which they went to Galvin's camp, where only about a dozen men remained. The *National Watchman*, June 29, stated the number of Fry's men as 200.

rived with part of his army about July 1,[1] and Randall, with fifty of his Chicago Commonwealers, about the middle of the month.[2]

On the Fourth of July there was another Commonweal parade. It included Coxey's contingent, representatives of the western armies led by "Jumbo" Cantwell and a commune of Indiana Commonwealers, with a Negro detachment bringing up the rear. Nothing extraordinary is reported of the celebrations at Fry's and Galvin's camp, but a public performance by Coxey's own army without some singular manifestation of the peculiarities of its leaders would have been disappointing, and on this occasion the army's reputation was maintained. The Commonweal enacted the death of liberty, with a charge for admission. A large and imposing goddess of liberty, after various symbolical performances, was borne swooning to the rejuvenated and redecorated panorama wagon, and was placed within its curtains. Presently there emerged a large man, gradually recognized by those of the Commonwealers who had not been involved in the proceedings, as their marshal, — now clean-shaven, for what goddess of liberty ever wore whiskers! Thus the Marshal of the Commonweal attained new notoriety as "Goddess of Liberty Browne." [3] Shortly after the death of liberty he started to New York with sixty men and his pan-

---

[1] Washington *Post*, July 2, 5, 1894.

[2] When 50 men of Randall's Chicago army arrived they went to Coxey's camp at Bladensburg. "They are about the toughest looking lot of men that has yet arrived, and appear to have had a hard time en route." — Washington *Post*, July 13, 1894. Randall arrived on July 17. He said that he would wait there until he heard from Coxey. — *Ibid.*, July 17. Some of the men of Sullivan's detachment of the Chicago army, and some of Vinette's second California regiment, arrived at about the same time. — *Ibid.*, July 18.

[3] Washington *Post*, July 5, 1894.

orama.[1] He had been to Washington, he said, to see
the servants of the bankers and brokers, and now he was
going to New York to see the bosses themselves.[2] It
was reported that his men were going to bathe at Atlantic City.[3] When Oklahoma Sam left to join Browne,
a reporter complained that there was "not a single star"
left in Coxey's aggregation.[4] What interest remained
in the plight of the industrials shifted to Fry's and
Galvin's camp, now located at Rosslyn, on the Virginia
side of the Potomac.

Kelly appeared unexpectedly on July 12.[5] His enthusiasm for the industrial army was unabated, and he
donated to the commissary two thousand dollars which
he had collected along the way. General Cantwell
added four barrels of flour, and several wagon loads of
produce were sent in by sympathizers. Altogether it
was "a great day for the commissary department."[6]
Kelly spoke at the meeting that night, the other attrac-
tion being music by his glee club and his cornet band.[7]
The Rosslyn camp was now at the height of its prosperity. The army seems to have constructed a very

---

[1] Chicago *Tribune*, July 11, 1894.

[2] Indianapolis *Journal*, July 23, 1894.

[3] Washington *Post*, July 24, 1894.

[4] *Ibid.*, July 16, 1894.

[5] "Lieutenant-General" Salisbury was at this time in command of the camp,
Galvin and Fry being out on the road to raise funds. Kelly soon left to meet Fry
at Manassas and Cantwell went to New York to address labor organizations
there. — *Ibid.*, July 11, 12, 14, 1894.

[6] *Ibid.*, July 12, 1894. Just before Kelly's arrival it was reported that "The
Commissary department is in fine shape, and has been so ever since the men have
been on Virginia soil." — *Ibid.*, July 11.

[7] *Ibid.*, July 12. Meetings of this kind were held frequently to advertise the
cause and to raise funds. On July 8, when a large number of people visited the
camp, Galvin made a short speech and Jumbo Cantwell "gave a recitation with
such dramatic effect that one of his listeners offered a load of provisions to the
camp." — *Ibid.*, July 9. There was an enthusiastic meeting on July 13, at which
Kelly, Fry, Salisbury, and other leaders addressed a crowd of 500 people. — *Ibid.*,
July 14.

respectable encampment out of the materials at hand. "The members," said an account in the Washington *Post*, "have improved the ways leading into the camp, and have constructed several pairs of stairs down the steep incline which leads to the camp ground. Cantwell's men have moved nearly a quarter of a mile from the main camp and to make shorter communications a roadway has been built through the marsh at the river front." [1] A spring was barreled up near the center of the camp. After Kelly's arrival new ground was cleared and new tents and thatched huts were erected for the accommodation of the large number of men who were expected to arrive soon afterwards.[2]

Men continued to arrive, but the problem of feeding them soon became a difficult one. The Coxey camp felt the pinch first. The men felt deserted after their leaders left, and by the middle of July there were few visitors coming to inspect the camp and pay admission. Jesse Coxey, who remained, said that his men picked and sold enough blackberries to buy food, but that there was nothing in sight after the blackberry season. Some deserted and went to Rosslyn to get better rations.[3] The plenty in the Rosslyn commissary, however, was transitory, and by July 23 there was no food in camp. Several of the men were arrested in Washington for begging from door to door. They were pitifully anxious to get the sack of food which they had collected back to

[1] Washington *Post*, July 12, 1894.
[2] *Ibid.*, July 14, 1894. "The sanitary conditions are good enough, and there is the entire Potomac River in which to bathe, but many of the men are averse to a good washing." — *Ibid.*, July 22.
At the time when Coxey's camp was broken up, it was described as containing about 40 acres, with about 40 tents and "improvised thatched roof shanties." — *Ibid.*, Aug. 10.
[3] *Ibid.*, July 16, 17, 18, 1894.

camp, where it was so badly needed. In the police court the judge told them that he thought they were honest men, who really wanted work, and that he did not want to send them to the workhouse, but that the terrorizing of women and children to get food, about which there had been complaints, must stop. The men were released. General Fry said that arrest had no terrors for him, for in jail he would at least get enough to eat. Kelly left for California to work for the cause there, promising that within two weeks he would send the army three carloads of provisions, but these provisions do not seem to have appeared in time to be of assistance.[1]

Meanwhile the number of mouths to feed grew. The Washington *Post* reported seven hundred men in the Rosslyn camp on July 17, eight hundred on July 21, nine hundred on July 23, and one thousand on July 26; and on the next day one hundred thirty men came over from the Coxey camp at Bladensburg. There were still a hundred men at Coxey's camp when the authorities broke it up on August 10. The maximum number in both camps in the latter part of July, therefore, must have been twelve hundred or more.

At the beginning of the starving time, General Coxey reappeared in Washington. His fame as the leader of the Commonweal had augmented his importance in Populist politics, and he was now the People's Party candidate for Congress in the eighteenth district of Ohio. It served him right, said the Chicago *Tribune*.[2]

[1] Washington *Post*, July 20, 21, 22, 23.
[2] Chicago *Tribune*, May 17, 1894; *National Watchman*, May 25, 1894. Dispatches in the Chicago *Tribune*, of June 23 announced that J. V. Lewis, manager for Congressman Ikert in the campaign two years before, had created a sensation by indorsing Coxey for Congress, and that Coxey's candidacy, at first considered a joke, might be serious, for workingmen of both parties were dissatisfied, and the

But Coxey was by nature an optimist. He spoke complacently about his candidacy, and said that some of his friends told him that he would be elected. He visited several of the national legislators to urge the passage of his Good Roads Bill. His recent speaking trip in Minnesota and elsewhere, he said, had been a "forage for subsistence", which had resulted in contributions of supplies for his army. He insisted that the "on to Washington" movement was growing, and that people everywhere were asking him about it, continuing:

I tell them to keep it up, and I tell the people that if they will only let it be known that they are collecting provisions and sending them on to Washington there will be plenty of hungry, out-of-work people of the country who will go down there and eat them. I tell them to get two and a half per cent. of the unemployed of the country in Washington and it will make 100,000 men, and such a crowd as that will force action on Congress. I tell them that they need not be afraid of the jail there, that I tried it and can recommend it as one of the best jails in the country, where they will be well fed and taken care of. The government has set the precedent and all they have to do to get in it is to walk on the grass. But I tell you in all seriousness, it wont be long before there are 1000 men here, and when the number gets a little over that they will begin to be felt.[1]

It was only a few days later that the number of men in the Rosslyn camp alone rose above a thousand, but the effect upon Congress was not noticeable. Within a

Democrats might support him. Although he was not elected, he remained a prominent figure in Populist politics. As the election of 1896 approached, Coxey's publications quoted newspaper suggestions that he would be an acceptable candidate for the presidency. — See *Cause and Cure*, Vol. II, No. 2, pp. 22, 23.

Michael D. Fitzgerald, of the New England industrial army, was nominated for Congress by the Socialist Labor Party in the 10th District of Massachusetts. — *Washington Post*, Aug. 22, 1894.

[1] *Washington Post*, July 20, 1894.

week Coxey announced that his affairs at home would require his attention for several months to come. Before leaving he advised his men to go to Washington, beg, provoke arrest, and thereby obtain food — advice which some had already acted upon, but which was distasteful to most of them.[1] Many went out to beg, and most of them eluded arrest, but they were not able to bring much back with them. Three of Galvin's men worked all day for a bushel of potatoes, which they brought back to camp. When a farmer offered a beef for the services of ten men for a day and a half, the offer was gladly accepted. When the meat was brought into camp the rain put out the fires, and it was devoured half cooked.[2] The Chief of Police finally permitted the army to send two wagons to the city every day to solicit food, but they were not able to obtain much.[3]

All the devices that the ingenuity of the leaders could suggest were tried to procure food. A census of the camp at Rosslyn showed that the army contained 86 Masons, 198 Odd Fellows, 354 Knights of Labor, 200 members of the Y. M. C. A., and about 50 Christian Endeavorers, and it was proposed to ask help of all these organizations. A representative of the Local Assembly of the Knights of Labor told the men that a thousand loaves of bread would be donated at the next meeting.[4] These efforts, however, did not produce enough to serve the purpose, and the men continued in a most pitiable condition. Yet, in spite of the hunger, a reporter recorded that the chickens from the neighboring farms wandered about the camp un-

[1] *Ibid.*, July 26, 1894.
[2] Washington *Post*, July 24, 25, 26, 1894.
[3] *Ibid.*, Aug. 1, 2, 1894.
[4] *Ibid.*, July 25, 1894.

molested. Colonel Galvin, however, wistfully regarding one of these birds, warned it that if the situation grew much worse he feared for its safety.[1]

This remarkable self-restraint cannot be attributed entirely to the influence of the leaders, for two days before Galvin contemplated the chicken in the presence of the reporter a democratic form of government had been adopted, based upon the consent of the governed. The absence of General Fry made something of the sort seem necessary. The ragged industrials, now dangerously near a state of nature, met and adopted a system of representation for all the men in the camp. Each organized contingent was to have a member on an advisory board, from which, each morning, an officer of the day was to be elected.[2]

The new advisory board made a final effort to get something out of Congress. A "Petition of the Unemployed" was drawn up, accompanied by a draft of "A Bill to provide work for American Citizens." The document was dated at Camp Rosslyn, August 1. On the next day it was presented to the Senate by Senator Peffer. It was the most complete statement of the demands of the combined industrial armies which their leaders drew up. The petition read as follows:

The United States Industrial Army is composed of many thousands of unemployed American citizens, and represents, by general consent, millions of unemployed or partly unemployed and underpaid workingmen. They have naught but their ability to labor to provide for themselves and families, and the average wealth possessed by them would not purchase a decent coffin.

[1] Washington *Post*, July 27, 1894.
[2] *Ibid.*, July 26, 1894.

A portion of this army is now encamped near Washington, thousands more are on the way and thousands now languish in jail who from hunger were driven to trespass on railroad property. For years they have peacefully and hopefully awaited for private and public enterprise to give them work, and their condition is now such that their loyalty to the laws of the land is being put to a very severe test, as witness the violent outbreaks that are becoming so alarmingly frequent and are so ominous of catastrophe to the nation. Political liberty is a mockery where economic slavery exists.

This army is organized in the interests of peace and, apart from the borrowing of transportation in an emergency, it has been, and will continue to be, law abiding, half starved and ragged as it is, thus showing to the world an example of patient endurance and determination that is unparalleled in history.

Had we the time and facilities we could have brought a ton's weight of petitions from the poverty-stricken masses.

They ask for immediate employment on public works at fair wages or else national assistance to supply their own wants by coöperative industry.

To have our leading industries nationalized and the product or service to be furnished at cost.

Free coinage of silver and a legal-tender currency issued direct to the people.

To have the immigration of foreign laborers stopped until there is a demand for their labor or until the serfdom of the wage earner is abolished.

Therefore, as the hour of adjournment approaches and our needs are urgent, we the undersigned, at the request of the army and the millions it represents, do respectfully petition your honorable body to pass some measure of immediate and temporary relief.

This petition was signed by the members of the advisory board — Fry, Galvin, Cantwell, Kelly, and five others.[1]

[1] 53rd Cong., 2d Sess., *Senate Miscellaneous Document*, No. 251, pp. 1, 2. The signers were: Lewis C. Fry, Los Angeles, Cal.; Arthur Vinette, Los Angeles, Cal.;

Two thirds of the members of the advisory board came from the Pacific coast, and none were from New England, but two of these requests — national assistance to coöperative industry and the complete nationalization of all industry — suggest the doctrine of Morrison L. Swift and the New Englanders rather than the original demands of any of the western armies. Probably this was in part a sop to the New England army, and in part because the leaven of radicalism had been working among the Westerners during their stay at Washington. The draft of the bill which was to furnish the immediate relief, however, was nothing more than a variation upon Coxey's Good Roads Bill. It proposed to authorize the Secretary of War to inaugurate a system of public works "for the creation of substantial wealth for the nation, and for the purpose of giving work to the unemployed citizens." All who applied where the work was being done, upon presentation of evidence of citizenship and of continuous lack of employment for thirty days, certified by a county clerk, were to be furnished with work by the day according to their physical abilities. The minimum wage was to be two dollars for an eight-hour day, and skilled labor to be paid "according to the average rate of wages prevailing in the neighborhood of the works." The Secretary of the Treasury was required to issue immediately $250,000,000 of legal-tender treasury notes, and thereafter an amount annually sufficient to meet the requirements of the bill. Since a number of public works were already begun, the bill was to go into effect

Thos. Galvin, Los Angeles, Cal.; Frank Cantwell, Seattle, Wash.; Chas. T. Kelly, San Francisco, Cal.; Geo. Howard, San Francisco, Cal.; S. H. Thomas, Cincinnati, Ohio; Chas. Clark, Minneapolis, Minn.; Allen Jennings, Indianapolis, Ind.

immediately upon its passage.[1] This final plea from the "petition in boots" failed to arouse Congress to any action favorable to the industrial armies.

By the end of July the most serious problem of the camp was to avoid starvation. The blackberry crop was exhausted and donations were few. The men realized that the promises which had induced them to make the journey were not to be fulfilled. When three members of western armies asked shelter for the night at the police station, they said that "When they enlisted it was pictured to them in glowing terms that the unemployed workmen of the country would flock to the National Capital in such large numbers that Congress would be so alarmed as to pass a bill for their relief." A man in the camp, who refused to give his name, told the *Post* reporter "that they had come to Washington under a false impression. They had been assured that there would be enough food here to live on, and that their petitions would receive attention from Congress. They had become convinced, he said, that both hopes were groundless." [2] The three hundred men of Kelly's army who were still in camp sent a committee to ask Representative Lafe Pence of Colorado for transportation back to his State, where, they said, they could make enough to tide them over the winter.[3] The Commissioners of the District of Columbia at last took steps to dissolve the army, influenced, no doubt, by a combination of compassion and of the desire to get rid of a nuisance, and moreover, it seems, by the intermediation of Mr. Frank Hume, a Washington merchant, who had

---

[1] 53rd Cong., 2d Sess., *Senate Miscellaneous Document*, No. 251, p. 2.
[2] Washington *Post*, July 24, 28, 1894.
[3] *Ibid.*, July 28, 1894.

become interested in sending the industrials home, and who had come to the assistance of the commissary when the men faced starvation.[1] Trains or cars were furnished to send the men to cities in the neighborhood, or at least in the direction, of their homes. Part of Kelly's men were sent to St. Louis on the last day of July and the first of August.[2] When a sermon was preached to the army on Sunday, August 5, the question was put to the men, and they all voted that they wanted to go home, but that they lacked the means to go unless they were sent.[3] Galvin's men accepted transportation to Los Angeles, and Thomas' to Cincinnati. "The men composing the Galvin and Thomas contingents," said the Washington *Post*, "were the backbone of the army, as they were all either mechanics or miners, and had no element of the tramp about them." Galvin was the only one of the better known leaders who stayed with his men to the end.[4]

Before their departure Galvin and Thomas gave out an open letter in which they expressed thanks to those who had given aid, especially to

Chief of police Col. Moore, who has proved himself a true and humane man; and also the District Commissioners, who

---

[1] Washington *Post*, Aug. 8, 1894.

[2] Sixty-six left on the Chesapeake and Ohio "in a second-class car on tickets provided by the commissioners of the District of Columbia" on July 31, and 80 or 90 more were expected to leave the next night. — *Ibid.*, Aug. 1, 1894.

[3] *Ibid.*, Aug. 6, 1894.

[4] *Ibid.*, Aug. 8, 1894. There had been a noticeable change in the tone of the *Post's* descriptions of the army soon after the first of August, on the part of both editors and reporters. Previously the accounts had been sympathetic and not unkindly. Now the men were described as shiftless tramps. Perhaps it was because the editors thought that the army had stayed too long, but there was probably truth in the statement that the better men had been leaving to get work and that the less desirable element remained, with a majority of "lazy, filthy tramps, who will not work or who want $2.50 to $4 for an eight hour day." — *Ibid.*, Aug. 4, 1894.

cheerfully responded when transportation was requested.
Last, but not least, do we express our sincere thanks to the
Hon. Frank Hume, through whose influence transportation
was secured and our commissary many times replenished
when we knew not where our next meal was to come from.
We desire the Governor of Virginia to understand that it is
not his threats nor fear of his militia that causes our departure. We depart through the request of Mr. Hume, for
whom we have the greatest respect, and also our own welfare. We are going to our homes, where we will continue
the fight for liberty and equality at the ballot box. We will
do all in our power to condemn the administration of Grover
Cleveland, and the actions of many of the so-called Senators
and Congressmen who have refused to act favorably upon
any of the bills presented for our relief.[1]

The allusion to the governor of Virginia referred to
a notice served by the sheriff that the army at Rosslyn
must get out of the State or the State authorities would
use force.[2] Both Virginia and Maryland now took decisive action. Governor Browne of Maryland ordered
the arrest of the hundred and two men who remained
at the Bladensburg camp. They were sent to the
Baltimore House of Correction, where the officers in
charge said they had the appearance of regular custom-
ers in such institutions,[3] and where, in the process of
enforced barbering at the expense of the State, Christopher Columbus Jones and Marshal McKee lost their
whiskers and their dignity.[4] A proclamation read by
the Adjutant General of Virginia at the Rosslyn camp
informed the industrials that they were a nuisance
which they must abate by their departure before noon of

---

[1] Washington *Post*, Aug. 8, 1894.
[2] *Ibid.*, July 28, 1894.
[3] *Ibid.*, Aug. 10, 1894.
[4] Washington *Post*, Aug. 17, 1894.

the following day. Upon their failure to abate, Governor O'Ferrall assembled three companies of militia — secretly, lest the District of Columbia police should prevent the crossing of the bridge — and drove the army across the Potomac into the District.[1]

Coxey returned to Washington, failed to get his men out of the workhouse by writs of habeas corpus, succeeded in salvaging his seven blooded horses, and left to attend the Populist State Convention in Ohio, which indorsed his Good Roads Bill and declared against interest-bearing bonds.[2] The last of the industrials were sent to St. Paul and to some of the eastern cities on August 15.[3] Governor Browne soon sent the imprisoned Commonwealers to their homes on condition of a promise not to return to Maryland as vagrants.[4] Coxey's Commonweal and the industrial armies had passed into the realm of history.

---

[1] Washington *Post*, Aug. 10, 11, 12. For a Populist opinion of these proceedings, see the editorial on "Russianized America" in the *National Watchman*, Aug. 17, 1894, which describes the arrest of men whose only crime was poverty as a "high-handed outrage."

[2] Washington *Post*, Aug. 14, 15, 17, 1894.

[3] General Jefferies, a recent arrival, and Colonel Vinette, refused an offer to send their men to Chicago, Indianapolis, or Kansas City. The men all voted against it. "They did not care to stop at any city east of Minnesota. They were well treated by the people of that state, while in all the other states east of this through which they passed the people were not so hospitable." *Ibid.*, Aug. 15.

[4] *Ibid.*, Aug. 17, 20.

CHAPTER XIII

THE MEANING OF THE MOVEMENT

The immediate cause of the industrial army movement was the unrest caused by unemployment after the panic of 1893. Large numbers of workingmen in desperate circumstances were willing to travel for long distances under uncomfortable conditions to obtain work or temporary subsistence. Many who had gone west in the time of prosperity joined the eastward movement of the armies in order to get back to their homes. Some joined from mere love of adventure, and the desire for travel and for a change, as Jack London did. To many who faced the alternative of starvation or reliance upon charity, the commissary department of an industrial army had strong attractions, and the collective importunity of these organizations was doubtless less humiliating to their members, and perhaps less strenuous, than individual begging. Professional vagrants were not unwilling to take advantage of these opportunities, but in the better armies, at least in Fry's and Kelly's, vigorous efforts were made to exclude them. These western armies seem to have represented the highest type of organization and personnel connected with the movement.

The evidence cited in the preceding chapters indicates that the industrial armies were composed, for the most part, of workingmen who in normal times would have worked for a living. They occasionally refused offers of work [1] because they believed in their mission, because they thought the pay was too low, because the jobs were distant or temporary, because they objected to replacing strikers who were holding out for higher wages, because they found life in the industrial army more satisfactory for the time being, or for other reasons.[2] Probably there was much truth in the statement that it was easy in the United States to get people to march because we are "a marching people, and we like to be in the procession." [3] It was asserted that there were anarchists, socialists, and criminals in the armies. Doubtless there were, but this does not necessarily mean that they differed in this respect from any group of several thousand workmen.

The armies could hardly have been moved about and fed as they were without a great deal of popular sympathy in their favor, but this was not the only thing that assisted them in their travels. They had "devised a new 'stand and deliver' process." [4] They were compared to the organ grinder portrayed in *Punch* who replied, when he was informed that there was a sick lady in the house, "Where there's sickness in the house I never move for less than a shilling." [5] An army was a source of much embarrassment to the locality in which it camped. It was expensive to feed it, but humanity

[1] New York *Times*, April 7, 28, 1894; Chicago *Times*, May 2, 1894; Chicago *Tribune*, May 13, 1894; *Our Day*, Vol. XIII, p. 278; Austen, "Downfall of Coxeyism", *Chautauquan*, Vol. XLIX, p. 452.

[2] See *Outlook*, Vol. XLIX, p. 818; *Review of Reviews*, Vol. IX, p. 650; *Ibid.*, Vol. X, p. 43; Major General O. O. Howard, "The Menace of Coxeyism: The Significance and Aims of the Movement", *North American Review*, Vol. CLVIII, p. 688 (June, 1894); *Journal of the Knights of Labor*, March 29, April 5, 15, 1894; *National Watchman*, June 8, 1894.

[3] M. M. Trumbull, "Current Topics", *Open Court*, March 22, 1894.

[4] Louisville *Courier Journal*, quoted in Chicago *Tribune*, June 22, 1894.

[5] M. M. Trumbull, "Current Topics", *Open Court*, Vol. VIII, p. 4061.

and local pride forbade that it should be allowed to
starve. An army was a potential danger, especially if
starved or thwarted into desperation. Workingmen
saw possible competition in a labor market already
sadly overstocked, and property owners feared depredations. Thus sympathy, where there was any, was reinforced by interest in the army's departure, and the
expedient course was to feed it and speed it on its way,
even if transportation had to be paid. Business men,
labor organizations, Populist farmers, and railroads,
impelled by various mixtures of philanthropy, fear, and
discretion, played their parts in this game of "passing
the buck", and the armies made the most of it. Some
of their leaders were very clever men.

So far as any immediate realization of its program
was concerned, Coxeyism was a failure. Of the hundred
thousand men who should have appeared in Washington on May 1 to make good Coxey's boast, or the four
hundred thousand predicted by Fry, there were never
much more than a thousand in the environs of the
capital, and never more than a number somewhere between five thousand and ten thousand on the road at
any one time in organizations that had Washington for
their destination. Congress did nothing more than
disregard or suppress those of its members who talked
about Coxeyism too charitably, and the police and the
local authorities did the rest. But to dismiss the subject as a comic performance with a farcical ending does
not explain it.

"We may laugh as we please at 'Coxey's Army,'"
said one writer, "but it is a symptom. Symptoms as
they appear on the surface may seem slight enough;
but they mean always internal disturbance; they mean

the possibility of diseases that may threaten the vitals."[1] The disease was one about which diagnosticians disagreed. It was, said the Springfield *Republican*, "a movement curiously adapted for reflecting to every crank and visionary and reformer a justification of his own particular hobby",[2] and the comments of conservatives were similarly colored by the predilections of the commentators. A doctor of the New York Board of Public Health regarded Coxeyites as so many spreaders of disease, and he was apprehensive that they would cause epidemics of smallpox.[3] The Superintendent of the New York Police Department looked upon them as vagrants who ought to be suppressed in the interests of law and order.[4] There was a theory that prominent silver men of the West, attracted by the idea of a petition in boots demanding free silver, and determined to throw the responsibility for the support of the Western unemployed upon the East, had organized the movement and financed it.[5] Thus various kinds of people gave to Coxeyism the interpretations to which they were predisposed.

The extreme of reactionary disgust that workingmen should act in a manner so inconvenient to railroads and so alarming to property interests was expressed in an

[1] Rev. M. J. Savage, "The Present Conflict for a Larger Life", *Arena*, Vol. X, p. 303.
[2] Springfield *Republican*, quoted in *Public Opinion*, Vol. XVII, p. 116 (May 3, 1894).
[3] Thomas Byrnes, "The Menace of Coxeyism: Character and Methods of the Men", *North American Review*, Vol. CLVIII, pp. 696–701.
[4] Alvah H. Doty, "The Menace of Coxeyism: The Danger to Public Health", *ibid.*, Vol. CLVIII, pp. 701–705.
[5] Yankton, [S. D.] *Press and Dakotan*, April 26, 1894. For a similar report about Hogan's army, see above, pp. 205, 206. The Chicago *Tribune*, May 3, 1894, stated that when Col. Redstone, the agent for the Coxeyites in Washington, was seen in conversation with Senators Stewart and Jones, a rumor was started that the silver men were at the bottom of the Coxey movement.

article by Judge N. M. Hubbard, the railroad lawyer who had made himself unpopular in western Iowa by his stand against Kelly's army. He complained that "Kelly and his tramps" had "appointed themselves a committee to tell Congress what to do"; that under the laws of every State they were vagabonds; and that the whole affair was "unlawful and without precedent"; yet no official of his State had "so much as politely requested Kelly and his tramps to disband and go to work." He thought that property owners should combine to prevent organized labor from fixing wages at a point that would give them more than their share of the productive wealth of the country, and that it was the labor organizations that were " sympathizing and urging forward these senseless Coxey movements." "This new form of anarchy," he concluded, "cannot be too soon rebuked and throttled." [1] Others who were less bitter than Judge Hubbard agreed with him about the composition of the armies, and refused to see anything but ordinary "hoboes" in them.[2] Still others expressed resentment at the tendency of "mobs" to claim that they represented the people. It was treason in a monarchy, said an editorial in the New York *Tribune*, to assume the power or the title of a sovereign, and it was a similar usurpation of prerogative in a republic when any body of men, acting otherwise than through the representative system provided by law, pretended that it must be obeyed because it represented the popular will.[3]

[1] N. M. Hubbard, "The Invasion of Iowa", *Midland Monthly*, Vol. I, pp. 588–590 (June, 1894).

[2] See editorials in New York *Times*, April 8, 22, 26, 29, May 4, 1894; Indianapolis *Journal*, April 20, May 12, 1894; *Nation*, Vol. LVIII, p. 306.

[3] This editorial in the New York *Tribune*, May 7, 1894, was quoted and approved

The natural tendency of conservative interests was to condemn Coxeyism more or less severely, but this tendency was modified by politics. The Democratic Party was in power, and its opponents held it responsible for everything undesirable. Republicans admitted that the situation was distressing, that unemployment was a real problem, and that honest workingmen were driven by their sufferings into this mistaken attempt at self-help; and they attributed it all to the misgovernment and free trade policies of the Democrats.[1] The trouble began, said Senator Hoar, when the elections showed that the Democrats would control Congress; it was intensified by the Democratic administration, and the hard times followed because of fear of an attack upon the policy of protection: hence Coxeyism.[2] Republicans generally were able to sympathize with the grievances of the Coxeyites without approving of their remedies, and to make political capital out of this sympathy.

Some of them went farther. Ex-President Harrison had said in February of 1894: "It is generally accepted now as a right principle that our city councils, our county commissioners, our State legislatures, should legislate to create work for the unemployed." He added that the "Republican theory has been all along that it was right to so legislate as to provide work, employment, comfort, to the American workingman. We believe that the national government has a duty to perform in this respect as well as the city council

by General O. O. Howard, "The Menace of Coxeyism: Significance and Aims of the Movement", *North American Review*, Vol. CLVIII, pp. 688, 689.

[1] See *Nation*, Vol. LVIII, pp. 322, 323 (May 3, 1894); editorials in San Francisco *Chronicle*, April 6, 1894; Indianapolis *Journal*, April 24, 1894.

[2] Chicago *Tribune*, May 1, 1894; *Our Day*, Vol. XIII, pp. 257, 258.

and the board of county commissioners." [1] The standard Republican remedy for industrial disorders was the protective tariff. The anti-protectionist editor of the *Nation* concluded that "protection and socialism are one in principle", and he soon added Coxeyism to the list of synonyms.[2]

Democrats cheerfully indorsed this view of the relation between Coxeyism and protection. In reply to the assertion that Coxeyism was caused by the Cleveland administration and the Wilson bill for the reduction of the tariff, they asserted that any one who wanted a job could get one, and that the industrial armies were composed of professional tramps, the scum of the population, who were entitled to little sympathy from respectable persons. It was only the Republican demagogues, they said, who wanted the votes of these vagrants, who were trying to make it appear that Coxeyites were respectable workingmen.[3] "The followers of Coxey," said one, "learned the lesson from the Republicans. Representatives of class interests boasted that they had written the laws by which they exacted tribute of the consumers. The Coxeyites are simply applying this mischievous lesson. They wish to see certain legislation perfected and they propose to go to Washington and put it through." [4]

The prevailing unrest and discontent, said another, was caused by the dangerous drift towards paternalism,

---

[1] *Nation*, Vol. LVIII, p. 131.

[2] *Ibid.*, Vol. LVIII, pp. 131, 282, 322, 323.

[3] *Nation*, Vol. LVIII, pp. 322, 323; New York *Times*, April 9, 22, 29, 1894; *cf.* Pittsburgh *Press*, May 1, 1894.

[4] Louisville *Courier-Journal*, quoted in *Public Opinion*, Vol. XVII, p. 95. For collections of editorial opinions representing various phases of the reaction to Coxeyism see *Public Opinion*, Vol. XVI, pp. 595, 621; Vol. XVII, pp. 15, 24, 43, 70, 94, 116, 136, 161.

which led all sorts of visionaries and their followers to demand that the Federal Government should put their schemes into operation. It was fostered by Republican legislative policies based upon the doctrine "that good wages, steady work, big dividends, and business prosperity were the incidents of legislation." Republican writers and orators who proclaimed that the "black pall of distress and discontent" that had descended upon the land was caused by the proposed reduction of the tariff, did not really believe it themselves, and admitted that they were only working up a partisan scare. "Patience, thrift, economy, and industry" were the only effective remedies, and they must result from individual action, not from legislative aid.[1]

The same Democratic editor discussed with evident relish the money inflation phase of Coxey's plan. He pointed out that the last Republican State convention in Pennsylvania had adopted a resolution demanding that the Federal Government should increase the amount of currency to forty dollars per capita. This would call for an increase of a billion dollars — twice as much as was called for by Coxey's Good Roads Bill. The object of Coxey's scheme was a desirable one, and as for his demand for more money, he at least was more moderate than the Republicans. The editor had heard rumors that Senators Cameron and Quay were prepared to put a free silver plank in the platform of the next Republican State convention. The inference seemed to be that as money inflationists the Republicans were worse than Coxeyites.[2] It was only natural that the members of each major party who disapproved of

---

[1] Editorial in Pittsburgh *Post*, April 6, 1894.
[2] Editorials, Pittsburgh *Post*, March 29, April 5, 1894.

Coxeyism should try to throw the blame for its existence upon their political opponents, and use it as a text for odious comparisons.

This division between the two major parties was not maintained consistently because cutting across it was the division between conservative or timid persons who viewed with alarm any tendency of the lower strata of society to assert themselves, and on the other hand, those who were prone to sympathize with the under dog, who wanted society reformed to uplift its lowest members, or who scented capitalism or the "interests" in any criticism of the unfortunate. By no means all the latter class were in the Populist Party, but naturally it was in the Populist Party that Coxeyism found its strongest support.

Populism, of course, was much broader than Coxeyism, but Coxeyism was, for the most part, Populism, and the sympathy of the farmers, laborers, and Populist leaders was too plain to be mistaken. The demands of the unemployed armies were demands incorporated into the platforms of the People's Party and of allied organizations, and of the Democratic Party after its accession of Populism in 1896. Money inflation was a fundamental tenet of Coxey and of the industrial armies; as it was of the earlier Greenback and labor parties, of the Farmers' Alliances,[1] of the People's Party, and of the Democrats in 1896.[2] Interest-bearing bonds were condemned by the Populists, the Democrats, and the National Silver Party in 1896, and by the Fusionist Populists and the Farmers' Alliance and In-

---

[1] Haynes, "Third Party Movements", p. 233.
[2] Edward Stanwood, "History of the Presidency" (2 Vols., Boston and New York, Vol. I, 1898, Vol. II, 1916), Vol. I, pp. 511, 543, 551; Vol. II, p. 40.

dustrial Union in 1900.[1] The Populists in 1892 had
condemned the banking system [2] against which Carl
Browne delivered his tirades from Massillon to Washington, and the Democrats repeated the condemnation
in 1896.[3] Government employment on public works
was advocated by the Populist platform of 1896.[4]

These planks covered the principal features of Coxey's two bills, except for the one which appeared to
conservatives to be the least objectionable — the ad-
vocacy of good roads — which found a place somewhat
later in the Republican platform of 1900.[5]

Of the measures peculiar to the western armies, opposition to unrestricted immigration or alien landowner-
ship appeared in the platform of the Farmers' Alliances
in 1889 and 1890, in the Populist platform of 1892,[6] in
the Democratic platform of 1896, and in that of the
Silver Republicans in 1900.[7] Chinese or Japanese exclusion was commended by the Democrats, [8] by the
Fusion Populists and by the Silver Republicans in
1900; [9] and the irrigation of western lands by both the
Democrats [10] and the Republicans in the same year.[11]

None of the armies seems to have been dominated by
any thorough-going socialistic schemes except for the
small New England detachments. The more radical
labor parties had less in common with Coxeyism than

---

[1] Stanwood, "History of the Presidency", Vol. I, pp. 544, 552, 556; Vol. II, pp. 33, 39, 40.
[2] *Ibid.*, Vol. I, p. 510.
[3] *Ibid.*, Vol. I, p. 544.
[4] *Ibid.*, Vol. I, p. 554.
[5] *Ibid.*, Vol. II, p. 49.
[6] *Ibid.*, Vol. I, p. 512; Haynes, "Third Party Movements", p. 233.
[7] Stanwood, "History of the Presidency", Vol. I, pp. 544, 546; Vol. II, p. 66.
[8] *Ibid.*, Vol. II, p. 63.
[9] *Ibid.*, Vol. II, pp. 42, 68.
[10] *Ibid.*, Vol. II, p. 63.
[11] *Ibid.*, Vol. II, p. 49.

did the Populists. The Socialist Labor Party demanded
in 1892 and 1896 a reduction of the hours of labor in
proportion to the increase of facilities for production;
but the resolution of the Populist convention of 1892,
demanding shorter hours of labor and a rigid enforcement of the eight-hour law on government works, more
nearly approximated the eight-hour day provision of
Coxey's bill. The Socialist Laborites demanded Government control of the railroads; so did the Populists.
The demand for the repeal of "all pauper, tramp, conspiracy, and sumptuary laws" seems to have been the
only formal Socialist Labor demand suggesting Coxeyism which was not also made by the Populists.[1] The
plank of the Social Democrats in 1900 for the "inauguration of a system of public works and improvements for the employment of the unemployed",[2] was
similar to the Populist plank in 1896. A radical socialist publication condemned the whole industrial army
movement, with the comment that more foolish things
than this would continue to be done until private property was abolished.[3]

This examination of party platforms, therefore, indicates that the remedies for unemployment proposed
by unemployed armies after the panic of 1893 were, in
the main, Populist measures. They were measures
commonly suggested throughout a period of some years,
both before and after that event, to allay economic distress among those classes that were less successful in
the struggle for a livelihood, whether they were farmers

---

[1] For the Socialist Labor platforms of 1892 and 1896, see Stanwood, "History of
the Presidency", Vol. I, pp. 513, 514, 540. For the corresponding Populist demands,
see *ibid.*, Vol. I, p. 512.

[2] *Ibid.*, Vol. II, p. 36.

[3] *The Altruist* (St. Louis), Vol. XXVI, p. 14 (April, 1894).

or industrial laborers. Coxey's bills were merely an ingenious combination of ideas which prevailed among many of these people. The western armies wanted some things peculiar to the regions from which they came, as well as to the classes from which they sprang.

These classes felt that they were victimized by a vicious system. Farmers thought that if they were industrious they ought to be able to sell their crops for enough to pay their mortgages and to live comfortably; industrial laborers felt that if they were willing to work, they ought to have an opportunity to work for a sufficient wage; something must be rotten in the State if this could not be done. They laid the blame at the door of capitalists or plutocrats, — those who, according to the Omaha platform, had boldly stolen the "fruits of the toil of millions" to "build up colossal fortunes for the few." The Populists did not want to change the form of the Government, but they wanted it administered in the interests of the people, meaning themselves. Distrusting the two old political parties, they organized to remedy the prevailing conditions, hoping by the use of the ballot to get control of the Government and to inaugurate their reforms. The ballot was too slow for Coxey, for the suffering from unemployment was acute, and he proposed to influence Congress immediately by his "petition in boots."

The existence of Coxeyism, in so far as it was separate from the larger movement, was short-lived. But its effect in stimulating Populism was probably considerable. It was spectacular enough to attract more attention than ordinary political speeches or writings. The newspapers to which the Omaha platform referred as "the subsidized press" made fun of it, it is true, and emphasized its picturesque and ridiculous features more than its ideas, but a modicum of these ideas appeared even there. With Populist or Labor publications it was different; they explained to their readers what the movement was supposed to be about, and their tone, whether they agreed with it all or not, was usually very sympathetic. A workingmen's movement that stood for Farmers' Alliance or Populist measures was an important connecting link between labor and the agrarian discontent. The armies, morever, were impressive as visible manifestations of the evil conditions about which Populists complained. The leaders — Coxey, Browne, Kelly, Fry, and the others — addressed audiences and aroused much enthusiasm at the places along their line of march where their ideas were liable to take root. The methods of the revival meeting and of the circus were thus combined for the spread of Populistic propaganda.

The sympathy of prominent members of the People's Party for oppressed humanity led them to support the industrials both in speech and in action. When the unemployed were swarming on the railroads in the autumn of 1893, Governor Hogg of Texas was informed of the arrest of fifty tramps from California who had arrived at San Antonio by freight. He condemned the arrests and offered to pardon the tramps. "Food, not fines", he said, "will be the treatment of the law-loving, law-abiding element in this state, when men commit no greater crime than travelling as tramps for lack of work." [1] His encouragement to Fry's army was as outspoken as his condemnation of the Southern Pacific for its treatment of the industrials.

[1] *Journal of the Knights of Labor*, Oct. 19, 1893.

Hogg's action in the case of the fifty tramps was followed two months later by an extraordinary letter from Governor Lewelling of Kansas to the boards of police commissioners of that State.

In this country — it began — the monopoly of labor-saving machinery and its devotion to selfish instead of social use, have rendered more and more human beings superfluous, until we have a standing army of the unemployed numbering in the most prosperous times not less than 1,000,000 able-bodied men; yet, until recently, it was the prevailing notion, as it is yet the prevailing notion of all other classes than the working people themselves and those of other classes given to thinking, that whoever, being able-bodied and willing to work, can always find work to do. . . .

The vagrancy laws, he said, denied equal protection of the law to the poorer classes.

The right to go freely from place to place in search of employment, or even in obedience to a mere whim, is part of that personal liberty guaranteed by the Constitution of the United States to every human being on American soil. . . . I am aware of no power in the Legislature or in the city councils to deny him the right to such happiness in his own way, so long as he harms no other person.

He urged that "simple poverty cease to be a crime", and announced that he expected police authorities to "carry out the spirit as well as the letter of the foregoing suggestions." [1] Governor Lewelling spoke of the Coxey movement as "a spontaneous uprising of the people", "an earnest and vigorous protest against the injustice and tyranny of the age", which showed "that this ghost of the hunger demon will not down at the bidding

---

[1] *The People*, Dec. 17, 1893. See also San Francisco *Chronicle*, Dec. 7, 11, 1893, which stated that the police authorities intended to carry out the governor's recommendation, and that as a result hundreds of tramps were making for Kansas.

of plutocracy", and he recommended to the people of Kansas that they hold meetings and petition Congress to give the industrials food, shelter, and a fair hearing.[1]

Governor Waite of Colorado expressed similar sentiments about the Commonweal armies. "Their cause is just," he said, "and they should be aided in their march instead of hindered. Were I called upon to order out the militia against them, as Governors Jackson of Iowa, and West, of Utah, did, I probably would do so, but it would be only as a commissary department." [2] He invited Kelly's army into his State. When industrial armies were stealing trains in Oregon, Governor Pennoyer refused to call out the militia with the remark that he "didn't care a whoop" whether the industrials or the United States Troops came out ahead.[3]

Perhaps these Populist governors were slightly sobered by a sense of their official responsibility; but not so Secretary of State Osborne of Kansas, who, when commenting upon the arrest of Coxey and Browne, uttered the awful warning:

I want to make this prediction, that there will be no overt act until the next election, then, simultaneous with the returns, flames will shoot into the air from the Atlantic to the Pacific and every palatial residence be destroyed in the uprising of the people. Woe unto them who have sought to stay this tide of the past six months. The farmers are preparing for this; they are selling a horse or a cow and buying Winchesters, and the mechanics are doing the same.[4]

[1] Indianapolis *Journal*, April 23, 1894.
[2] *Ibid.*, April 23, 1894.
[3] *Nation*, Vol. LVIII, p. 356 (May 17, 1894).
[4] *Weekly Iowa State Register*, May 4, 1894. The *National Watchman*, June 8, 1894, prints an excerpt from the *Virginia Sun* under the headline "A Confederate Field Officer Shows How Citizen Soldiers Can Learn War in One Lesson." It expressed fear of the drilling of the militia, plutocracy's army, in Washington,

There were other predictions of revolution if plutocracy remained intractable.[1] Even General Weaver, when he wrote an article in favor of Coxeyism, referred to revolution as a distinct possibility; whether the movement expended itself at the ballot box or broke into violent disorder, he said, would depend upon whether it was met with kindness or repression.[2] The manner in which Populist senators and representatives defended Coxey and his lieutenants in Congress and in the police court has already been described.

Unfriendly critics described Coxeyites as Populists of the lowest grade,[3] or complained of the way in which People's Party leaders were "urging the poor deluded trampers on", encouraging their outbreaks of disorder, and defending Coxey in the courts, in the expectation of winning votes.[4] So far as the last statement was true, it might be taken as an admission of the popularity of the movement. "The Coxeyites," said W. T. Stead, "ridiculed by the classes, have the sympathy of the masses. Organized labor, and labor not organized, has

and told how easy it was for the opposing forces to prepare. It concluded: "Let the plutocrats and their tin soldiers beware! 'They who take to the sword shall perish by the sword.'" See also Major Sam. L. Leffingwell, "Militiamen *vs.* Industrialism", *American Federationist*, Vol. I, p. 27 (April, 1894), and B. O. Flower, "Plutocracies' Bastiles: or Why the Republic is Becoming an Armed Camp", *Arena*, Vol. X, pp. 601 *ff.* Flower wrote to L. H. Weller of Iowa, June 13, 1894, a letter in which he described the armories being built in the East by private subscription, showing, he said, "that the plutocracy is not only alarmed but is determined", and added: "After the imprisonment of Coxey for stepping on the grass and the arrest of Fitzgerald for free speech in Philadelphia and other outrages of recent occurrence, the people can see plainly what they have to expect." L. H. Weller, MSS., Wis. Hist. Soc.

[1] *Weekly Iowa State Register*, May 4, 1894; San Bernardino, California, *Industrial Journal*, quoted in *National Watchman*, May 25, 1894; Scott City, Kansas, *Scott County News*, quoted, *ibid.*, June 29, 1894.

[2] James B. Weaver, "The Commonweal Crusade", *Midland Monthly*, Vol. I, p. 590 (June, 1894).

[3] *Nation*, Vol. LVIII, p. 358 (May 17, 1894).

[4] Indianapolis *Journal*, May 3, 1894.

cheered the armies on their way." [1] The story of the progress of the armies shows that organized labor gave both sympathy and more substantial support. "There is something so abhorrent to human reason," Stead continued, "in the waste of a million willing workers in a continent which has not yet made decent roads through its most populous districts, that everyone must sympathize with the attempt by pacific, although irregular, methods, to force the subject upon the attention of the government." He argued that since in case of war the United States would be able to feed its recruits, it ought to be able to do something when the enemy was hunger; and that perhaps the industrial armies would make such action necessary. The movement, he said, was assuming menacing proportions, and he feared for the result. [2] Stead was not the only foreigner who exaggerated the danger, partly because of European failure to understand that the mock-seriousness in the accounts of the movements of the various armies was a part of the joke with which the American press was trying to enter-

---

[1] W. T. Stead, "Coxeyism", *Review of Reviews*, Vol. X, p. 52; *Outlook*, Vol. XLIX, p. 733. For expressions of the sympathetic attitude of organized labor, see *American Federationist*, Vol. I, pp. 53, 69, 76; *Journal of the Knights of Labor*, April 26, May 3, 17, 1894. Opponents of Coxeyism quoted the unfavorable opinion of Hugh O'Donnell, leader of the Homestead strikers in 1892. See Austen, "Downfall of Coxeyism", *Chautauquan*, Vol. XIX, p. 451; Chicago *Tribune*, May 8, 1894.

Sympathy for Coxeyism was by no means confined to the laboring classes. General Howard wrote that "The most significant feature of the Omaha and Council Bluffs sojourn [of Kelly's army] was the indorsement this Industrial Army received from prominent citizens, as well as from thousands of workmen in these cities." — "The Menace of Coxeyism: The Significance and Aims of the Movement", *North American Review*, Vol. CLVIII, p. 691.

[2] W. T. Stead, "Coxeyism", *Review of Reviews*, Vol. X, p. 56. Stead wrote to Henry Demarest Lloyd, May 23, 1894: "I must confess that I am amazed at the indifference of the average observer to appreciate the significance of Coxeyism." On June 6 Stead wrote that he could not understand why his American editor made light of the movement and implied by his editorial that Mr. Stead "was an idiot for attaching any importance whatever to the armies of the Commonweal." Henry Demarest Lloyd MSS., Wis. Hist. Soc.

tain its readers.[1] It required a knowledge of American
background and American characteristics, greater than
many Americans themselves possessed, to understand
how these things could be without great danger to the
State.

There was to be found in the men of the industrial
armies certain apparently contradictory qualities which
foreigners, and many who were not foreigners, did not
seem to comprehend — a superficial lawlessness, combined with deep-seated capacity for self-government
and respect for certain fundamentals of law and order.
Most of them were frontiersmen or the descendants of
frontiersmen. They were self-reliant, they knew what
they wanted, and they adapted available means to
their ends without being much embarrassed by consideration for the fine points of the law. When they wanted
to go somewhere on a mission that they thought was
worth while, when trains were available and they
thought that the railroads ought to carry them (the
railroads represented plutocratic monopoly, anyway)
they took the trains and used them when they could.
Even when this was done without the consent of the
owners, the trains might be considered borrowed rather
than stolen. They seldom took anything else, except,
occasionally, food when they were starving. They followed leaders who were able to obtain their respect by
their personality and ability, and who offered to help
their followers to obtain the desired ends. They sub-

---

[1] "Hence in Europe, where American humor, if unlabelled, is seldom understood,
the belief spread that the United States had fallen into anarchy. The Republic
was to be overthrown by a great uprising of its own citizens. The movement of
Coxey's prowling tramps was gravely likened to the famous march of the mob
from Paris to Versailles. English leader-writers awaited solemnly for the crash
of a wide-spread revolution." — H. T. Peck, "Twenty Years of the Republic",
p. 374.

mitted to a discipline which, in the best organized of
the armies, at least, was a marvel to those who observed
it. If some of them submitted to the rules of good behavior only because they knew that their leaders knew
what they were about, and because this was the best
means of getting their food and transportation, it was
at least an intelligent submission.

They adopted extra legal "constitutions", forms of
government, and other regulations, and they made them
work. Some of these regulations expressly bound the
men to respect the constitutions and laws of the United
States and of the States through which they passed.
Most of the industrials had no idea of overthrowing the
Government. They merely wanted to get something
out of it. They believed in popular government. They
believed that they represented a large part of the people, and as representatives of the downtrodden masses,
they merely wanted to improve the operation of the
Government according to their own lights — rescue it
from a plutocratic minority, some would have said —
and thus prevent these unfortunate masses (themselves
included, of course) from suffering as they had suffered.
Their solutions of the problem may have been all
wrong: certainly they were one-sided, but they contained many suggestions that were worth while. In
this they were representative of the whole Populist
movement, of which they were a part. There was
fighting blood in these men, and when they were
thwarted or mistreated, the results were sometimes
deplorable. But the remarkable thing was not that
they made so much trouble, but that, under the circumstances, they made so little. When all is said, the
story of this much-ridiculed movement is hardly less

than a distinct tribute to the capacity for self-government and self-restraint of those American workingmen.

The frontier had always had certain contradictory
characteristics. Individual self-reliance and initiative
had been combined with reliance upon the central Government to give the frontiersmen what they needed or
were unable to supply for themselves, especially in such
fields as cheap money and easy transportation. Paternalism was distasteful in so far as it interfered with
individual initiative, but the kind of paternal assistance
that provided for keeping open the fields of endeavor
in which individuals wanted to exercise their initiative
was much desired. This was the attitude of the industrial armies when they demanded the right to earn their
own livings through work created by the Government
for this purpose, at wages satisfactory to the workers.
The farmers still regarded the old internal improvement
question in terms of transportation — railroad rates
and good roads. The Coxeyites saw it principally in
terms of work and wages. According to a writer who
heard Kelly and his subordinates speak at Ogden, their
"prevailing idea seemed to be that whenever a man
cannot for himself find work at two dollars a day, it is
the duty of the Federal Government to find it for him
and keep him in it. Paternalism in government was the
watchword, not self-help." [1] But to ask the Government to provide work and to ask for bread were very
different matters. Populists denied that the former was
paternalism at all.[2]

[1] *Our Day*, Vol. XIII, p. 278.

[2] A Populist writer, replying to an article by Senator Kyle in the *National Wash-
ingtonian* of April 13, 1894, made a distinction between the proper sphere for social
action and the proper sphere for governmental action; the Populists, he said, did
not try to invade the former, and therefore Populism was not paternalism. "Paternalism is bad; it destroys all self-reliance and manliness among the people, and

The means of providing work, according to Coxey's scheme and according to the ideas of most of his sympathizers, were to be furnished by an issue of fiat money; their plan was thus based upon what is commonly considered an economic fallacy. Nevertheless, if the judgment of Thorstein Veblen was correct when he classified fiat money schemes in the same paternalistic group with fiat prosperity by means of a protective tariff, the Coxeyites were hardly in a minority in the degree of their paternalism.[1] What workingmen who voted for protection wanted was the same thing that Coxeyites wanted — a chance to work for wages that would enable them to live up to what they believed, and their party orators told them, was an American standard of living. Both wanted the Government to provide the opportunity.

These ideas, so far as they prevailed, were vague and inarticulate in the minds of most people until some one came along with a formula that seemed to express them. They followed the leaders who described the panaceas that sounded most promising and that offered to supply their immediate wants. The people, said a Middle Western periodical,

are not doing much philosophizing on the situation, and yet they are sorrowfully aware that many conditions do exist which should not. . . . These conditions are unfortunate, for, divested of prejudice, can any reasonable mind reject the general proposition that labor as well as capital

creates instead a servile dependence upon the Government. But the failure of the Government to perform its functions, delegating its power to individuals and corporations, is worse than paternalism. The granting of franchises, in the opinion of the Populists, is the greatest of governmental crimes." — C. B. Morton, "Populism Not Paternalism", *National Watchman*, Vol. IV, p. 801.

[1] T. B. Veblen, "The Commonweal Army", *Journal of Political Economy*, Vol. II, p. 460.

has claims which governments are bound in duty and in self-interest to respect and, within reasonable limits, to allow. This brings us face to face with the real question behind the general confusion of ideas and conditions. . . . Why should not government apply to the labor market the same business common sense which it applies to the money market for the prevention of disaster? [1]

Coxeyism answered this question in the affirmative, and suggested a plausible means of accomplishing the desired result.

On the one hand Coxeyism contained symptoms of this tendency to demand of the Government greater activity in supervising the welfare of citizens and in providing them with opportunities. On the other hand it suggested an enlargement of the field of natural rights — an addition to the doctrines of Locke expressed in the Declaration of Independence. "The classic phrase," said Veblen, "is no longer to read 'life, liberty, and the pursuit of happiness'; what is to be assured to every free-born American citizen under the new dispensation is 'life, liberty, and the *means* of happiness.'"[2] The right to work at good wages was added to the older conception of property rights. At the meeting of the American Federation of Labor in December, 1893, a resolution was adopted "That the right to work is the right to life, that to deny the one is to destroy the other. That when the private employer cannot or will not give work the municipality, State or nation must." [3] "The right to life, liberty, and the pursuit of happiness," said President Samuel Gompers at the same meeting,

---

[1] Editorial comment in *Midland Monthly*, Vol. I, pp. 612–614, quoted in Haynes, "Third Party Movements", pp. 341, 342.

[2] T. B. Veblen, "The Army of the Commonweal", *Journal of Political Economy*, Vol. II, p. 458.

[3] "Proceedings of the American Federation of Labor", 1893, p. 35.

"should be a guarantee that employment, remunerative, safe and healthful, is accorded to all." [1] Some resolutions written for a Populist convention in 1894 by Henry Demarest Lloyd contained the significant statements:

The same Declaration of Independence which yesterday made the people their own governors will make them today their own employers. To be compelled to buy the necessities of life of monopolies at their own price, to have to sell labor and the produce of labor at the prices monopolies choose to give is taxation without representation. . . ." [2]

A new phase of the struggle for economic freedom was bringing forth a new interpretation of the old declaration.

The frontier, which has been held responsible for so many distinctively American characteristics, disappeared, according to the census reports, only a few years before the pilgrimage of the Commonweal. The "economic revolution", which had been developing while the frontier was disappearing, had brought on, in certain parts of the United States, conditions similar to those of older and more crowded European countries.

[1] "Proceedings of the American Federation of Labor," 1893, p. 1. A meeting of the unemployed in Cincinnati passed a resolution "That as sovereign citizens we demand that the municipality, the State and Federal Government furnish work to the unemployed, or suspend distraint for rent and establish depots to provide them with provisions on credit, or loan them money for their support until they are reemployed." — *Journal of the Knights of Labor*, Sept. 14, 1893. See also San Francisco *Chronicle*, March 30, 1894, for the assertion by "one of the Industrial Army agitators" at Los Angeles that it was the duty of the city council to furnish work for the unemployed.

J. J. McCook objected to recognition of "the 'right to employment' of which we have heard so much of late." "But a little while ago a theory, it has already been advanced to its second stage of development. First it was 'Right to living wages.' Now it is 'Right to Union Wages.'

"Step number three will be 'Right to living wages at congenial work.' And number four will be 'Right to congenial work at Union wages.'" — J. J. McCook, "The Unemployed", *Charities Review*, Vol. III, p. 238 (March, 1894).

[2] H.D. Lloyd MSS., *Wis. Hist Soc.* The document is headed: "People's Party Convention at Springfield, Ill., July 4, 1894. Written by Henry D. Lloyd."

The pressure was intensified by the removal of the safety valve of free land. Marxian socialism was introduced, and it began to make some headway before 1894.[1] But Coxeyism, like the whole Populist movement, was mainly an indigenous growth, the descendant of anti-monopolism, greenbackism, Granges, and Farmers' Alliances, rather than of anything European. There was something of a class struggle between those who had less property and privileges, and those who had more, as there had been in the time of Jefferson or Jackson. There was often bitterness in the attitude of those who called themselves the people against those whom they called capitalists or plutocrats, but because they used the word "capital" in something like a Marxian sense, it did not necessarily follow that they all believed in a complete socialist revolution. There was a widespread belief that the rich had too much and the poor too little, and that something ought to be done about it,[2] but although the Knights of Labor indorsed the

[1] Davis R. Dewey, "National Problems", p. 249.

[2] "As near as the bizarre characters in which it is written can yet be deciphered, the message of the Army of the Commonweal says that certain economic concepts are not precisely the same to many people today that they have been to the generation which is passing. 'Capital,' to this new popular sense, is the 'capital' of Karl Marx rather than that of the old school economists or of the market place. The concept of 'property' or of 'ownership' is in the process of acquiring a flexibility and a limitation that would have puzzled the good American citizen of a generation ago. By what amounts to a subconscious acceptance of Hegelian dialectic it has come about that an increase in a person's wealth beyond a certain ill-defined point, should not, according to the new canon of equity, be permitted to increase his command over the means of production or the processes which these means serve. Beyond an uncertain point of aggregation, the inviolability of private property, in the new popular conception, declines. In Hegelian phrase, a change in quantity, if it is considerable enough, amounts to a change in kind. A man — still less a corporation — must no longer do what he will with his own, if what is classed as his own appreciably exceeds the average. It is competent for his neighbors to appeal for his guidance to the corporate will of the community, and in default of an expression of the corporate will the neighbors in question may properly act vicariously for the community." T. B. Veblen, "Army of the Commonweal", —*Journal of Political Economy*, Vol. II, pp. 457, 458.

"Coöperative Commonwealth", in which the people should control the means of production, most of the discontented cast their votes for Populist candidates rather than for the candidates of the more radical labor parties. What most of them wanted was not the complete Marxian revolution, but merely government action that would make it easier to do things for themselves. They preferred to work through the medium of the existing representative institutions. Coxey himself did not advocate anything more violent than an unusual but peaceable method of impressing upon Congress the necessity for certain measures that he thought the people desired and needed.

There were extremists both for and against Coxeyism. There were those who viewed with alarm and those who pointed with scorn, and there were plenty of each who wanted strenuous repression. There were overzealous sympathizers whose words or acts furnished ammunition for the enemy. But neither the Judge Hubbards nor the Secretary Osbornes had their way. Except for the frequent seizures of trains, most of the industrial armies behaved themselves with exemplary moderation, and those in authority did likewise to such an extent that the Coxeyites got only a very moderate amount of martyrdom out of their pilgrimages — much less than they would have had if the Judge Hubbards had been in control. Consequently the Coxeyites were less dangerous than they might have been. The mass of the general public was sympathetic, amused, or mildly concerned, but, on the whole, not greatly excited about it.

The gloomy forebodings of our visitor, the editor of the English *Review of Reviews*, as to what might happen if Coxeyism were repressed, were not justified by the outcome. Coxeyites were treated with more kindness than cruelty. The complacent optimism of the editor of the American *Review of Reviews* perhaps showed that he understood his countrymen better. He spoke of the industrial armies as "bodies of American pilgrims bound on a merely fantastic and adventurous journey, under the leadership of ill-informed and visionary men whose energy and capacity for organization happen to find an outlet in this plan." The performance of Coxey or Kelly, he said, "is apropos of nothing in particular. It is merely a fresh evidence of the elasticity of the American spirit." [1] But although this American editor may have understood the response of Americans to this sort of thing better, he did not show that he understood the causes of the movement as well as Mr. Stead did, or that he attributed enough importance to the symptoms of these causes. Coxeyism was important for what it signified rather than for anything it accomplished. The fact that it did not turn out to be dangerous does not mean that it was not worth studying. It was one of the symptoms of the rapidly developing economic revolution in the United States. More specifically, it showed certain reactions of the American frontier spirit to the growing industrialism which was replacing the old order.

[1] *Review of Reviews*, Vol. IX, p. 650. W. T. Stead wrote to Henry Demarest Lloyd, June 6, 1894: "I think you will be interested in . . . the new number of the English *Review of Reviews*. My American editor, I see, has pooh poohed Coxeyism and generally declared that I am an idiot in attaching any importance whatever to the armies of the commonweal. What he will think when he reads the pages of my article I don't know, but I send them to you in advance of their publication in order that you may glance over them. I think it probable that you may be more in agreement with me than my New York Editor." — H. D. Lloyd MSS., *Wis. Hist. Soc.*

CHAPTER XIV

EPILOGUE

In the spring of 1928, when Mr. Coxey again figured prominently in press dispatches, a reporter remarked that the Commonweal General of 1894, "far from being a dead duck or a mere forgotten notable of long ago" was just as good copy for the newspapers as ever: he was "the same old Coxey." [1]

Ever since the march upon Washington in 1894 Coxey has continued to agitate his reforms and to make them his platform in the political arena. In his contest for Congress in 1894 he polled twenty-four per cent. of the votes cast in his district, receiving more than five times as many votes as the Populist candidate two years before.[2]

Not long after this election Mr. Taubeneck, chairman of the People's Party national committee, called a conference of Populists at St. Louis. According to one of Coxey's publications the Commonweal General played a prominent part in this conference. A resolution was adopted making the non-interest bond plan an issue in the coming presidential campaign of 1896. This plan was ignored, however, when the national committee issued its address to the people.[3] Coxey remained prominent as a Populist leader, and some newspapers men-

[1] *Literary Digest*, Vol. XCVII, p. 45 (May 19, 1928).
[2] *Cause and Cure*, Vol. II, No. 2 (April, 1896), p. 26.
[3] *Ibid.*, Vol. II, No. 2 (April, 1896), p. 26.

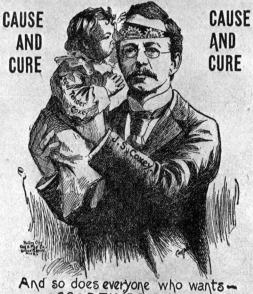

A REDUCED REPRODUCTION OF THE COVER
OF GENERAL COXEY'S MAGAZINE, "CAUSE
AND CURE," DECEMBER, 1897

tioned him as a presidential possibility.[1]   It is
interesting to note that the Illinois reformer, Henry
Demarest Lloyd, author of "Wealth Against Commonwealth", wrote on July 10, 1896, of the coming nomination: "My own preference for a ticket would be Coxey
and Debs. Those are the two men who have done something, and have made the record that proves them in-
domitable and incorruptible." [2]

Possibly if the People's Party had not fused with the
Democrats, and if William Jennings Bryan had not
captivated the Democratic convention and most of the
Populists by his eloquent appeals for free silver, Coxey
might have been better known in some other capacity
than that of a leader of an unemployed army. He was
strongly opposed to the fusion, and he insists that in a
separate Populist Party lay the salvation of the country.
Bryan, says Coxey, was the man who wrecked the
Populist organization, and who put an end to further
education of the people on the money question when
he shifted the issue to imperialism in 1900.

Although the non-interest-bearing bond plan failed
to attain the prominence of a major issue in national
politics, it continued to be agitated by its energetic
sponsor, and it found a place in the Populist platforms
of several State conventions.[3]

[1] See editorials in Cleveland *Plain Dealer*, Jan. 20, 1895; Washington, [D. C.]
News, Jan. 10, 1895; Massillon, [Ohio] *Independent*, Jan. 28, 1895, all quoted in
Cause and Cure, Vol. II, No. 2 (April, 1896), pp. 21–23. According to Mr. Coxey,
the *Plain Dealer* editorial was written by Charles Grant Miller, then a disciple of
the financial ideas of Don Piatt. After a conversation with Coxey, Miller wrote
the editorial and lost his job as a consequence.

[2] Caro Lloyd, "Henry Demarest Lloyd", Vol. I, p. 259.

[3] According to Coxey's *Cause and Cure*, Vol. III, No. 22 (Dec., 1897), it was incorporated into the Populist State platforms in Ohio in 1894, 1895, 1896, and
1897, and in Iowa in 1896. It also states that in 1896 a representative was elected
in the third congressional district in Kansas after he had made this plan an issue
and Coxey had "stumped" his district.

In 1897 Coxey was a candidate for the office of governor of Ohio. His platform was now more comprehensive, demanding, in addition to non-interest bonds, a service pension to all old soldiers, the direct election by popular vote of the president, vice-president and senators, and the initiative and referendum.[1] He next purchased a tent one hundred by two hundred feet, and a baggage car, painted white, with his platform inscribed upon it in full in red, white, and blue letters. With this paraphernalia he set out to tour the country, lecturing in the interest of good roads and more money.[2]

The hard times after the panic of 1894 presently passed away. Mark Hanna had announced his friend William McKinley as "the advance agent of prosperity", and after McKinley assumed the presidency, prosperity, which was now due to set in, presently arrived. The People's Party, which had thriven on hard times, was already split into "Demo-Pops" who supported Bryan and "Middle of the road" Populists who tried to keep the party organization intact. Coxey favored the "middle of the road" policy, but that wing of the party was decidedly on the decline, and his prospects for election to office on his non-interest bond program were not encouraging.

By 1914, however, a situation had developed which bore many resemblances to that prevailing in 1894. Industry lagged, and many workers were unemployed and destitute.

Meanwhile Coxey had developed new items in his program. His scheme to furnish public improvements

[1] *Cause and Cure*, Vol. III, No. 22 (Dec., 1897).
[2] *Ibid.*

at cost and to relieve unemployment by means of the
non-interest bond bill remained unchanged. A second
proposal was intended to furnish the people with an
easy means of making private improvements — buying
or improving farms, building homes, or developing
their business. The Federal Government was to establish a system of banks — one in every municipality,
town, or village with a population of one thousand or
more, and to carry on the same functions through the
postoffices in villages with a population between five
hundred and one thousand. These banks were to make
loans of legal-tender currency secured by real or chattel
property, up to its assessed valuation or its market
price, as the case might be. Even live stock and such
farm products as wheat, corn, or cotton, and raw
materials which had acquired value through labor expended upon them, were included among the securities
which might be offered for these loans. Long-time
loans, to enable agriculturalists to buy farms or workingmen to acquire homes, were to be repaid in installments
of not less than four per cent. per annum. As in the
case of the bonds in Coxey's earlier plan, this would
retire the principal within twenty-five years. Meanwhile, in lieu of interest, a tax of two per cent. per annum was to be paid on the loan.[1] Thus, by paying six
per cent. or less on the original principal, for twenty-
five years, the borrower could pay all charges and retire
the principal as well.[2]

A third item in the revised program involved the
purchase by the Federal Government of all the railroads

[1] Coxey estimated the cost of the administration of this system at one half of
one per cent. of the loans. The rest, he said, would be clear gain for the government.
[2] "Coxey: His Own Story", p. 65.

and other means of transportation and communication. Coxey believed that if the corporations controlling the railroads were unwilling to sell for a fair price, their value ought to be determined by a jury, just as in the case of a farmer whose land was condemned for a railroad right of way by the right of eminent domain. The property was to be paid for by legal tender notes.[1] Coxey summed up his plan in the threefold slogan: "Medium of exchange without cost; public bonds without interest; common carriers without private profit"; and he demanded the passage of three bills for these purposes as a cure for hard times.[2]

Coxey regarded the Glass-Owen Bill to establish the Federal Reserve System as a device of Wall Street bankers to perpetuate their system. He asserted that Congress, in passing this measure, had "completely surrendered to the 25000 banks and placed 99% of the people in serfdom through interest worse than that of the black men and women prior to the Civil War." The people, he said, "will finally wake up out of their slumber of deceit, pretense and sham and will find that their idol, William Jennings Bryan, has sold not only his but their birthright for a mess of potage [sic] (Power and the Almighty dollar), and has minted his cross of gold for a basis for the New Banking System and is now feeding the people the thorns from his crown."[3] On October 23, 1913, Coxey appeared before the Senate Committee on Banking and Currency to urge the substitution of his plan for Federal banks and non-interest bonds for the banking and currency reforms of the

---

[1] "Coxey: His Own Story", pp. 13–15, 33–35.
[2] *Ibid.*, first and fourth unnumbered pages at the beginning of the pamphlet.
[3] *Ibid.*, pp. 7, 8.

proposed Glass-Owen measure. He explained his views and was requested to submit a draft of his bills in writing. No one except Senator Knute Nelson of Minnesota seemed to take a sympathetic interest in the scheme, and the Glass-Owen Act included no part of it.[1] During this hearing Coxey showed himself to be a true fiat money man when he said, "I contend that the only real money is the fiat of the Government. Money is simply an idea of Congress enacted into law. It is a representative of value, and should never have a value of or in itself." [2]

Carl Browne, after the episode of the Commonweal of Christ was concluded, returned to California. In a shack at Sacramento he worked upon a flying machine through which he hoped to make his fortune. When this invention was completed he took it to Washington for a demonstration. "On that long-protracted mission Brown [sic] became a well-known figure in the halls of the Capitol and on the streets of Washington, where he was a frequent speaker in open-air meetings." [3] Throughout the remainder of his life he worked faithfully in agitating Coxey's reforms. Browne died on January 23, 1914, too soon to participate in an event from which he would doubtless have derived great satisfaction. According to an obituary notice written by Coxey, Browne's whole effort during the last two years of his life was devoted to gaining the support of the Socialist Party for Coxey's revised program.[4]

In 1914 General Coxey planned a second march of

---

[1] The report of this hearing is reprinted, in "Coxey: His Own Story", pp. 53–67. *Cf. Literary Digest*, Vol. XCVII, p. 49 (May 14, 1928).
[2] "Coxey: His Own Story", p. 57.
[3] Samuel L. Gompers, " Seventy Years of Life and Labor ", Vol. II, p. 12.
[4] "Coxey: His Own Story", p. 94.

the unemployed. It was to start from Massillon on April 16, Coxey's sixtieth birthday, and to arrive in Washington on May 21 to demand the passage of Coxey's three measures.[1] With a small band of marchers Coxey made the journey. It caused no such excitement, however, as it had twenty years before. This time Coxey made his speech from the Capitol steps without hindrance, and marched his army back to Massillon.

Meanwhile General Charles T. Kelly of San Francisco was trying to repeat his earlier performance. At Sacramento, however, he was arrested and sentenced to serve a term in the county jail. During his enforced leisure, in thinking over his past activities and ideas, he concluded that his radical attitude was unsound. Upon emergence from his captivity he gave up his career as a radical agitator, and devoted himself to social service work, becoming secretary of a workingmen's Christian association in San Francisco. In 1924 he published an article in the New York Times Current History entitled "Are Radicals Insane?" in which he discussed the mental outlook and capacity of those who favored violence and revolution, and diagnosed the causes of their attitude. In discussing these causes he gave a prominent place to unemployment. He suggested a remedy — the utilization of unemployed labor in the construction of public works such as irrigation dams and public highways, under the direction of the War Department — that was suggestive of the industrial army demands in 1894.[2]

Although Kelly was arrested, some of his men persisted in their pilgrimage to Washington. A body of

---

[1] "Coxey: His Own Story", fourth unnumbered page at beginning of pamphlet.
[2] Current History, Vol. XX, pp. 205–210 (May, 1924).

them passed through Massillon after Coxey and his little band had returned. Mr. Coxey relates that he suggested that he would like to entertain them for a day or two in a building at his quarries while they rested for a continuance of their journey. As they marched out of Massillon toward the quarries it occurred to him that a draught of cooling pre-Volstead beer might not be unacceptable to them, and he drove ahead to make arrangements at the last saloon along the line of march. When he halted the army and extended the invitation, however, the men declined it with thanks. They explained that before leaving San Francisco all the members of the army had taken an oath that they would not take a drink until they had arrived in Washington.[1]

In 1916 Coxey conducted an active campaign for nomination as United States Senator, with no more success than before.[2] He continued to agitate his non-interest-bearing bond bill before Congress, and occasionally he succeeded in having it introduced there.[3] He also made his appeal to the chief executive. On April 14, 1922, he was granted an interview with President Harding. According to a sympathetic newspaper account, Coxey on that occasion "probably spoke more frankly . . . than any man who has yet had a White House audience."[4] He urged the President to believe that the business depression with its starving workmen and suicides was caused by the bankers and the Federal Reserve System. All this could be remedied, he in-

[1] Coxey.
[2] *Ibid.*
[3] In 1919 Coxey printed a pamphlet without title giving the text of his revised bill, with comments thereon. The bill H. R. 1473 was introduced May 21, 1919, and in revised form, as printed in the pamphlet, it was introduced on Aug. 8, 1919.
[4] Article by Leo R. Sack in Cleveland *Press*, April 17, 1922, quoted in leaflet "Coxey Makes Appeal to Harding."

sisted, by the adoption of the Coxey monetary reforms. "If you will help," he said, "we can have every wheel turning at full speed in thirty days' time" after the adoption of a series of proposed laws.

To begin with, as a preliminary step, Coxey wanted the Department of Justice to bring criminal indictments under the anti-trust laws against the "invisible government" consisting of J. P. Morgan and Company; Kuhn, Loeb and Company; The Guarantee Trust Company; and the National City Bank, all of New York, and the Mellon Bank of Pittsburgh; also ex-Secretary of the Treasury Houston and the Federal Reserve Board. Having thus cleared the way, a series of Coxey bills was proposed.

First, the non-interest bond bill.

Second, a bill providing for the issue of legal-tender paper money to buy the vessels owned by the Emergency Fleet Corporation, and for the conversion of these vessels into a permanent American merchant marine by their sale to private concerns on fifteen years' credit without interest.

Third, a bill to provide an issue of legal-tender notes for a soldiers' cash bonus.

Fourth, a bill directing the Secretary of the Treasury to refund all interest-bearing obligations of the United States, as they matured, in legal-tender currency, and to prohibit the Treasury from issuing any more interest-bearing bonds.

Fifth, to float the railroads and other transportation companies out of their difficulties on bonds and paper money. The proposal was that when a transportation company needed new equipment or other improvements it might issue twenty-year non-interest-bearing bonds and deposit them with the Secretary of the Treasury as security for a loan of legal-tender notes, the amount needed to be determined by the Interstate Commerce Commission. The railroads were to be prohibited from issuing any more capital stock, and from paying annual dividends exceeding six per cent.[1]

Coxey submitted his proposals in writing, and in due time they were referred to S. Parker Gilbert, Junior, Undersecretary of the Treasury. Mr. Gilbert informed Mr. Coxey that the adoption of his program was "entirely out of the question", and stated his reasons. There ensued a lengthy correspondence between Mr. Coxey and the Undersecretary, which shortly found its way into the *Congressional Record*, where any one who so desires may read it.[2] Coxey also tried to convert Senator James Couzens of Michigan to his money plan, but the senator pointed to the recent experiences of European countries and refused to be convinced.[3] Not long afterward the General attempted to gain the support of Mr. Henry Ford. Although the *Dearborn Independent* showed signs of marked interest in Coxeyism, its sponsor does not seem to have developed into a complete Coxeyite.[4]

Coxey has continued his political activities as persistently as he has lobbied for his bills. In 1924, and

[1] "Coxey Makes Appeal to Harding." The first three proposals were incorporated in bills already introduced in the House of Representatives (H. R. 4576, 10530, 10890).

At the end of this leaflet Coxey appealed to the voters of Ohio to place his name on the ballot as non-partisan candidate for the United States Senate.

[2] Coxey reprinted this correspondence, under the title "Legal Tender Notes Secured by Bonds", from the *Congressional Record* of June 29, 1922.

[3] Couzens to Coxey, Jan. 24, 1924; Coxey to Couzens, Jan. 26, 1924; Couzens to Coxey, Jan. 30, 1924. MSS. letters loaned to the author by Mr. Coxey.

[4] Coxey reprinted articles from the *Dearborn Independent* of Feb. 27 and Aug. 14, 1926, as a campaign document, under the caption "Ford Endorses Coxey's Ideas."

again in 1926 he was an "independent progressive" candidate for Congress, and in 1928 he filed his candidacy for the Senate.[1]

The third high spot in Coxey's career as a leader of the cause of the jobless developed in 1928. The unemployment situation was again serious enough to attract wide-spread attention. Coxey maintained that conditions were even worse than in 1894. He attended meetings of the unemployed and of farmers' organizations, preaching his gospel of money at cost. In New York he suggested that the city rush work on the subways, financing it by non-interest-bearing bonds. His slogan was "unhorse the coupon clippers." When the question of leading another army of the unemployed to Washington was broached, he said that his business required his attention, and that he was too busy.[2]

Then, in March, came the rumors that Coxey was to lead another army to the capital. It was reported that James Eads Howe, the "millionaire hobo", planned such an expedition. At the national congress on unemployment Coxey told the hoboes that he would go to Washington to urge the passage of his bill for their relief. If he failed, he would inform them and the unemployed might take a referendum on the march. The General would lead them.[3] It was asserted that the march was prevented at this time only because Coxey offered to act as the representative of the unemployed at the Capitol.[4]

---

[1] "Money at Cost." A six-page pamphlet issued by Coxey in 1924 as a campaign document; also a single large sheet issued under the same title; "Ford Endorses Coxey's Ideas"; New York *Times*, June 9, 1928.

[2] *Ibid.*, Feb. 7, 11, 14, 1928.

[3] New York *Times*, March 19, April 26, 1928; *Literary Digest*, Vol. XCVII, p. 45. May 19, 1928).

[4] New York *Evening Post*, quoted in *Literary Digest*, Vol. XCVII, p. 45.

Coxey's bill — the old "non-interest-bearing bond bill" — had again been introduced "by request" by Representative Guy E. Campbell of Pennsylvania. Secretary of the Treasury Mellon wrote a letter to the House Committee on Finance, attacking the Coxey plan. It was a fiat-money scheme, he said, which would cause dangerous inflation of the currency. He objected that since there was nothing to prevent municipalities, counties, and States from issuing bonds secured by the same property, the total might run as high as two and a half times the assessed value of the property, instead of merely half of this value because of the "overlapping of the government subdivisions." The House did not act upon the bill. The unemployed have not marched.

Mr. Coxey was described by one who marched in his army in 1894 as "a man of wealth, a dreamer of dreams, and a breeder of blooded horses." [1] To-day he drives his car instead of his team, but he is much the same. To quote a recent newspaper description:

The "general" is an affable gentleman who far from looks his age of seventy-three. He is drest like a business man, which, as the owner of a stone quarry, he is. A stand-up collar and silver-rimmed spectacles give him an old-fashioned appearance. He still has a thick head of hair, tho it is gray, and his face shows few wrinkles. His eyes are the eyes of a dreamer rather than of a man of action, the eyes of an enthusiast who sees through what he considers a world of injustice to Utopia — a Utopia to be reached by following his directions." [2]

[1] Griffin, "Secret Service Memories", *Flynn's*, Vol. XIII, p. 915.
[2] Howard Erilsson of the Omaha *World-Herald*, quoted in *Literary Digest*, Vol. XCVII, p. 45.

APPENDIXES

APPENDIX A

[This text is taken from Coxey's publication, *Cause and Cure*, Vol. II, No. 2, pp. 5, 6, as they were introduced in the House of Representatives somewhat later than they were introduced in the Senate by Senator Peffer.]

1. The Good Roads Bill. — 53rd Congress, 2d Session, H. R. 7438, June 12, 1894.

A BILL to provide for the improvement of public roads, and for other purposes.

Be it enacted by the Senate and the House of Representatives of the United States of America in Congress assembled, That the Secretary of the Treasury of the United States is hereby authorized and instructed to have engraved and have printed, immediately after the passage of this bill, five hundred millions of dollars of Treasury notes, a legal tender for all debts, public and private, said notes to be in denominations of one, two, five, and ten dollars, and to be placed in a fund to be known as the "general county-road fund system of the United States," and to be expended solely for said purpose.

Sec. 2. That it shall be the duty of the Secretary of War to take charge of the construction of the said general county-road system of the United States, and said construction to commence as soon as the Secretary of the Treasury shall inform the Secretary of War that the said fund is available, which shall not be later than sixty days from and after the passage of this bill, when it shall be the duty of the Secretary of War to inaugurate the work and expend the sum of twenty millions of dollars per month pro rata with the number of miles of road in each State and Territory in the United States.

Sec. 3. That all labor other than that of the office of the Secretary of War, "whose compensations are already fixed by law," shall be paid by the day, and that the rate be not less than one dollar and fifty cents per day for common labor and three dollars and fifty cents for team and labor, and that eight hours per day shall constitute a day's labor under the provisions of this bill, and that all citizens of the United States making application to labor shall be employed.

2. The Non-Interest-Bearing Bond Bill. — 53rd Congress, 2d Session, H. R. 7463, June 15, 1894.

A BILL to provide for public improvements and employment of the citizens of the United States.

Be it enacted by the Senate and House of Representatives of the United States of America in Congress assembled, That whenever any State, Territory, county, township, municipality, or incorporated town or village deem it necessary to make any public improvements they shall deposit with the Secretary of the Treasury of the United States a non-interest-bearing twenty-five-year bond, not to exceed one-half of the assessed valuation of the property in said State, Territory, county, township, municipality, or incorporated town or village, and said bond to be retired at the rate of four per centum per annum.

Sec. 2. That whenever the foregoing section of this act has been complied with it shall be mandatory upon the Secretary of the Treasury of the United States to have engraved and printed Treasury notes in the denominations of one, two, five and ten dollars each, which shall be a full legal tender for all debts, public and private, to the face value of said bond and deliver to said State, Territory, county, township, municipality, or incorporated town or village ninety-nine per centum of said notes, and retain one per centum for expense of engraving and printing same.

Sec. 3. That after the passage of this act it shall be compulsory upon every incorporated town or village, munici-

APPENDIX B

(From Vincent, "Commonweal", pp. 163–165)

Whereas, The evils of murderous competition; the supplanting of manual labor by machinery; the excessive Mongolian and Pauper immigration; the curse of alien landlordism; the exploitation, by rent, profit and interest, of the products of the toiler, has centralized the wealth of the nation into the hands of the few, and placed the masses in a state of hopeless destitution.

We have only to look upon the history of the past — like causes produce like results. These same causes led to the downfall of Persia, Greece, and conquering Rome. The end came when two per cent of their population owned all the national wealth.

We have reached that point on our own road to ruin where three per cent of the population own seventy-six per cent of all the wealth. Witness the abandoning and selling of children by their parents in San Francisco, on the western shore, and the protest against the slave traffic in children from Italy by New York, on the eastern shore of our nation.

This is one of the signs, history tells us, that preceded the downfall of all the past great nations.

The daily grind of pinching poverty, linked with the thought of a hopeless future, kills even the deep maternal instinct. The greatest crime perpetrated by a nation is to allow her people to be idle and sink into debauched servitude. The strange tragical questions confront us on every hand.

Why is it that those who produce food are hungry?

Why is it that those who make clothes are ragged?

Why is it that those who build palaces are houseless?

pality, township, county, State or Territory to give employ-ment to any idle man applying for work, and that the rate be not less than one dollar and fifty cents per day for common labor and three dollars and fifty cents per day for team and labor, and that eight hours per day shall constitute a day's labor under the provisions of this act.

Why is it that those who do the nation's work are forced to choose between beggary, crime or suicide, in a nation that has fertile soil enough to produce plenty to feed and clothe the world; material enough to build palaces to house them all, and productive capacity, through labor-saving machinery, of forty thousand million man-power, and only sixty-five million souls to feed, clothe and shelter. Recognizing the fact that if we wish to escape the doom of the past civilization something must be done, and done quickly.

Therefore we, as patriotic American citizens, have organized ourselves into an Industrial Army, for the purpose of centralizing all the unemployed American citizens at the seat of government (Washington, D. C.) and tender our services to feed, clothe, and shelter the nation's needy, and to accomplish this end we make the following demands on the government:

1st. Government employment for all her unemployed citizens.

2nd. The prohibition of foreign immigration for ten years.

3rd. That no alien be allowed to own real estate in the United States.

CONSTITUTION.

ARTICLE I. — NAME.

Section 1. This organization shall be known as the United States Industrial Army.

Sec. 2. It shall have the power to make its own Constitution and By-Laws and elect its own officers.

ARTICLE II. — HOW COMPOSED.

Section 1. This army shall be composed of American citizens over sixteen years of age, or those who have declared their intentions to become such.

ARTICLE III. — OFFICERS.

Section 1. The officers of the army shall be a general, five aids, a quartermaster-general, brigadiers, colonels, captains and sergeants.

Sec. 2. The general, quartermaster-general and five aids shall be elected by the army; brigadier by his brigade; colonel by his regiment; captain and sergeant by their company.

ARTICLE IV. — THE GENERAL AND STAFF.

Section 1. The general and staff shall have the supervision over the army, and see that the constitution is carried out; grant commissions to recruiting sergeants, and have power to revoke the same.

Sec. 2. The general and staff shall constitute a court-martial. The accused to have a right of an appeal to a vote of the army against their decision.

Sec. 3. Officers to hold office during good behavior.

ARTICLE V.

Section 1. Fifty men shall constitute a company; ten companies a regiment; five regiments a brigade.

ORDER OF DISCIPLINE.

Roll call twice a day, when practicable. Drill once a day, when practicable. Any disobedience of orders shall be sufficient grounds for expulsion from the army. Each regiment to have its own rules of order not in conflict with the order of the army.

Adopted at Los Angeles, Cal., March 5, 1894.

APPENDIX C

[Extracts from the dispatches of Marshal William Mc-Dermott, sent from Helena, Montana, to the Attorney-General of the United States, June, 1894. — 53rd Cong., 2d Sess., *Senate Executive Document*, No. 120, pp. 15, 16, 18.]

June 4 — On the morning of May 19 my attention was called to the fact that about 160 Coxeyites, or so-called "industrials," had forcibly taken possession of a train of cars belonging to the Northern Pacific Railroad Company, at Heron Station, Montana, 274 miles west of here. These lawless vagabonds took the conductor, engineer, and fireman of the train and locked them in one of the cars, put two of their own number on the engine to run it, and started east with the train. Upon consultation with the court, I hastily organized a posse of 45 deputies, who started west on a special train and captured 152 Coxeyites at Arlee, 152 miles west of here, and turned the captured train over to the railroad company. The 152 Coxeyites I held prisoners at Arlee.

May 22 I received intelligence that Coxeyites had captured another east-bound train at Heron, Mont. I had 25 other special deputies sworn in, and recaptured the stolen train at Tuscan Siding, near Thompson Falls, with 52 Coxeyites. I had the train turned over to the railroad company, and imprisoned the Coxeyites at Thompson Falls. The 152 Coxeyites became so disorderly and riotous that I was obliged to call upon the United States troops. A company under command of Capt. Wilson was sent from Fort Missoula to guard them. A few days later I had the 52 prisoners removed from Thompson Falls to Arlee, where all the prisoners were placed in the same camp.

There were and are several hundred Coxeyites scattered along at different points of the Northern Pacific Railroad between here and Spokane, Wash., and I adopted the same course as that pursued by the United States Marshal of Idaho, namely, having deputy marshals running on all trains in Montana west of Helena to prevent Coxeyites from capturing trains. I have about 80 such deputies now on duty.

Since adopting this course I have been successful in preventing train stealing, except the capture of a train 71 miles west of here on June 2, but the Coxeyites were only in possession of the train a few hours, when it was recaptured by special deputy marshals. The retaining of these special deputy marshals is a great expense to the Government, and I shall dispense with their services just as soon as I am warranted in doing so.

June 7 — Coxeyites are giving me lots of trouble and putting the Government to big expense. Have just brought in 66 prisoners from the West and 60 more have possession of a train of the Northern Pacific Railroad east of here. Troops here refuse to aid me unless my efforts fail. Deputy marshals are expensive, and I have no money on hand. Would like your advice. Shall I continue the employment of special deputies or can troops be used instead? [In reply the Attorney-General sent $1,000 for fees and expenses and promised $500 more the next week.]

June 15 — If this "industrial" movement continues, even $40,000 would not be enough to cover my expenses, as I cannot get my pay rolls in quickly enough to get credit, and special deputies are a hard lot to contend with, and must be paid when discharged.

APPENDIX D

[From Stead, "Coxeyism", *Review of Reviews*, Vol. X, p. 51.]

All members must submit to its discipline, be orderly, peaceful, and law-abiding.

Every member must obey promptly the directions and orders of those who have been elected or appointed to places of authority over them.

A guard will be detailed every day for the succeeding twenty-four hours of a sufficient number of men, to be divided into three reliefs, which shall be under the command of the officer of the day.

Every day a sufficient number of men will be detailed to act as police, to see that the camp, barracks, or other place of shelter is kept clean, and to direct men who are thoughtless and careless about their persons to keep as clean as possible.

Every man must keep his person and his immediate portion of the quarters clean, and refrain from boisterous, profane, and obscene talk, and conduct himself in such an orderly, sober, and dignified way, whether in or out of quarters, as will inspire the public everywhere that we are American citizens; that we take a pride in our country; that we have a just sense of our rights under the laws of the land; and that we are banded together to make the whole people as a jury listen to our grievances.

No person will be allowed in camp except members of the Commonweal army and those who have permit of the countersign.

No speechmaking shall be allowed in camp without consent from the commanding officer.

As all the men in the army have joined for "pot luck" and expect to take it, let there be no grumbling over rations or the quarters furnished to us, no matter what be the quality of the one or the inconveniences of the other. We are patriots, and must endure our lot, whatever it may be.

BIBLIOGRAPHY

Books

Andrews, E. Benjamin, "The History of the Last Quarter Century in the United States, 1870–1895." New York, Scribner, 1896. Useful as a contemporary account of conditions in the United States in the early nineties.

Black, Jack. "You Can't Win." With a foreword by Robert Herrick. New York, Macmillan, 1927. The story of a reformed criminal. Contains graphic descriptions of tramp life in the nineties.

Dewey, Davis R. "National Problems, 1885–1897" (Vol. 24 of *The American Nation: A History*, edited by Albert Bushnell Hart). New York, Harper, 1907.

Gompers, Samuel L. "Seventy Years of Life and Labor. An Autobiography." 2 Vols., New York, Dutton, 1925.

Haynes, Fred E. "Third Party Movements Since the Civil War with Special Reference to Iowa." Iowa City, Iowa, State Historical Society of Iowa, 1916.

Lloyd, Caro. "Henry Demarest Lloyd, 1847–1903. A Biography." 2 Vols. New York, Putnam, 1912. An account of a leading Illinois Populist and reformer. Useful for the study of Populist ideas.

London, Charmian. "The Book of Jack London." 2 Vols. New York, Century Co., 1921. Contains some very interesting material on Jack London's experiences with tramp life and travel, and a chapter on his march with Kelly's army.

London, Jack. "The Road." New York, Macmillan, 1907. A collection of stories that had appeared in the *Cosmopolitan* in 1907.

Olcott, Charles S. "William McKinley." 2 Vols., Boston, 1916.

Peck, Harry Thurston. "Twenty Years of the Republic, 1885–1905." New York, Dodd, Mead & Co., 1907.

Rhodes, James Ford. "History of the United States from Hayes to McKinley, 1877–1896." New York, Macmillan, 1919.

Stanwood, Edward. "History of the Presidency." 2 Vols. Boston and New York, Houghton Mifflin, Vol. I, 1898, Vol. II, 1916. Contains party platforms.

Tully, Jim. "Beggars of Life." New York, A. and C. Boni, 1924. Experiences of a tramp.

Vincent, Henry. "The Story of the Commonweal." Chicago, W. B. Conkey Co., 1894. Written by the official historian of the Commonweal, who marched part of the way to Washington with Coxey's army, and helped organize the Chicago Commonweal. His attitude is sympathetic and moderate. Published at about the time Coxey reached Washington, it contains only the history of the movement up to the end of April, 1894, and accounts of armies far removed from the author's personal observations are sometimes hasty compilations with a few discrepancies and inaccuracies. It is the fullest and most comprehensive "inside" history of Coxeyism, during the period it covers, and, with the exceptions noted, an accurate one.

Articles

Austen, Shirley Plumer. "Coxey's Commonweal Army." *Chautauquan*, Vol. XIX, June, 1894, pp. 332–336. "The Downfall of Coxeyism." *Chautauquan*, Vol. XIX, July, 1894, pp. 448–452. Give an intelligent and somewhat critical account based largely upon personal observation.

Bemis, Edward W. "The Convention of the American Federation of Labor." *Journal of Political Economy*, Vol. II, March, 1894, pp. 298, 299. Chicago.

Brown, James M. "How the City of Toledo Provided for her Unemployed." Part III of "The Unemployed: A Symposium." *Arena*, Vol. X, October, 1894, pp. 715–720. Boston.

Byrnes, Thomas. "Character and Methods of the Men." Part II of "The Menace of Coxeyism." *North American Review*, Vol. CLVIII, June, 1894, pp. 696–701. New York. By the Superintendent of the New York Police Department.

Closson, Carlos C., Jr. "The Unemployed in American Cities." *Quarterly Journal of Economics*, Vol. VIII, January, 1894, pp. 168–217. Cambridge, Mass.

Denny, C. S. "The Whipping Post for Tramps." *Century*, Vol. XLIX, March, 1895, p. 794. New York. An open letter by the mayor of Indianapolis.

Doty, Alvah H. "The Danger to Public Health." Part III of "The Menace of Coxeyism." *North American Review*, Vol. CLVIII, June, 1898, pp. 701–705. By the Chief of the Bureau of Contagious Diseases, New York Board of Health.

Duryea, Reverend Joseph T. "The 'Industrial Army' at Omaha." *Outlook*, Vol. XLIX, May 5, 1894, pp. 780 *ff*. New York.

Flower, B. O. "Plutocracy's Bastiles: or Why the Republic is becoming an Armed Camp." *Arena*, Vol. X, October, 1894, pp. 601–621. Shows a radical editor's fear of militarism and of oppression of the proletariat by the forces of capitalism.

Flynt, Josiah. "Tramping with Tramps." *Century*, Vol. XLVII, November, 1893, pp. 99–108.

"What to Do with the Tramp." *Century*, Vol. XLVIII, September, 1894, pp. 794–796.

Frank, Henry. "The Crusade of the Unemployed." *Arena*, Vol. X, July, 1894, pp. 239–244.

Garret, Garet. "The Driver." *Saturday Evening Post*, Vol. CXCIV, December 24, 1921, pp. 3 *ff*. Philadelphia. The first installment of this novel opens with a description of the march of Coxey's army which is for the most part accurate historically.

Griffin, Matthew F. "Secret Service Memories", *Flynn's Weekly*, Vol. XIII, pp. 906–927, Vol. XIV, pp. 86–98. Reminiscences of a secret service operative who marched with Coxey's army from Pittsburgh to Washington.

Hall, A. Cleveland. "An Observer in Coxey's Camp." *Independent*, Vol. XLVI, May 17, 1894, pp. 615, 616. New York.

Hofer, E. "The Tramp Problem." *Overland Monthly*, Vol. XXIII, June, 1894, pp. 628–632. San Francisco.

Hooker, G. E. "The Unemployed in Boston." *Independent*, Vol. XLVI, April, 1894, pp. 487, 488.

Hooper, Osman C. "The Coxey Movement in Ohio."

Ohio State Archeological and Historical Society Publications, Vol. IX, pp. 155–176. Columbus, Ohio, 1901. The fullest non-contemporary historical account of the Ohio movement, with illustrations showing the Commonweal badges and other insignia.

Howard, Major General O. O. "Significance and Aims of the Movement." Part I of "The Menace of Coxeyism." *North American Review*, Vol. CLVIII, June, 1894, pp. 687–696.

Hubbard, N. M. "The Invasion of Iowa." *Midland Monthly*, Vol. I, June, 1894, pp. 588–590. Des Moines, Iowa. A violent attack upon the industrial armies by a conservative railroad lawyer who had had trouble with one of them.

Kelley, Charles T. "Are Radicals Insane?" New York Times *Current History*, Vol. XX, pp. 205–210. May, 1924. By a former leader of an industrial army.

London, Jack. "A Jack London Diary. Tramping with Kelly through Iowa." *Palimpsest*, Vol. VII, May, 1926, pp. 129–158. Iowa City, Iowa. Kept by Jack London during his trip with Kelly's army.

"My Life in the Underworld. A Reminiscence and a Confession." *Cosmopolitan*, Vol. XLIII, May, 1907, pp. 17–22. New York.

"Holding Her Down. More Reminiscences of the Underworld." *Cosmopolitan*, Vol. XLIII, June, 1907, pp. 142–150.

"Pictures. Stray Memories of Life in the Underworld." *Cosmopolitan*, Vol. XLIII, September, 1907, pp. 513–518.

"The March of Kelly's Army. The Story of an

Extraordinary Migration." *Cosmopolitan,* Vol. XLIII, October, 1907, pp. 643–648.

"Hoboes That Pass in the Night." *Cosmopolitan,* Vol. XLIV, December, 1907, pp. 190–197.

The articles describing tramp life and travel are valuable for an understanding of part of the background of the industrial army movement. The parts relating to Kelly's army are based largely upon London's diary.

Loomis, Reverend Samuel Lane. "The Tramp Problem." *Chautauquan,* Vol. XIX, June, 1894, pp. 308–313.

McCook, John J. "A Tramp Census and its Revelations." *Forum,* Vol. XV, August, 1893, pp. 753–766. New York.

"Tramps." *Charities Review,* Vol. III, December, 1893, pp. 57–69. New York.

"The Unemployed." *Charities Review,* Vol. III, March, 1894, pp. 236 *ff.*

Preston, S. O. "Provision for or Treatment of the Unemployed." *Charities Review,* Vol. III, pp. 218–225.

Parsons, Frank. "Lessons of Last Winter." Part II of "The Unemployed: A Symposium." *Arena,* Vol. X, October, 1894, pp. 712–715.

"The Relief of the Unemployed in the United States during the Winter of 1893–94." *Journal of Social Science, Containing the Transactions of the American Association,* Number XXXII, November, 1894, pp. 4 *ff.* A report from the department of social economy made at the Saratoga meeting, September 7, 1894.

Savage, Reverend M. J. "The Present Conflict for a Larger Life." *Arena,* Vol. X, August, 1894, pp.

297–306. Contains some moralizing upon Coxeyism.

Shaw, Albert. "Relief for the Unemployed in American
Cities." *American Review of Reviews*, Vol. IX,
January, 1894, pp. 29–37.

Stead, W. T. "Coxeyism: a Character Sketch."
American Review of Reviews, Vol. X, July, 1894,
pp. 47–56. One of the best contemporary articles
on Coxeyism, by the editor of the English *Review
of Reviews*, who was visiting in the United States
at the time of the Coxey movement. It is followed
by a "Marching Itinerary of the Industrials" trac-
ing the movements of the principal armies.

Stetson, H. L. "The Industrial Army." *Independent*,
Vol. XLVI, May 31, 1894, p. 681. An account of
Kelly's army at Des Moines, by the president of
Des Moines College.

Tracy, Reverend Joseph V. "A Mission to Coxey's
Army." *Catholic World*, Vol. LIX, August, 1894,
pp. 666–680. An account of a mission to the army
while it was encamped near Washington after
May 1, by a Catholic priest. Contains a valuable
description of the character of the men.

Veblen, T. B. "The Army of the Commonweal."
Journal of Political Economy, Vol. II, June, 1894,
pp. 456–461. A critical and penetrating analysis
by a scholarly economist of the economic and social
ideas involved in the Coxey movement.

Weaver, James B. "The Commonweal Crusade."
Midland Monthly, Vol. I, June, 1894, pp. 590–594.
Shows the attitude of a Populist leader towards
Coxeyism.

Will, Thomas E. "Data, Theory and Bibliography."

Part I of "The Unemployed: A Symposium."
Arena, Vol. X, October, 1894, pp. 701–711. Includes a section on "The Tramp."

Periodicals

Aside from the articles cited above, the files of the
following periodicals are useful for editorial comments,
etc.

The Altruist. St. Louis. A radical socialist organ.

The American Federationist. New York. The official
mouthpiece of the American Federation of Labor,
edited by Samuel Gompers. Valuable in determining the attitude of labor towards Coxeyism.

The American Review of Reviews. New York. Editorial
comments on Coxeyism have the usual note of
genial optimism of the editor, Albert Shaw.

The American Law Review. St. Louis. Has notes and
editorials upon the use of injunctions and other
legal aspects of the Coxey movement.

The Independent. New York.

The Journal of the Knights of Labor. Philadelphia.
Extremely useful both in determining the attitude
of labor and for news items relating to the industrial discontent in general and Coxeyism in particular.

The Midland Monthly. Des Moines, Iowa.

The National Watchman. Washington, D. C., and
Alexandria, Va. Expresses a rather extreme Populist attitude.

The People. New York. A Socialist Labor organ.

Our Day, A Record and Review of Current Reform.
Boston and Chicago.